Transmigrational Writings between
the Maghreb and Sub-Saharan Africa

Transmigrational Writings between the Maghreb and Sub-Saharan Africa

Literature, Orality, Visual Arts

Hélène Colette Tissières

Translated by Marjolijn de Jager

University of Virginia Press

Charlottesville & London

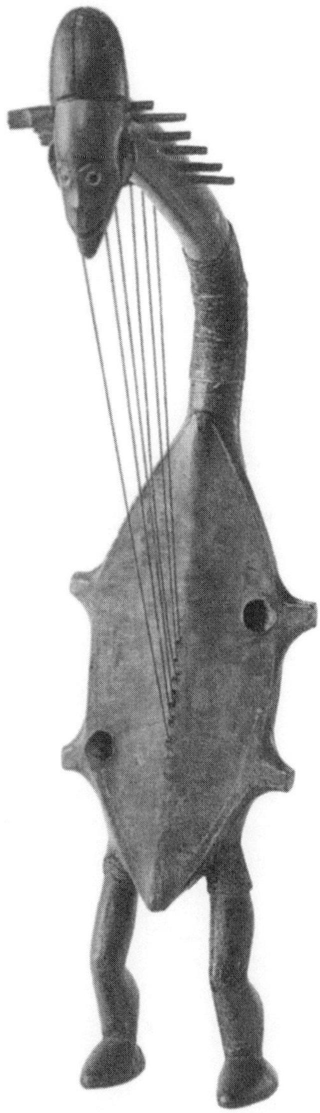

Originally published in French as *Écritures en transhumance entre Maghreb et Afrique subsaharienne: Littérature, oralité, arts visuels,* © 2007 Éditions l'Harmattan

University of Virginia Press

Printed in the United States of America on acid-free paper

First published 2012

9 8 7 6 5 4 3 2 1

Library of Congress Cataloging-in-Publication Data
Tissières, Hélène.
[Écritures en transhumance entre Maghreb et Afrique subsaharienne. English]
Transmigrational writings between the Maghreb and Sub-Saharan Africa : literature, orality, visual arts / Hélène Colette Tissières ; translated by Marjolijn de Jager.
p. cm.
"Originally published in French as Écritures en transhumance entre Maghreb et Afrique subsaharienne: Littérature, oralité, arts visuels, 2007 Éditions l'Harmattan"—T.p. verso.
Includes bibliographical references and index.
ISBN 978-0-8139-3209-5 (cloth : alk. paper) — ISBN 978-0-8139-3210-1 (pbk. : alk. paper)
1. African literature (French)—History and criticism. 2. North African literature (French)—History and criticism. 3. Oral tradition—Africa. 4. Oral tradition—Africa, North. 5. Performing arts—Africa. 6. Performing arts—Africa, North.
I. Title.
PQ3980.5.T5813 2012
840.9'96—dc23

2012009484

To my parents

For Zawadi

Contents

Acknowledgments

ACADEMIC RESEARCH is in dialogue with the thinking of the world, and I am very grateful to Antoine Raybaud, who made himself available to follow the journey I wanted to take, and to Michael Dash, for reading the manuscript when it was in its initial stage. They both shared their vast knowledge and encouraged me to pursue the circular movement that the themes generate, always spurring me to further the topics developed. I am also deeply grateful to John Conteh-Morgan for his invaluable suggestions and his academic rigor (unfortunately, he departed from this world in 2008, leaving behind a great void in the field of African literatures); to Alexie Tcheuyap for his friendship and the many viewpoints he shared; and to Marjolijn de Jager, who agreed to translate this work and tried to maintain the style, the rhythm, and the energy that the analyzed texts impart.

I am very thankful to Pascal Martin Léon of *Revue Noire;* to Orlando and Dolores Blanco of Éditart, who publish beautiful handprinted books; to Bassam Chaitou, collector of contemporary Senegalese art; and to the photographers Philippe Maillard, Mamadou Touré Behan, and Mohamed Sijelmassi for allowing me to reproduce their pictures. This made it possible to establish the importance of illustrating the connections made and of introducing often little known paintings and patterns. I would also like to express my gratitude to the Institut du Monde Arabe in Paris and the Museum for African Art in New York for their assistance.

Over the course of the years, various remarkable encounters have enriched my thinking: with Albert Aghazarian, Myrlie Evers-Williams, Abiola Irele, and Mamadou Mbodji. Their bold commitment, off the beaten path, motivated me to transgress the barriers erected. Finally, I must avow that this work would never have been completed without the steadfast support of my parents, who, when they were still of this world, always encouraged me to follow my academic passions; of my daughter, who enhances my peregrinations with her wondrous gaze; and of my longtime friend Pietro Santoro, who never ceases to lighten my daily life with his countless attentions.

Crucial on-site work was made possible and closely knit ties were created with colleagues, researchers, and artists thanks to several grants. Two of these came from the American Institute for Maghreb Studies, which allowed me to spend time in Morocco; one from the Fulbright Foundation, which permitted my affiliation with the Departments of Modern Languages and of English at Cheick Anta Diop University in Dakar, where I taught from 2003 to 2005.

Working on a theme that leads to a myriad of complexities produced by the circulatory movement itself, I found the viewpoints gathered and the support received essential. Thus, I am indebted to the writers, artists, and researchers who tackle these questions, among whom are Édouard Glissant, Abdelkébir Khatibi, and Abdelwahab Meddeb, to whom far more credit is due than this work will ever be able to demonstrate. They illuminate life in a world where withdrawal—a perpetual temptation—is sought for the appropriation of illusory rights. Butterflies or birds, as they glide through the air beyond the realm of wonderment, by the inscription of lines that cross or follow one another, that separate or vanish, their flight will have shaken one and become an elusive color on the pierced immensity of the sky—as a work of art that offers itself to the imagination to prevent one from being swept away or engulfed.

Introduction

The perspective of the works published on "francophone"[1] African literature, marked by separations and divisions, corresponds to equally as many implicit paradigms of study, which we can blame for renewing the mostly artificial schisms that colonialism created in matters of culture, as well as in the separation between the different regions of conquest. This separation still clearly exists between the two sides of the double culture of the intellectual and, specifically, of the writer and the artist in previously colonized countries, which is the separation between the acquired "metropolitan" culture and the inherited native culture. On the other hand, the division in the academic disciplines practiced in the West—literary criticism, art history, music and theater analysis—as well as the usual separation in all these disciplines between "modern" art forms and so-called archaic art forms, may have intensified those separations of ideological origin. The need of decolonized countries to claim an identity and their desire to identify with a nation have also contributed to the creation of schisms; by seeking to define themselves through elements that try to be unchanging and everlasting, beings become rigid and isolated.

The perspective at the heart of this work is different: it is an investigation of the movements[2] at work in the literary texts of Independence. These movements occur on different levels: geographic, between the Maghreb and sub-Saharan Africa; historical and cultural, between ancient and modern practices; verbal, between orality and writing; aesthetic, between writing and visual images. The indicators that pointed my study in this direction are of several orders, which answer to a generalized work of borrowings and grafts. Among these, I should mention:

- In literature the occurrence of a whole cultural context that may have been obscured and "delegitimized" (discredited), reduced to a state of mere survival by the colonial state but that, nevertheless, remained a vivid memory and a living form, actively communicative, of sharing, and of cohesion between social groups;

- Due to colonization, the transformation of this culture reduced to orality and undercover consciousness, stifled and marginalized, which constitute a repressed reserve the investigation of which leads to questioning not only the words of memory but also the unspoken language of mourning, closure, and sorrow;
- Parallel to the forms of communication that come under orality, the activity of an entire universe of graphic signs, such as calligraphy and tattooing; the plastic arts together with the forms practiced; the theater in rituals and social ceremonies; every form that arouses the interest and the investigative work of writers: Khatibi for calligraphy and tattooing, Liking for rites and rituals, Meddeb for the abstraction that Islamic art promotes;
- The interest displayed by writers in the organization of polyphony and of narrative dialogism as much as in the introduction of levels of experience and representation (including the typography of texts) for content, organization, and enunciation of orality;
- On both sides of the Sahara, the borrowings from each cultural region to the other via brotherhood rites or customs: the spread of Islam in the African environment; in the Maghreb the transmission of signs that stem from sub-Saharan African cultures.

I have arranged the research into two parts of four chapters each. The first part establishes my approach in developing the issue that came out of the notion of movement. In this section, the first chapter lays out the patterns that allow me to argue against a division between the Maghreb and sub-Saharan Africa by showing that numerous authors collect and express the multiple components that sustain them and validate the range of elements that characterize them and are the result of encounters, displacements, and sharing. The second chapter deals with the elements that authors disseminate throughout their novels and that refer to historic events that produce uncontrollable violence; to their ensuing effects, such as rupture and exile; to ancient practices such as rites or the development of an inner quest to break through any deadlock. These references are connections and circumlocutions that transcribe the movement of the passage and count on multiple meanings, while at the same time denouncing certain phenomena. For example, madness is used to evoke the consequences, sometimes dramatic, of violent behavior forced on individuals weakened by deadlock. In a literary context it is also used as a tool of subversion, bypassing the imposed norms and contributing to the project of writing, which deconstructs categories, closed systems, and rigid definitions. The third chapter emphasizes the contribution of techniques peculiar to orality: liveliness of speech, use of proverbs, myths, and epics, as well as the use of the storyteller or griot's methods, such as repetition or wordplay. The fourth chapter deals with the importance of the visual arts, which shatter the framework in an even more radical fashion, for by freeing itself from language the presence of the pictorial image in a work opens out onto a vast silence. Thus, some writers prolong or pursue this combination of the arts which has always existed throughout the continent, recording African cultural specificities and philosophical approaches, opposing boundaries, and shuffling methods.

The second part illustrates these observations by examining—in the light of the theme of the movements developed in the first section—the works of four authors: Abdelwahab Meddeb, Tunisian; Werewere Liking, Cameroonian; Tchicaya U Tam'Si, Congolese; Assia Djebar, Algerian. These four writers refer to history, to juxtapositions, to multilingualism, shattering the framework to record the political aspect, the psychological effects of violence, while deconstructing the narrative. They turn toward other forms of art, to orality and painting in particular. They dismantle borders as they follow the movement that the nomadic life engenders, circulating between territories and nations, between the Maghreb and sub-Saharan Africa, referring to different forms of art and ancient practices, and sharing imaginative worlds. Liking has a profound knowledge of the initiation practices of the Bassa of Cameroon, where she comes from. She inserts these rituals in her novels and plays, and does the same with orality techniques, while uniting them with other approaches. Meddeb inscribes in his texts a Sufi path and traces innumerable parallels between modern art and the value of abstract representation in Islam, drawing on various elements in sub-Saharan Africa. In his novels Tchicaya U Tam'Si evokes universal feelings and Congolese beliefs: the power of nature, visions, and divination. Djebar invests in the visual image and orality and presents different mnemonic signals, avoiding the exclusive use of one form and one language, questioning how the past has been viewed, and giving voice to women.

These intentions may create a void, since the authors share knowledge that is often unrecognized or unknown and that the reader must decode; offer interrogations and quests as they tackle hieratic concepts. These writers write neither in opposition to nor in line with Western movements, from which, furthermore, they have often been dismissed. In their writing the reader sometimes finds phenomena described by contemporary Western writers who take apart their narratives to follow the movement of a thought, thereby reproducing the contradictions of the human being, countering any absolutist vision. Nonetheless they are different: other elements help to build the text, such as calligraphy, the art of tattooing, orality, rituals, ancient signs, all practices in which this study is particularly interested.

Along the way we can ask ourselves numerous questions: Where does this intertwining lead us? Why does the author need to get away from language and the cogs of the written to place himself beyond language? What do these gaps and all the crisscrossing between speech and word, between language and visual image, contribute? The reference to orality will shatter the fabric, sending it back to a missing body language, a whole setting that the text relinquished. At the same time, visual image distances us from language to present us with forms, colors, and signs. Thus, starting with traces—fragments of knowledge—we will be able to clear a path and move toward sometimes uncommon spaces that regain the power of the oral, or sanction the unutterable by using the pictorial.

We will come to see that this movement leads to the interstitial space between arts, eras, world identities, where the writer invites us to examine the schisms in each genre in order to open out onto the heterogeneous, the errancy,[3] by becoming a nomad and escaping from any single interpretation that might immobilize the work. It puts demarcations into question, inciting us to trace new ways while encouraging us to go back to the knowledge developed through the centuries and to assemble the scattered fragments that, according to Toni Maraini, constitute "our vast patrimony." They seem like mysteries and demand that we find their function and significance once again in order to determine their meaning.

In her book *Journeys through the French African Novel,* Mildred Mortimer noted the importance of establishing the links between the Maghreb and sub-Saharan Africa and expressed the wish that they be more closely analyzed: "The purpose of juxtaposing Maghrebian and sub-Saharan fiction in four of the six chapters of this book is to disclose affinities between texts. While I do not attempt in-depth contrastive analyses in this study, I hope that my initial efforts will encourage critics to explore a neglected path" (14). Her analysis is based on many texts from the colonial period, while the geographic connections are founded on intersecting themes and on the writers' use of orality. This study continues the same approach, although it primarily examines authors of the next generation, who, by following the trails, interweave the arts and bring together knowledge and practices that extend well beyond any borders.

Even if the links between north and south of the Sahara are still being challenged or barely taken into account, there are ever more studies being done to tackle the problem and more institutions looking into these questions as well. The theoretical writing of Édouard Glissant, influenced by the views of Deleuze and Guattari, and the work of Abdelkébir Khatibi and Abdelwahab Meddeb are essential for grounding this problematic. On the other hand, in the Maghreb, research on slavery is beginning to respond to some interrogatives and has forced governments to make documents available that have long been kept under lock and key. By illuminating this past, the contributions of sub-Saharan Africa to the Maghreb will certainly be further developed, and consequently the interlacings will be discussed more frequently. But it is undeniable that numerous (critical as well as literary) African works and styles (those of griots or artists) continue to be dismissed or poorly distributed, obstructing the issue of wide flows of movement that still remain covered and underground.

PART ONE

Circulatory Movement and Flow

1 Circulatory Flow between Maghreb and Sub-Saharan Africa

Geographic, Historical, and Artistic Links

The commonly applied division separating the Maghreb from sub-Saharan Africa causes innumerable problems, since it denies the diverse intertwinings and influences, not only political, cultural, and religious but linguistic and aesthetic as well, that exist between the two areas. The Algerian writers Kateb Yacine and Nabile Farès refer to sub-Saharan aspects in their work. Hampâté Bâ, the Malian writer whose texts are infused with Sufism, a mystical branch of Islam, and Cheikh Hamidou Kane, a Fulani from Senegal, present themes that are quite similar to those of authors from the Maghreb. The Moroccan poet Abdellatif Laâbi uses images drawn from sub-Saharan Africa, while the painter Farid Belkahia, also from Morocco, is interested in the music of the Gnawa, descendants of former sub-Saharan slaves, and incorporates techniques that come from black Africa as well. Thus the juxtapositions and shifting that the continent has known result in a communication of thought on which the arts and literature build. On this subject let us quote the writer Édouard Glissant, from Martinique:

> For the question, indeed, is this: the sublime and deadly notion that the peoples of Europe and the cultures of the West have exported throughout the world, namely that every identity is an identity with its own unique root, wholly separate from the next. This view of identity contradicts today's "real" idea of identity, in heterogeneous cultures, as a factor and result of creolization, that is to say identity as a rhizome, identity no longer as a unique root but as a root moving toward other roots. (*Introduction à une poétique du divers,*[1] 23)

This phenomenon has been around for a very long time. It has allowed populations to mix, to develop, to survive, while at the same time delineating the special features that are theirs alone.

The African continent consists of more than fifty states that were born in the course of the twentieth century and of approximately one thousand languages[2] grouped together under a few categories. The criterion of language does not define a writer in terms of culture and even less of country. For practical reasons we speak of French, Indian, Chinese, or francophone African literature, but these are deceptive labels giving rather little insight into the work, even harmful to it at times, and provoking any number of preconceptions that do almost nothing to elucidate the text. We speak of English literature and recognize the fact that it differs from American literature. But here, too, we run into problems, since some authors place themselves between several cultures.

In most African countries more than a few languages are spoken, hundreds even (in the Democratic Republic of Congo alone there are more than three hundred). The creation of states brings together many ethnicities whose cultural differences are often great. Consequently, the choice of a language and its use are essential. They demonstrate an act that is marked both by the fervent desire to share thoughts within a community and by the pain that any choice in a multilingual context causes. We are familiar with the position of the writer Ngugi wa Thiong'o, originally from Kenya and now living in the United States, who stopped writing in English in favor of Kikuyu in order to facilitate his people's access to his texts. However, few among the population are accustomed to reading literary works. Nevertheless, this decision is above all a political and cultural act inducing a profound change that can only be evaluated with time.

Salman Rushdie, in his *Imaginary Homelands,* declares himself against the creation and preposterous use of certain terms that marginalize writers. He is opposed to the expression "Commonwealth literature," which tries to consolidate work written in English by Pakistani, Australian, Caribbean, and Canadian writers. This approach puts authors who are not English on the periphery and gives rise to the vaguest of definitions. Arguing that literary barriers cannot be set up according to linguistic or national criteria, Rushdie goes on to say:

> One of the most absurd aspects of this quest for national authenticity is that—as far as India is concerned, anyway—it is completely fallacious

> to suppose that there is such a thing as a pure, unalloyed tradition from which to draw. [. . .] Eclecticism, the ability to take from the world what seems fitting and to leave the rest, has always been a hallmark of the Indian tradition, and today it is at the centre of the best work being done both in the visual arts and in literature. (67)

The label "francophone literature" raises just as many problems for which no solutions have yet been found, and it produces serious inconsistencies that Roger Little points to, for example, in his article "'La francographie': A New Model for la 'francophonie'":[3]

> Simenon and Cohen on the other hand appear to be deemed worthy of entering the French canon, just as from earlier times Rousseau and Constant have been thoroughly absorbed. Why should this not be true of Depestre and Dib, of Sembene or Senghor, to say nothing of Marie Ndiaye? And what of writers from the *départements d'outre-mer?* Politically, they are French, but in literature they are Francophone. As to *Beur* writers, they are set apart, neither French nor Francophone. In short, the absurdity of such a crude categorization suggests strongly that it should be abandoned or, at the very least, considerably refined. (32)

Referring in an article to Khatibi's reflections in his work *Figures de l'étranger dans la littérature française,* Réda Bensmaïa also brings up the problematics of definitions differentiating texts that circulate beyond borders:

> For a long time we have been accustomed to thinking of literature in ethnic, national and, obviously, linguistic terms. [. . .] If writing in French links a writer to a linguistic "community," this does not necessarily subordinate him to an ethnic or national community. This is the position that led Khatibi to formulate some unsettling questions, which he posed in "Nationalisme et internationalisme littéraires." I quote: "What is the writer's homeland? Is it solely his language, the hospitality of his writing language, whether that be native or not? Is it the ideal unity between a land, a language, and a culturing [*sic*] identity of mind and body? Is it the mosaic of exile and of a universal trans-nation?"
>
> As the text from which I have taken this quotation clearly shows, for Khatibi the "homeland" of a writer does not reflect a given soil, land or culture, but rather a certain *circulation*—a migration even—between lands, between languages and cultures. ("Géographie politique de la littérature," 114)

These positions proceed from the thoughts of Gilles Deleuze and Félix Guattari on minor literature. It was also they who coined the term "rhizome," taken up by Glissant, to describe its multiple roots: "The three characteristics of minor literature are the deterritorialization of language, the connection of the individual to a political immediacy, and the collective assemblage of enunciation" (Deleuze and Guattari, *Kafka,* 18). The question of deterritorializing is crucial, for it places the writer in the space of circulatory flow. On the other hand, as we shall see in the next chapter, this literature is often linked to the political.

We are experiencing a period of displacements, of globalization in which human beings migrate, for personal, political, or economic reasons, thereby accumulating a variety of perspectives and participating in the porosity of boundaries. In addition, the writer is made to face the necessity of favoring one language, a decision that is not always motivated by choice but rather by a given situation. In many countries colonized by Europe, a foreign language was grafted onto the mother tongue, not a written language, and thus was substituted for the dialect. Consequently, the use of a language is hardly illustrative of cultural specificity, since those who live at the crossroads of cultures are many and languages travel beyond borders. However, the danger Ngugi wa Thiong'o encountered is to have submitted to the use of a dominant language, like English, that carries with it an entire way of life, an approach to the world, and pursues the practice of colonization—certainly not to be minimized—thus forcing other cultures to gradually disappear, as much by enacting the laws of "globalization" as by promulgating literary, pictorial, cinematographic, and social values.

> The defense of languages assuring Diversity is thus inseparable from restabilizing relations among communities. How is it possible to come out of seclusion if only two or three languages continue to monopolize the irrefutable powers of technology [. . .]? This dominant behavior blocks the flowering of imaginations, forbids one to be inspired by them [. . .]. (Glissant, *Poetics of Relation,* 108)

Glissant develops a perspective that lies anchored in the Caribbean context, but that corresponds to the present situation in the world, as he mentions in his writing.

> In my opinion, we make an error every time we expressly link the problem of language to the problem of identity, because what characterizes our

> time is precisely what I call the imagination of languages, that is to say the being present to all the languages of the world. [. . .] All writing used to be monolingual. Today, even when a writer does not know any other language, in the process of his writing he takes the existence of the languages around him into account, whether he knows it or not. (*Introduction à une poétique du divers,* 112)

He implies that when a language vanishes, the whole earth loses an irreplaceable element. An indispensable link vanishes, a process that was elaborated at length—the tool of an entire community. Its disappearance threatens the planetary balance, which in order to endure should see a diversity and variety of languages coexist so that even in imperceptible ways the many forms of knowledge, developed across the centuries, can be in touch with each other.

Thus, in order to provide a presence for languages that are unknown or cast aside, some authors choose to write in their dialect or mother tongue, others insert particularities of their language into the adopted language, and still others strive for innuendos, reversals, silences, and detours, thereby fragmenting their stories.

Surprising differences exist throughout Africa, shaped by a wide range of customs, processes, and philosophies. But the usual division Maghreb–sub-Saharan Africa[4] conceals the important share that black Africa has in Morocco, in Algeria or in Tunisia, and thereby participates in the obliteration of a complex contribution. On the other hand, it denies the movement of thought, art, and signs across the entire continent. Abiola Irele mentions the danger of erecting such barriers that do not correspond to the situation and obliterate the complexity of the context:

> [A]part from the relationship that is already postulated between the oral and the modern literature, there is also the problem posed of drawing firm lines between the various areas of the written literature: that written in the various African languages, as distinguished from that in the European languages, that of black Africa as distinguished from North Africa, or the settler communities; and even within the narrow area of black Africa, that of the important distinctions that could be made between the emerging national literatures and the connections within them between the oral tradition, and between the written literature in the indigenous languages and the new literature expressed in the European languages. (*The African Experience in Literature and Ideology,* 10–11)

Boundaries are useful and allow for working inside a setting that offers a certain structure and facilitates access to the texts. But this process that slices Africa in two conceals the extraordinary combinations that have been created over the centuries. Either we would then have to consider every community or every country as one entity—and there we run into the artificial boundaries drawn when Europe was dividing up Africa—or we must view the totality of the continent as in constant flux. In his writings, Elikia M'Bokolo reminds us of the difficulties that division creates:

> North Africa comprises some ten States. [. . .] In the first place it involves the very strong awareness of belonging to the Arab world, even if that awareness is not the precise reflection of racial and cultural realities, for each of these States has, besides the Arab component, elements of Berber and black origins. Then it has to do with being part of the Muslim community: having provided the leaven for the resistance to colonial domination, Islam appears since the time of independence as the inspiration for innovative political experiments. According to the authors, the Sahel-Sudan states were attached to West, Central or North-Eastern Africa. Each one of these couplings is debatable, for these states do not belong to any one of these zones exclusively. The Sahara, which is an important part of their territory, has never been an insurmountable obstacle, neither for people nor for ideas. (*L'Afrique au XXe siècle,* 53)

The intersections are considerable and onerous, giving rise to forms of resistance, injury, and repression. Some displacements are the result of migrations to escape from bad weather, drought, and famine. Others flow from religious and colonial conquests. Still others stem from traffic in slaves, practiced for centuries along the roads of the Sahara as far as the Middle East, India, and Europe. Displacements were many, and the populations that were moved, voluntarily or against their will, put the mark of their practices, their cultures, and their languages on the new location:

> In Tunisia, as elsewhere in the Maghreb, communities of Blacks were established that began with the descendants of former slaves from sub-Saharan Africa. Following the example of mystic brotherhoods, these communities founded ethno-religious congregations and put themselves under the patronage of *Sidi Bilal,* an emblematic figure in the Muslim tradition. [. . .] Bilal worship, which in Tunisia is known as *Stambali* or *Bori,* in Algeria as *Diwan,* and in Morocco as *Derdeba,* gradually adapted

itself to the system of performances and to the magic-religious practices that characterize popular Sufism in the Maghreb. [. . .] Nevertheless, it preserves the characteristics and principles of African religiosity whose most representative aspects are related to the worship of spirits. (Rahal, *La communauté noire de Tunis* [The black community of Tunis], 9)

For a long time the Sahara has been a place of intense exchanges where over the centuries various populations have come in contact. A thematic issue of *Autrepart* brings together articles attesting to the countless activities that existed throughout the Sahara "even before the Roman era" (Grégoire and Schmitz, "Afrique noire et monde arabe" [Black Africa and the Arab world], 6). They mention the numerous commercial exchanges that allowed goods to flow (the Maghreb provided fabrics, leather, perfumes, spices; sub-Saharan Africa brought ostrich feathers, ivory, gold, and slaves). Merchants followed the caravan routes, along which various alliances were made in order to confirm the movements and the transportation of the merchandise. Later on, with the spread of Islam, pilgrimage routes to Mecca were laid out going across the Sahara and linking Senegal with Egypt. More recently, and at the risk of losing their lives, Senegalese, Malians, and inhabitants of Burkina Faso and Niger have been trekking through the desert to find work, often only temporary, in the Maghreb.

The studies in this issue of *Autrepart* clearly show that a great many such activities took place, and persist today, despite the Sahara's inhospitable features. Even if the exchanges diminished during colonialism and the partition of Africa—"trans-Saharan commerce suffered from the creation of these new political entities demarcated by arbitrarily traced frontiers" (ibid., 8)—the Sahara remains a vast region in which large numbers of exchanges are made that violate the restrictions decreed by the states among which it is divided. Thus displacements brought the Maghreb and black Africa closely together. For example, one can find Moroccan practices in Senegalese culture in many areas, from cooking, where dishes borrow flavors that are then transformed; to the way tea is prepared, creating an atmosphere where people can exchange ideas; to the use of henna on the body and the wearing of the *djellaba, babouches,* or fez.

The proliferation of Islam in West and East Africa saw the birth of Sufi brotherhoods, which established many connections between places. In 1964 King Hassan II of Morocco had the Grand Mosque built in Dakar, where he sent his architects, thereby prolonging a longtime relationship between Moroccan and Senegalese brotherhoods, including the one created by Sidi Ahmed Tidjani, who is buried in Fez and was the founder of the Tidjani *Tariqa,* which has had powerful ramifications beyond the Maghreb. Parallel to these processes of conversion and religious tendencies, so-called Animist beliefs were preserved in the Maghreb, Islam notwithstanding, and have survived in daily practices. Across Africa the prevailing role of diviners, talismans, signs, and motifs on the body continues. Thus, procedures became mixed, and nomadic populations living between regions transported various forms of knowledge.

> Where Morocco is concerned, it seems important to remember the Afro-Saharan esthetic traditions (still not well known) that precede Islam and, therefore, the relationship geometry/abstraction and the symbolic/icon image that Islamic art incorporated in its own grandiose vision and that until very recently were perpetuated by the popular and rural arts in their regional artistic production. (Maraini, *Écrits sur l'art* [Writings on art], 11)

Furthermore, not only have some researchers shown that writing systems have existed there for a very long time, in contrast to the colonial position that claimed it was bringing a previously nonexistent asset to the continent, but they have also found similarities between signs used by populations that the West thought were separated by the immensity of the desert.

> Lebeuf (1965), challenging the idea that writing does not exist in Black Africa, points out the presence of systematic metaphysical thinking among the Dogon, the Fali, etc. and shows that such systems also exist among certain North African Berbers. He thus clips the wings of the other contemporary prejudice which separates North Africa from Black Africa culturally, denies "vernacular" cultures a world vision and an African contribution to humanity, and ignores its writing systems: Could this be the beginning of a new type of relation? (Battestini, *African Writing and Text,* 95)

At the time of the Muslim conquest, the use of Arabic writing became widespread and was used to transcribe African languages. To a great extent this propagation of Islam is due to the Tuareg, who were in control of the commercial routes across the Sahara. During Musa's reign (1312–37), Timbuktu became a center of Islamic knowledge, of flourishing commercial exchange, and attracted thinkers from the Near East, the Maghreb, Egypt, and sub-Saharan Africa. It was a crossroads of thought that encouraged a multitude of viewpoints:

> Thus, Fes seemed to have a certain cultural influence over Timbuktu during the reign of the Songhai Empire. The learned went there to complete their education in *fiqh* and *malekite* law, theology and grammar. The Timbuktu *medersa* were modeled after those of Morocco. [. . .] During his stay in Morocco, Ahmed Bâba contributed to the culture of Islam in the Maghreb. The cultural relationships between Morocco and Sudan then developed at the same rate as the political and economic changes that marked the region. (El-Moujahid, "Le Maroc et l'Afrique," 52)

In a work on the arts and crafts of Senegal, Abdou Sylla mentions the same phenomenon when describing the connections made throughout the years:

> Having left for Mecca in 1324, accompanied by a large escort of scholars, friends and relatives, of 10,000 soldiers and 500 slaves, Kankan Moussa returned with Arab architects, poets, and experts and initiated a policy of cooperation with the Arabic countries, especially with Egypt and the Middle-East. It was during this period that the intellectual influence of famous cities began, such as Timbuktu, Walara, Djenne, Gao, and Mopti, for instance. Between 1396 and 1397 Askia Mohamed, too, made the pilgrimage to Islam's holy places and upon his return developed a brilliant and original Islamic civilization, whose principal centers were Timbuktu and Djenne, spurred on by scholars such as Ahmed Baba, Gao Zaccaria, Ahmed Ben Omar, Mahmoud Kali, etc.
>
> Then, between 1890 and 1920, Arab-Berber merchants from the Maghreb first, followed by well-educated Senegalese Muslims and marabous, introduced painting on glass to the country [. . .]. (*L'artisanat sénégalais* [Senegalese artisans], 52)

With regard to the written word and languages, two phenomena appear: in West Africa a large number of languages, such as Fulani, Hausa, and Wolof, use Arabic script to transcribe information and ideas. The name of this practice is *Ajami.* In East Africa a new language emerges—Swahili—which is a combination of languages, corresponding to intercultural cross-fertilization and borrowing Arabic characters for the written word.

These cross-fertilizations had profound consequences, interweaving traditions, religions, and philosophies. Ideas came together, creating a mosaic of structures. Mnemonic techniques, the use and dissemination of signs, orality, musical methods, rhythms, and the invention of instruments circulated, even if each community preserved its own particular characteristics. Borrowing and exchanging enable humans to interact, allowing them to be perfected and deepened. One finds characters in tales, accounts, and masquerades that testify to these amalgams.

Later, North Africa and black Africa were sometimes subjected to identical forms of colonization, to which was added a military, judicial, economic, and cultural system. Colonial procedures differed from country to country. Still, similar procedures were put in place, such as the propagation of a European language and the establishment of an institutional and bureaucratic system that confronted the colonized peoples with new organizational forms that frequently caused rifts, such as the introduction of European school systems to replace traditional schools.

Then resistance movements sprouted, which sometimes unified the entire African continent—Nasser's Pan-African project, Fanon's demands, and Senghor's assertions. In many texts collected after his death in a book entitled *Toward the African Revolution,* Frantz Fanon stressed the importance of a union between African countries in order to fight French colonial oppression more assertively. The objective of this political strategy was the consolidation of the continent in order to get rid of a common enemy and to take advantage of France's destabilization caused by the Algerian War.

The Algerian revolution provided a valuable model for action, motivating the demand for independence across Africa. Having led to the elimination of French occupation, it expedited the process of decolonization. At a meeting in Accra under the aegis of Kwame Nkrumah, Fanon remarked that the bonds were extensive:

> The meeting in Accra brought together the political and trade union organizations of the African continent. Their common ideology was a national will opposed to foreign domination: their tactic, to weaken the colonizers one after another; their strategy, to frustrate the oppressor's maneuvers and attempts at camouflage.
>
> What struck the observer at Accra was the existence at the most spontaneous level of a solidarity that is organic, even biological. (*Toward the African Revolution,* 153–54)

In 1960 Fanon proposed circumventing the Tunisian and Moroccan frontiers, which were under strict French surveillance, in order to provide the FLN with supplies via Mali. For it was by supporting the Algerian revolution and by ensuring its success that Africa would be able to liberate itself:

> We are off. Our mission: to open the southern front. To transport arms and munitions from Bamako. Stir up the Saharan population, infiltrate to

> the Algerian high plateaus. After carrying Algeria to the four corners of Africa, move up with all Africa toward African Algeria, toward the North, toward Algiers, the continental city. What I should like: great lines, great navigation channels through the desert. Subdue the desert, deny it, assemble Africa, create the continent. (Ibid., 180–81)

The objective of Pan-Africanism as conceived by Nkrumah is similar: consolidating the African countries in order to solve comparable concerns and solidify links that would facilitate self-determination, thereby reducing Western intervention.

Nkwame Appiah, a philosopher and critic, still sees the strength of Pan-Africanism not in eradicating the continent's enormous differences but in building a network of financial, technical, and rural cooperation:

> We [the African people] share a continent and its ecological problems; we share a relation of dependency to the world economy; we share the problem of racism in the way the industrialized world thinks of us (and let me include here, explicitly, both "Negro" Africa and the "Maghrib"); we share the possibilities of the development of regional markets and local circuits of production; and our intellectuals participate, through the shared contingencies of our various histories, in a common discourse whose outlines I have tried to limn in this book. (*In my Father's House,* 180)

Contacts of a geographical, economic, and political nature have given birth to innumerable forms of cultural, social, and philosophical interlacing, which in turn invent new systems, adapting them to present needs and blurring their origins. In their work, artists are causing many signs and influences to reemerge, expressing temporal and thematic combinations, concerns that are modified according to events and changes.

As Glissant suggests, "The interrelationships emanate mainly through fractures and ruptures. Perhaps it is even their nature to be fractal: that is why our world is a chaos-world" (*Traité du tout-monde,* 24). Thus, in the period of independence, "francophone" African writers of the Maghreb and of sub-Saharan Africa intertwine the arts and fragment their writing. Sometimes similar historic events leave their imprint on these writers, as do exile, multilingualism, and the encounter of different (at times opposing) ideas. Often they have had a French education that has stood in juxtaposition to their own culture, they write in French, and they direct themselves to the same audience. In some cases, they invoke gaps that are the site of both a creative gesture and a metaphysical flight, a space interrogating the past, thereby removing themselves from the pitfalls of history and language—a trick the writer uses and which calls on other arts via the unspoken and enriches the poetic with the visual, connecting African and European concepts, mixing traditions, eras, and approaches, all the while bringing to the work a unique vision.

In a play entitled *Un Touareg s'est marié à une Pygmée* (A Tuareg married a Pygmy) (1992), Werewere Liking describes the itinerary of a Tuareg named Firoun in the heart of the continent—the staging of a Pan-African project—where he meets and marries Ngolobanza, a Pygmy woman. The text emphasizes the importance of creating connections across Africa in order to find a new equilibrium. Through her knowledge and her ability to find water, Ngolobanza will bring a vital element to the Sahara. In her novel *Orphée-Dafric,* Liking interweaves Greek and Egyptian myths with references to Orpheus, the musician, and Thot, the god of writing, master of transformation.

As he goes through the Musée des Arts d'Afrique et d'Océanie, the protagonist in the novel *Phantasia,* by the Tunisian writer Abdelwahab Meddeb, ponders his relationships and his feelings when faced with African objects, identifying himself with sub-Saharan ideas:

> African statuary affirms the primitive in me. It will have been rediscovered by my eyes, which prefer that art not represent feelings or ideas according to principles of reason and moderation, but that it appear in profusion, in cries and pain, captured on the other side of madness where you die before dying, whence you return overwhelmed by the millennia, your voice changed, strangely calm, marked by the end of organic constraint. (152)

In a veiled way, the text also evokes the black community's rites and procedures as they—descendants of former slaves from sub-Saharan Africa—perpetuate Bilal worship:

> The brotherhood has three groups of musician-healers that lead the ritual ceremonies. These groups intervene in the process of healing upon the request of families when one of their members has been affected by black genies. Each group has one or several *arifa* (seer), a *maâllem* (a *gumbri* player) and two or three *chkachki* (rattle players). (Rahal, *La communauté noire de Tunis,* 28)

Trance, which allows an individual to abandon consciousness and connect with the sacred, is an important practice of the brotherhood. The dream scene in *Phantasia* mentions the instruments that are used during the rite of possession and the dances that end in the trance: "A frenetic dance shakes the kingdom of the djinns, who wave their arms and legs around in a disorderly fashion. A couple of black djinns strike rattlesnakes of steel and Basque drums" (74).

In a dialogue published in the catalogue of the exhibition *Rencontres africaines* (African encounters), Abdelwahab Meddeb states that such practices circulate and enrich the Maghreb:

> In his Maghreb presence, the black person is a being who remains marked by exile. This exile is expressed in song, in music, and on the stage where the trance takes place. It is probably the major contribution of the black person to Maghreb scenography: this dance, this song, this music, this cosmogony, this therapy through trance they call *gnawa* (Guineans) in Morocco and *stambali* in Tunisia. It is one way of preserving the pagan, animist part within monotheistic belief. ("Dialogue," 61–62)

Blood and the theme of sacrifice are also frequently present in the work, since they are part of both the Muslim religion and the pagan rites of Stambali at the same time.

In an interview with Tahar Bekri, published in *Notre librairie,* Tchicaya U Tam'Si mentions that the separation in literary studies between the Maghreb and sub-Saharan Africa picks up on a general attitude that comes out of the "logic of apartheid": "We fight apartheid and we practice it" (Tchicaya U Tam'Si, "Dialogue Sud-Sud," 59). Later, he remarks that this split does not correspond to the reality he has known:

> Still, I had the pleasure of enjoying the excited surprise of the first Moroccan students attending the University of Rabat who had registered for a course on black African Literature. They were expecting to encounter a different world and there they were, not feeling at all on foreign soil. In Tunis I applaud a monthly journal, still in limbo, intending to be *Lettres Africaines* and open to every form of expression of the continent. One should remember that the Sahara never was a frontier. Some day, those of us who turn their backs upon each other ought to confront one another and face . . . Face what? The future of the South-South dialogue, of course. (59)

In another issue of *Notre librairie,* I. C. Tchého goes back to the bonds between Maghreb writers and Tchicaya and mentions that Tahar Djaout

> praises his ability to stay faithful to a unifying vision of multiracial Africa. Tchicaya *"refused to accept that the Sahara constituted a barrier, just as he refused to accept that the Congo River should split the land of Patrice Lumumba in two disunited regions,"* Djaout writes. (Tchého, "Échos maghrébins de Tchicaya U Tam'Si," 59)

We should mention that the review *Souffles* (1966–72), established in Morocco under the direction of Abdellatif Laâbi, was concerned with uniting the arts and politics throughout Africa around similar concerns and objectives.

The connections are endless and extend across cultures in all their forms of expression. In music, examples abound: Ray Lema, from the Democratic Republic of Congo, finds the rhythms of his country back again among the Gnawa of Morocco—descendants of former slaves from the southern Sahara who came together in brotherhoods and practice music as well as song and dance in order to end up in a trance:

> Yes, the ritual repertoire of the Gnawa is the result of a syncretic mixture of African contributions, of music from the Maghreb (Berber in particular), and of the culture of the marabou. From Islam the Gnawa have taken the popular worship of Saints such as Abdel Kader Jilali and Moulay Brahim, while preserving the supernatural beings who hold on to the unmistakable remembrance of their Sudanese origin in their names. (Barlet, "Les Gnawa, thérapeutes de la différence" [The Gnawa, therapists of difference], 16–17)

The Senegalese singer Youssou N'Dour inserts Arabic rhythms and melodies into his compositions. His album *Sant Allah,* which came out in 2003 and was recorded with the Symphony Orchestra in Cairo, draws a parallel between his Muslim religion, strongly marked by a Senegalese approach (valorizing the marabou), and Egyptian music. This project openly reflects mixtures in which traditions blend.

In painting, many Maghreb artists are inspired by black Africa or unconsciously transmit a complex knowledge that draws its roots from sub-Saharan Africa:

> A painting of signs has been mentioned. Indeed. Most often coming from pictographic iconography, signs constitute the multiform repertory "of an ancient and solemn memory, whose fragments continue to live on in the artist's spirit" as Klee wrote. African and Eastern knowledge is there to feed this *painting of recollection,* on the condition, however, that the

plenary pictorial and plastic sense defeats its "epigrammatic logic." (Maraini, *Écrits sur l'art,* 68)

Farid Belkahia, the Moroccan painter mentioned above, incorporates sub-Saharan elements in his paintings, giving the title *Trance* to some canvases or, as Maraini notes, by referring to black Africa through the choice of materials and forms of his work:

> Through a strange phenomenon of cultural correspondence, these works, arranged in hieratic compositions, almost sculpted totems/idols in a way molded in round, oval, broken or superimposed surfaces that break through the regular framework, sometimes remind us of the famous little funerary sculptures in copper, bronze, and wood, they call Kota or Mahongwe (Gabon, Congo) [. . .]. (Maraini, "Farid Belkahia," 36)

Later we read: "According to an Upper Volta tradition, the skin, the material of chaos mastered, covers the cosmic abyss and gives birth to the drum, a ritual object whose sound is supposed to be that of the vibrations of the world's creation" (36–38). And in *Écrits sur l'art,* when speaking about Ahmed Cherkaoui, a Moroccan painter (1934–67), Maraini mentions the influence of African art on his work: "From that period onward, one can note the presence of direct references to African art" (156).

In 1994 Mohammed Kacimi created a public painting entitled *La mémoire du corps* (The body's memory) on a beach in Benin in homage to the slaves. In an edited volume on the painter we find a quotation from Kacimi that claims a trajectory made of many belongings and elements: "Seeking the substance of my identity and its roots, I discovered that I belong to a many-sided and intricate tradition. My identity is upheld by this spirit of the multiple and that is how I claim it" (Briot, "Chronobiographie," 176).

Conversely, artists from black Africa use techniques that remind us of practices in the Maghreb. In Senegal, artists have been practicing painting "under" glass[5] (*sous verre*) since the nineteenth century, taking up again Islamic figures while inserting charismatic local personalities such as Cheikh Bamba. "The first Senegalese reverse-glass [*sous verre*] paintings were executed around 1900 [. . .]. The technique was already popular in central Europe and north Africa, where it was influenced by Turkish portraiture [. . .]" (Roberts and Roberts, *A Saint in the City,* 88).

Here is another example: the work of the Senegalese painter Chalys Lèye, who makes his paintings according to a *khatem.* This supposedly comes from an ancient Arabic practice also used in the Maghreb brotherhoods and which might also incorporate Chinese methods.

> In Senegal, the mystical forms and powers of letters and numbers converge in what is called a *khatem*—a loanword from Arabic that refers to mystical closure and literally means "seal," hence the calligraphic names and blessings pressed into wax as one closes a letter. *Khatem* is related to the Fulani word *hatumere,* which one also hears sometimes in Senegal and elsewhere in west Africa [. . .]. These ancient devices may have been discovered by Chinese mathematicians more than four thousand years ago and were developed by Muslim theorists [. . .]. (Ibid., 174–75)

As for the writers, they broaden this contribution in their work by using a language that draws from vast knowledge imbued with contacts and exchanges with the various elements around them, which interweave and thus grow richer. The artist inhabits many worlds, which he brings out and combines through his sensitivity and his creation. Both in his work and in interviews, the Algerian writer Kateb Yacine has mentioned the importance of black Africa to the Maghreb: "We are African. Tamazight is an African language: cooking, craftsmanship, dance, song, life style, all of it shows us that we are Africans. The Arab Maghreb, and all that, are inventions, ideology, and are created to make us turn away from Africa" (*Le poète comme un boxeur* [The poet as boxer], 109). In his novel *Le polygone étoilé* (The starry polygon), he expresses the need for an African union in order to consolidate political aims, bonds that are sometimes denied, in order to come out of the darkness:

> But we were not aware of the basic point. We could not know that the dust of the Numidians, the decadent Maghreb of the Orientalist tales, held another oracle in reverse for us, [. . .] and that old genies were awakening from this new rush, genies who had been left for dead in the nameless land, not just one nation, not two, not four, not an oilfield, not a layer of gas, but that an immense continent, all of Africa was liberating itself from North to South, making Algeria its springboard, its home, its tenet, its Maghreb star, in order to get through the night [. . .]. (141–42)

In his writing, we find animal metaphors (lion, rooster, baboon, toad) that remind us of the tales and proverbs of black Africa, as well as such names as "Hospital Face," "No Luck," "Bad Weather" to designate a character—a widespread device in sub-Saharan Africa whose function is to fend off bad luck or to direct an individual's destiny.[6] The presence of the black protagonist, through his almost silent appearances, inscribes a mystery in the web and indirectly evokes history. The fragmented text gathers together disparate elements, events, and influences, bringing them in touch with each other. Moreover, Nedjma, the central character of the novel, symbolizes intertwining. Abandoned by her mother, a French woman, and by her presumed father Si Mokhtar, an Algerian, she represents heterogeneity, which according to the text goes beyond these specific origins to incarnate the enigma, a liberty, and a fascinating beauty:

> You knew Nedjma without knowing her, since from secondary school on she had escaped from more than one clan, more than one caste that would have liked to make her into its brood mare. [. . .] and in the end brandish her as a challenge to the superior race, which would snigger and always respond with the same arguments: "Of course, quite a marvel, the result of who knows what mixtures [. . .]." (*Le polygone étoilé,* 152)

Her origins and facets are many:

> Wild?
> Yes
> Her native blackness had reappeared
> Her face hard smooth and sharp (148)

And it is a black man who gains possession of her, in Nadhor, where Mokhtar had brought her back, back to her birthplace.

Kateb Yacine fragments his writing as he inscribes the history that has shaken Algeria. He shows the need for Africa to unite in order to strive for common aspirations. And the central figure, Nedjma—a polygon—through her partially unknown origins symbolizes a force that dismantles frontiers.

In an article entitled "Kateb Yacine et le monde noir" (Kateb Yacine and the black world), Tchého analyzes the issue of the figure of the black individual in the writer's work. He notes that in the novel *Nedjma,* the black person possesses both stereotypical attitudes circulating in the Maghreb and superhuman qualities that cannot be renounced:

> [. . .] after reminding Nedjma that he is no longer a slave, he confirms with great assurance that all the Keblouti "have come forth from the same tree / Beginning with myself the avenging black man / The slave freed in spite of you in spite of me." (87–88)

A little later, Tchého continues with the following observation:

> Thus, in Kateb, dynamic thought is reconstructed in the deconstruction of fragments of the black people's myths. From this a whole new modern mythology is created that is above all anti-establishment and, at any rate, relies on new political and other parameters in today's North African space. (89)

What filters through these words is the presence and importance of the black person in Kateb Yacine's writing, which refers first of all to his role in the Maghreb—a role that cannot be reduced to clichés, since the author instantly transgresses them, which grants him an irrefutable power. Tchého also suggests conceiving of a rift between this character and Islam, since he incorporates ancient pre-Islamic practices to which Kateb Yacine, of Berber origin, was quite attached. Thus his presence fulfills several functions. He provides mystery, while at the same time, recalling historic data and pointing out that he is part of the Maghrebian identity.

There are many intertwinings throughout Africa. They pick up themes, while varying them and making them into new contributions for the reasons mentioned earlier. Tchicaya U Tam'Si calls on nature, on the animal world, to reinforce the malevolent atmosphere that spreads and eats away at the existence of the protagonists. For instance, toads begin to roar as a reflection of the strange anxiety that has spread: "He was getting up when the choir of frogs and toads burst into their song and the dogs started howling, here, there, everywhere!" (*The Madman and the Medusa,* 149). In *L'exproprié,* the Algerian Tahar Djaout uses similar images: "Then the toads had a second wind; they started to laugh noisily, to rant against the sun once more" (131). These similarities show that either the authors are drawing from an imagination imbued with matching elements, tales, or philosophies, or they are influencing one another. They certainly have common concerns, but it is striking to note the sometimes intersecting approaches they use. Djaout's *L'exproprié* shows a cruel, bloody world, orgiastic desire, and grotesque reversals (thereby distancing him from the work of Tchicaya U Tam'Si), which remind us of the work of another Congolese writer, Sony Labou Tansi, whose writing is filled with death, excesses, and violence that lead to a profound rift.

In his collection *Les songes impatients* (Impatient dreams), written between 1992 and 1995 in several different places—Paris, Copenhagen, Tunis, Dakar, Boston—the Tunisian poet Tahar Bekri weaves Africa together.

Throughout the poem "Book One" we find allusions to the slave trade and the displacements that were its result:

> The colors of the earth come back,
> the black ancestor would nourish the rings
> beneath the eyes like a rebus, caravans
> would display gold on the fabric of dreams
> at oblivion's edge. (31)

In his novel *Mémoire de l'absent* (Memory of the absent one), Nabile Farès retraces the threads that make up the web of collective Algerian memory. The narrator turns away from the prejudices that lie anchored in society, among which is the importance given to genealogy, which, according to him, sets up an illusion and condemns the deletions that mask history. He reports the importance of influences originating in the south, in sub-Saharan Africa, as a result of slavery. "The absent one" in the title of his work refers to everything that has been denied and repressed and that, in spite of the refusal to recognize it, is made up of basic elements found in culture and humanity.

> The Black child?
> He who lives there, sitting beneath us, and coloring our skin.
> The Black Child?
>
> A few words are coming from the land of the South.
> From the frontiers of the land of the South. (68)

The text restores the influences underlying the culture and upon which it developed, creating social and linguistic *métissages* that have renewed, crossed, enriched, and given new life to the foundation of the culture.

> In school, they do not teach mixing.
> No. They build above it. In an idiotic way, as if nothing mattered. As if nothing existed. As if the mix were not important.
> Mistake. The mix exists.
> It is what cultivates the world. Gives life to the world. (79–80)

According to Farès's text, in rejecting combinations, the human being denies part of himself and, prisoner of an illusion, shuts himself off from the world.

why is the slave
white?
Because he denies
the Black child?
Would that then
be the end
of the mystery? (73)

Nabile Farès supports the contribution of interlacing in various ways. In his text, through the use of fragmentation, he interweaves disparate elements, going back to many sources of his imagination, pursuing—as will be discussed in chapter 4—cave art, drawings, in order to state what words cannot manage to translate. He invokes patterns that join writing at its beginning and takes up elements that originate in distant places. Thus, he dismantles the rifts between the Maghreb and black Africa and links other forms of art to the text.

The writer Pius Ngandu Nkashama of the Democratic Republic of Congo (formerly Zaire), taught for several years at the University of Annaba in Algeria before settling in France. In his novel *Des mangroves en terre haute* (Of mangroves on the highlands), published in 1991, he is inspired by the Arabic poem *Majnun and Layla,* which goes back to the theme of eternal love. He blends numerous characteristics of the Maghreb and of sub-Saharan Africa, blurring spaces. Descriptions of landscapes and customs place the story beyond a single country or region, frustrating the reader's expectations. Elements of black Africa such as the mangroves (as in the novel's title), "the calabash" (9), "huts" (10), "sorghum" (65), and "the bush" (72) are interwoven with names, places, or vegetation of the Maghreb: "Nadhor" (20), "dried up wadis" (20), "olive groves" (23), and so forth. Ngandu Nkashama clarifies his objectives in the text itself:

> Your fingers curled around the knots of the weaving. Ropes and twists of dried straw are tangled to make the threads into a solid fabric. Thus the words that produced the universe were woven, arranging it into high land and low marsh grounds. Lianas would lengthen and diffuse the light, diffracted since the language of the first Creator. We are born from the work of weaving, Aneidia. (26)

The writer follows the weaver's model. He interweaves what is practical (ropes and lianas) to make them into a work of art and to create an open space that receives the many roots. He reconnects the continent by bringing together languages (several African languages appear in the text), practices, and a variety of places.

The volume *Faces of Islam in African Literature,* edited by Kenneth Harrow, brings together various articles dealing with the influences of Islam and Sufi practices on the literatures of sub-Saharan Africa. What appears repeatedly in this book is the presence of a syncretism in which Animist and Muslim traditions are closely intertwined. Denise Asfar shows that *Kaïdara,* the Peul initiation tale as retold by Hampâté Bâ, reveals close links between the Fulani tradition and Sufi concepts through the use of symbolism (stages in a quest, significance of numbers, etc.). "The quest tales of Fulani initiation provide strong evidence of the confluence of Islam and traditional African religion" (Asfar, "Kaïdara," 153). For example, she observes that the three-part story reproduces the stages of Sufi initiation, based on the position of Hampâté Bâ himself, who sees a continuous thread between Animist tradition and Islam:

> This savanna country [Mali] is a country of Bambara, Peul, Dogon, and Malinke traditions, some of which gave birth to great empires in the past, before their encounter and sometimes their fusion with Islam produced the appearance of a new kind of traditional behavior toward God, more as a prolongation, however, than as an opposition to what preceded [. . .]. (Bâ, *Aspects de la civilisation africaine,* 113–14)

Again in *Vie et enseignement de Tierno Bokar* (The life and teaching of Tierno Bokar), Bâ describes how the great Sufi master refers to Peul tales when explaining the Koran:

> In Tierno's home the most beautiful story in the world was told, the story of creation and how man came into being. [. . .] He would speak of God and relay His Word in an interminable conversation, embellished with images, rich in examples from Peul tradition or other local traditions [. . .]. (41)

In this work he also mentions the influence of the Maghreb *zaouïas* (Sufi gathering places) on sub-Saharan Africa:

> We know that the Tidjaniya, a brotherhood born in Algeria within the purest of Sufi traditions, had penetrated the black world from three directions: one came directly from the north, moving down from Algeria

> toward Sudan and Timbuktu; the other came from the west by the Senegal River; and the third came from the east with El Hadj Omar who brought it back from Mecca. (55)

Also in *Faces of Islam in African Literature,* Eric Sellin pursues these ideas by referring to the article "L'Islam 'noir' ou les preuves d'une grande tolérance," published in the Moroccan magazine *Matin du Sahara* (April 1989, 16–23), which states:

> Indeed, Islam does not reject a certain syncretism. It is not opposed to animism. It compromises with it. Animism and Islam frequently live within the same individual. Islam imposes rites that Animism often and easily integrates (ritual animal sacrifice, circumcision, prayer gestures, etc.). (Sellin, "Islamic Elements in Camara Laye's *L'enfant noir,*" 235)

In this light Sellin analyzes Camara Laye's *L'enfant noir,* clarifying elements that come from different sources. In his article, Thomas Hale studies the *Tarikh el-Fattâch,* chronicles from Mali, which give an account of the exploits of Askia Mohammed and his desire to spread the Muslim faith. Hale comments, however, that some versions, especially oral ones, insert concepts of traditional Songhai cosmogony. Although he does not deny that tensions arise when sometimes irreconcilable thought systems are juxtaposed, Hale emphasizes those segments that produce combinations and, while obscuring the text, also create its depth.

Whereas Islam may be described by some writers (Sembene Ousmane, Yambo Ouologuem, Birago Diop in some of his tales) as a form of excessive constraint, according to Mbye Cham's article in *Faces of Islam,* others express a harmonious coexistence between practices, which comes both from the ability to adapt and from the tolerance these cultures[7] practice.

In literature, transcription of the interweaving between the Maghreb and sub-Saharan Africa obviously does not show up only in "francophone" African works. It appears in many texts written in various languages used across the continent. Tayeb Salih, a Sudanese who writes in Arabic, transcribes the Arab-Black experience (Abdelwahab Meddeb discusses this briefly in an interview in the journal *Africultures* 13, entitled "L'Africanité du Maghreb"). In *Saison de la migration vers le Nord* (Season of migration to the north), the theme of intermixing and interlacing appears in manifold ways throughout the text. It is first invoked by the narrator and by the protagonist Moustafa Saïd, both of whom have studied and traveled abroad. Then it is mentioned in tackling the descriptions that situate the narrative in a Sudanese context crisscrossed by multiple procedures: ancient practices (excision, slavery, patriarchy), the importance of Islam (prayers, recitations, and gestures linked to it), colonization (as well as the systems that derive from it). Finally, the blendings show through in the discursive structure, which combines several genres—poetic, epistolary, narrative—and inserts poetry fragments (coming from an unknown Englishman, from Abu Nuwas) and sayings.

The narrative development shows the village is fossilized. The customs destroy Hasna Bint Mahmoud and bring her to commit suicide—her father having forced her, after the death of her husband Moustafa Saïd, to marry a man some forty years older than she. Still, a poorly handled exposure to the world also leads to death. Moustafa Saïd, who has traveled far and wide, cannot cope with his experiences and seems to have put an end to his life in spite of the stability he acquired. Thus, the text advocates the position of the narrator, who was better able to grasp his various experiences and to counter alienating customs.

Numerous literary texts build on influences, borrowings, exchanges, and displacements, reflecting a complex cultural and historical situation in which methods and experiments have intermingled. They motivate the imagination and, drawing from this broad expanse of knowledge, the author is inspired to create in turn new and invigorating structures, which shake up entrenched ways of thinking.[8]

Mildred Mortimer has charted a previously overlooked path by analyzing works from the Maghreb and sub-Saharan Africa in her study *Journeys through the French African Novel.* She examines the theme of travel in some dozen texts, showing the contributions of orality and outlining parallels between the two regions:

> In the early 1950s, Maghrebian and sub-Saharan African writers, formed by a common French colonial school system, began to describe the life of the African hybrid whose double acculturation—European and African—resulted in an ambiguous adventure. It is not surprising that Camara Laye's *L'Enfant noir,* as a cultural document of a vanishing Africa and a psychological portrait of a cultural hybrid, bears a striking resemblance to an Algerian autobiographical novel of the same era, Mouloud Feraoun's *Le Fils du pauvre.* Both works express the writer's debt to oral tradition. (13)

In four of the six chapters, Mortimer draws a parallel between two authors, one of the Maghreb and one of black Africa. She takes into account works both from the colonial period and from after Independence, texts written by both men and women, noting, however, that for women the fight is waged not only against the repression of the dominant power but also against a suffocating patriarchal attitude. Thus, she links the Ivoirian Ahmadou Kourouma's *The Suns of Independence* with *La traversée* by the Algerian Mouloud Mammeri, around a feeling of disillusion regarding the road taken by governments in the postcolonial period. Or else she brings Sembene Ousmane's *God's Bits of Wood* together with *Nedjma* by Kateb Yacine, showing how the two writers—one Senegalese, the other Algerian—refer to a similar context, that of colonization, to then go beyond the conflicts generated by history: "Sembene and Kateb transform the individual journey to self-understanding into a collective. In the same vein, they stress the importance of historical events that promote a new sense of communal identity replacing tribalism with nationalism" (70).

Mortimer puts Mariama Bâ's *So Long a Letter* together with Assia Djebar's *Fantasia: An Algerian Cavalcade.* The former shows the need to go inward, while the second work invokes the importance of clearing a path for oneself on the public stage. Still, for both these authors the aim is to write in order to find themselves and to unite women, which is of utmost importance to each of them: "Bâ and Djebar consider female bonding essential to the struggle against male domination and view the act of writing as a process that leads to healing, liberation, transformation, and self-understanding" (164). Finally, in the last chapter, Mortimer draws parallels between Ken Bugul's *The Abandoned Baobab: The Autobiography of a Senegalese Woman* and Leila Sebbar's texts dealing with the rupture caused by the juxtaposition of opposing cultures.

Mortimer uses narrative evolution as a basis for developing above all else the thematics of the journey, the expanding of the I, claiming the use of techniques borrowed from orality. By pointing to the presence in the literary texts of themes, needs, and techniques that are similar in sub-Saharan Africa and the Maghreb, she clears a path, raises a number of questions, and invites us to consider and pursue important analogies.

The forms of interlacing between the Maghreb and sub-Saharan Africa are broad and rooted deeply in the collective unconscious, as Toni Maraini noted in *Écrits sur l'art.* They have been formed over the centuries from a variety of events—a vast network—the result of relationships and ruptures, influences, insertions, and rejections. The latter, less visible, less tangible, have been reorganized and evoked by writers, artists, and musicians for all the world to hear, from its distant trembling, its subtle components, fracturing exclusive perspectives, illusions, and failures. They emerge in particles, are adrift. Sometimes these elements lie buried in the silences scattered throughout the work, unexpectedly reappearing and revealing both the collective "patrimony" and the individuality of the writer, the painter, the musician.

Thus, we can state that since Independence numerous African artists have given expression to these contributions and have described the amalgam of current experience in the world. They are transmitting ancient concepts, linking human beings in spite of themselves, beyond allegiances, refuting the artificial divisions traced when Europe partitioned Africa, as they invite us to enjoy the intertwining, the inventions of signs that are able to inscribe knowledge encountered along the way as they passed through History, and that have traveled across the continent.[9]

محمد

2 On-Screen and Off-Screen Connections

The Spoken and Its Flaws

A FRAGMENTED LITERATURE, one that links different horizons, abruptly changes themes, and rearranges eras, creates innumerable silences that the reader will have to understand. These silences mimic the working of thoughts that move from one subject to another, formulating the individual's contradictions, which are marked at the end of the twentieth century by uncertainties, inscribing into the rupture questioning, wavering, and moments of emptiness. In African texts written in French, especially those of the period of Independence, they also refer to a context located between cultures, languages, and places, transcribing problems, urges, and preoccupations, determined by the dynamics of errancy.

On the other hand, silences can refer to implicit givens. For writers they are a powerful way of indirectly evoking the political context in which they live or have lived, using them as detour. Some of these, Frantz Fanon and Édouard Glissant in particular, mention the ensuing psychological effects, showing that alienation, isolation, and rejection result in madness. In other cases, this madness can be used to dismantle the demarcations, shake up the established norms, pursue the marking of an ambiguous route—ideas developed by Deleuze and Guattari, which Glissant pursues. Still others use silence to introduce rites or a metaphysical quest, as does Werewere Liking, who structures her narratives on the model of the ritual in order to transform the individual and society, endowing emptiness with multiple forms. The writers who are discussed or mentioned in this book often pass from one space into another, playing with what is possible, passing from word to silence, from meaning to the absurd. In their book on Kafka, Deleuze and Guattari, speaking about a literature they specifically describe as minor, refer to the work of deterritorialization done to the language:

> Even when it is unique, a language remains a mixture, a schizophrenic mélange, a Harlequin costume in which very different functions of language and distinct centers of power are played out, blurring what can be said and what can't be said; one function will be played off against the other, all the degrees of territoriality and relative deterritorialization will be played out. (*Kafka*, 26)

Even if they are interlaced in many works, we will consider the three areas—history, madness, and culture—separately as a reflection of the complexity of everyday life, marked by a variety of events and practices that extend from the political framework to a composite of customs, describing the resulting psychological effects, while defying the context so as to bypass the difficulties.

Historic Context

It should be remembered that African countries gained independence largely thanks to the decolonization movement, unleashed in Ghana in 1957 by Kwame Nkrumah, who played a major role for all of Africa and benefited from the determination of the Algerian people fighting for their independence (the war in Algeria lasted from 1954 to 1962). Most of the countries obtained their independence between 1962 and 1969, a recent phenomenon and one that all too often continues the practices established by the colonizers. The governments formed at that time were not always elected by the population, and outside pressures frequently supported specific leaders while ousting others. In the course of the decolonization process, many of the countries went through wars, problems, insurrections, or coups d'état (Algeria, Togo, Sierra Leone, Nigeria, Ghana, Liberia, Guinea-Bissau, the Democratic Republic of Congo, Congo, and so forth, and more recently Niger, the Comoros, and the Ivory Coast). The disintegration of states, exposing the political stalemate, should stimulate an examination of the infernal cycle that was created.

The inequalities have hardly disappeared with Independence. International interventions have often increased the tensions, feeding the conflicts because of financial interests (arms sales, the purchase of precious metals and oil). In Senegal, French industrialists have taken over key companies (communication, water, and so on). After the CFA franc suffered serious devaluation in 1994, foreign companies obtained their goods at a very low price.

Thus, Western governments have continued to exercise control: political, by supporting specific leaders to the detriment of those elected by the people; economic, by supporting certain regimes and neglecting others; cultural, by financing particular artistic productions and not others (films, publications, exhibitions). Many factions were armed by Europe, the United States, the former USSR, to the detriment of the country as a whole and inciting wars and unimaginable genocides. Algeria lived through the ordeal of a civil war when the elections of December 1991 were canceled. The population of Rwanda has endured a carnage that is still shrouded in perplexing silence. In Sudan, the fighting is endless, perpetuating practices of subjugation and exploitation, slavery, and the recruitment of child soldiers. In Chad, 40,000 political murders were committed and 200,000 people tortured under the dictatorship of Hissène Habré (1982–90), who wasn't charged until much later. Other dictators, such as the Ethiopian Mengistu and the Ugandan Idi Amin, were granted immunity from prosecution.

Economic and political stability has not been established. Wars still ravage many countries and famine continues to be an extremely serious problem. The prisons that were built under colonialism now house untold numbers of opponents to the regimes, while countless writers and journalists have been imprisoned there as well, among them those who rose up in Morocco against the king's policy for the Western Sahara or those who criticized the government in Kenya. Lumumba, Cabral, Sankara, and a great many others who were elected by their own people were "mysteriously" eliminated shortly after coming to power. As for women, they continue to be discriminated against and dominated by a system that, more often than not, they have not chosen and that keeps them silent. They are the object of a multitude of constraints, and in many regions they still struggle to acquire an education and obtain positions of power.

For a range of reasons that may be linked to economic, political, and ideological factors, the postcolonial situation drives people into exile and nomadism. Lack of resources and finances, or the precariousness of distribution, motivates artists and intellectuals to leave Africa, thereby creating the departure of an important contributing group. On the other hand, many journalists and writers have to face serious constraints. The tragic death in 1993 of the Algerian writer Tahar Djaout attests to the violence committed against writers, musicians, and artists. Large numbers of intellectuals have left their country to pursue their work, find employment, publish their writings, and participate in international dialogues. After the death of Lumumba, with whom he had collaborated as director of the newspaper *Congo,* Tchicaya U Tam'Si (1931–88) decided to leave Africa to work in Europe. Abdelwahab Meddeb, born and raised in Tunis, settled in Paris to engage in the world at large and pursue the forms that were important to him, taking a critical look both at his native country and at the West. The Cameroonian Werewere Liking settled in the Ivory Coast, where she runs a theater group. However, for several years now she has been confronted with the momentous problems that the country is experiencing and that seriously threaten the realization of her projects. Ngandu Nkashama lives in the West, having left the former Zaïre for political reasons when it was ruled by the dictator Mobutu.

In a multicultural and multilingual context, sometimes made up of a variety of philosophical and religious systems, no matter where the writer moves, he/she has the difficult task of warding off censorship and totalitarian positions; of sharing thoughts that also capture repressed voices; of adjusting the past to present demands, balancing disparate forces, channeling absurd gestures, and, through it all, avoiding clichés and an involuntary return to old values.

> Tradition is valuable only when it requires as much activity and energy as progress does. Maintaining a living tradition amounts to combining ancestral values with a modernity that is open and most of all inspired by something authentic. (Ben Jelloun, "La mémoire déroutée" [Memory defeated], 160)

In *Face à l'islam* (Confronting Islam), Meddeb speaks of the crucial need for preserving elements that go far back in time (which he calls archaic), while simultaneously joining them with modernity—our present identity being based on these diverse components. In order to do this, he speaks of the importance of accepting the contradictions that such forms of coexistence engender. He encourages being open to otherness, posing questions so as to embrace the diversity of the imaginary that has appeared, and thus permitting the refinement of his own positions in a world where a myriad of approaches continue to circulate both underground and above the surface.

Consequently, to come back to the intent of this chapter, the literature of the so-called postcolonial period[1] inscribes a series of practices, of settings pieced together that frequently express a reaction to history and to the political situation, which Khatibi clearly calls to mind:

> When historic violence provokes upheavals between countries, civilizations, and languages, one cannot avoid the matter of trauma and its being read as *conflictual inscriptions* in the memory of the text. I am borrowing this expression from Claude Ollier: "Let's say," he writes, "that every act of writing etches into the moment a collection of organized socio-cultural conflicts in series of simplistic oppositions." The order and the disorder of the text are inscribed on the crystallization of these conflicts. (*Figures de l'étranger* [Foreign figures], 117–18)

Writers express complex juxtapositions that have been interwoven between countries and continents, between religions and thinkers. The result doesn't always make it possible to determine their components.

Raybaud, speaking of Kateb Yacine's writing in *Le besoin littéraire* (The literary requisite), reminds us that the literary text—in view of a twentieth century marked by wars, genocides, disappearances, and imprisonments—can in no way describe all the horror, which for him is part of the "unspeakable" in that it goes far beyond language. As a result, writers fragment their narrative, making countless silences emerge—switching paths where the reader trips, gets lost, and swerves.

> A new emergence of history results that consists neither of the epic nor of the solid fabric of the nineteenth-century European historic novel, but of a *historic palimpsest:* vestiges reemerging as pieces of "broken mirror," the appearance of new and significant work with disparate and eclectic fragments, multiple hybridizations [. . .].
>
> A new perspective should be added to this, to the credit of the new modernity that I see outlined [. . .]. The abandonment of a complete story, that is to say one that issues forth from the objective to assimilate violence and the unpredictability of history in a revitalizing myth (progress, national identity, the emergence of a new society or a new world). And, in return, an attempt of a different order, or rather of a different disorder, shattering in every sense of the word: to narrate what cannot be recounted. [. . .] The non-recountable, that which goes too far beyond the norm to bear recounting [. . .]. (113–14)

A multitude of things left unsaid recall the events of the twentieth century. First of all, the silence of the colonized in the face of endless injustices, inequalities, and discrepancies that the West imposed while at the same time extolling the values of the Enlightenment. This accumulation of contradictions causes a wound in the colonized individual that Fanon and Memmi discuss at length in their analyses.

Then come revolt and the forming of nations. The postcolonial African subject overthrows the clichés and confirms political independence from Europe. He demands self-determination for his territory, economic and administrative management of its goods, and a validation of its culture. But he will have to connect a long complex trail composed of many juxtapositions: the past and traditional values, the history of colonization, the phenomenon of modernity (globalization, technology, individuality). In leaving tradition partially behind so as to adhere to this modernity, vertigo, uncertainties, and fissures set in.

> Historicity, globalization, technology are new perspectives that manage to deconstruct the traditional mental universe and begin its reconstruction according to more inclusive lines of force, more rigorous to the mind. New points of grounding in what is real, a qualitative expansion of the intellectual spirit of each individual, but also greater psychological insecurity and emotional distress because the break between the person's universe, faith, and the political space has been activated. The religious imagination is more and more disconnected from the public domain. Personal conscience is summoned to invent unlikely agreements where there had always been harmony. (Hussein, "L'individu postcolonial" [The postcolonial individual], 170)

This postcolonial situation is marked in the West by a difficulty in critical analyses of colonization. Moreover, to this day great silence hovers over the Algerian War, and over the role of the West in any number of other conflicts or coups d'état. On the other hand, this phenomenon puts the "former" colonized in a tense situation in which he or she must reconcile modernity based on individualism, the secularization of the state, the free market, science and technology, with a past that was based on the collective and the metaphysical. In addition, the image of the Muslim that the West reflects prolongs the misconceptions around Islam—lacunae, prejudices, and distortions—creating many denials and additional tensions.

As for the exploitation of cheap labor, the West perseveres in the disequilibrium that was put in place at the time of colonization. Illegally hired, the African immigrant is of profitable economic value: "The dream of European capitalism is that the immigrant labor force be usable as a pure power of value creation, without a soul or a conscience, without traditions or culture—a kind of contingent material, devoid of any subjectivity" (Naïr, "Les deux regards" [The two ways of looking], 23).

Consequently, through writing, the fragment is a way of trying to tackle the difficulties encountered, the contradictions lived. In order to report the rifts caused, denounce the abuses, and stand up to an arbitrary policy by questioning its legitimacy, the writer resorts to stylistic techniques such as irony, sarcasm, and parody (Ahmadou Kourouma, Sony Labou Tansi, Tchicaya U Tam'Si); an overabundance of clichés, situational and verbal reversals, denunciation (Ousmane Sembene, Abdellatif Laâbi); placement of empty spaces—places where violence erupts—in an enunciative and explosive montage (Mohammed Khaïr-Eddine, Tahar Djaout). The fragmented linguistic design expresses the absurd through the breaks inscribed in the writing and the violence of the images.

> I was born among cactus flowers. The same ones that Club Mediterranée brochures and official photographers so highly praise. Among railroad workers' strikes, scorpion fights, obsolete trickery, babysitters' diaper pins, and rusted brooches. They don't want to get rid of the travel agencies yet, as they find the workingman to be an ideal target! They drown him in sun, the beautiful sordid sun of southern beaches! They execute him with his own savings by showing him around so-called temperate regions although their people (whose hackneyed genius and folklore they still celebrate) are kept on a leash, nailed to the floor, weighed down by regulations that the West itself does not, or hardly ever, admit on its raft. (Khaïr-Eddine, *Le déterreur* [The excavator], 14)

The references to sharp objects ("pins," "brooches," "nailed"), to venomous insects ("scorpions"), to thorny plants ("cactus"), translate the flaying. Many exclamation points and the accumulation of images attest to irritability and the emptiness that emanates from the context. The substitutions, such as "cactus flowers" that replace human arms welcoming the newborn child, open out onto a menacing environment. Nature is destructive (the sun kills) and the people are slaves to the whims of the West. Through the use of caricature and condensation and by a displacement of meaning, the images depict tensions that lead to the absurd.

Many of the Independence texts describe the accumulation of bruises, voids, non-sense experienced by untold numbers of people caught in the toils of history and in maneuvers beyond their reach. The theme of endlessly extending violence is frequently described by Sony Labou Tansi:

> Mallot-the Tiger's-Child's regime lasted for seven years. There were sixteen wars of secession, sixteen wars against the Darmellia—and sixteen retaliatory wars by Jean Canon who was now known as the Terrible Sergeant. In fact, as soon as he returned from his studies, Jean Canon decided that the Darmellian army ought not to have any rank higher than that of sergeant. He said that colonels, generals, and field marshals were nothing more than titular soldiers growing fat, fighting around young girls and sparkling wines, building night clubs and villas, wallowing in the most inhuman meat and, when the foreign power that supplied the guides decided the time had come, they would take power and choose a ruler's name; then they would open nauseating bank accounts at the banks of the foreign power that supplied the guides. Every now and then, in some inaugural speech or other, they would "parrot-whisper" verses their ancestors had created. (*La vie et demie* [Life and a half], 174–75)

Repetition highlights stagnation. Warlike responses and counterresponses lead to nothing. The use of vague terms ("some inaugural speech or other"), and of redundancies such as the number sixteen, useless palaver ("he said"), the choice randomly made ("would choose a ruler's name"), show the arbitrary nature of any decision; a pouring-out of gestures devoid of any significance. A verbal buildup that mimics the heaping of nourishment and pleasures: "growing fat," "young girls," "sparkling wines," "night clubs," "villas," and "wallowing in meat." The recourse to "verses their ancestors had created" has no motive other than to launch an illegitimate power. Torrents of insane acts, sarcasm, and the indeterminate prevail and threaten the society's stability as a whole.

In the play *Je soussigné cardiaque* (I, the undersigned, heart patient), Sony Labou Tansi diverts the common use of the language, accumulating expressions, images, sketching unexpected parallels, illustrating the very expression of the protagonist Maillot, who fights to denounce injustices: "I am THE IMPREGNABLE FIRST-MAN" (101). The presence of the scream allows the language to be shaken up—which in the above-mentioned book on Kafka (whose texts were written in German), Deleuze and Guattari qualify as follows:

> He will push it toward a deterritorialization that will no longer be saved by culture or by myth, that will be an absolute deterritorialization, even if it is slow, sticky, coagulated. To bring language slowly and progressively to the desert. To use syntax in order to cry, to give a syntax to the cry. (*Kafka*, 26)

This unconventional passage is crucial here: it allows one to leave the very structure of language, to toss around the norms, and to attack power structures without in return adopting the totalizing characteristics criticized.

The brutalities that are practiced on every level, the unjustifiable murders, foreshadow uncontrollable violence. Horror is numbing in the books by Pius Ngandu Nkashama:

> Josiane had never again known any peace. And yet, she had so beckoned it, that peace. Even when that mouth twisted with grimaces, that irate mouth of the director of her school had jammed her into a corner on that June evening when she was preparing the party for the Congregation! . . . She had fought back while coarse, scaly hands tightened around her neck. Tightened to smother her. Since then she'd been wandering. The faces of the dead were superimposed on the grimaces and pursued her to all the places she was entrenched. It actually seemed to her she'd been wandering ever since she'd come into the world. Ever since the universe resembled this wrecked circle. Nowhere had she been able to take root.
>
> This evening, too, when the sun had just been dissolved in a cloud of sulfur, napalm, and fire. In the middle of a conflagration that spread from one corner to the other. She had wanted it so badly! But what was she actually wishing for, now that she was being buffeted on a godforsaken sea and her shipwreck did not conjure up a single island to which she could cling? (*Le pacte de sang* [The blood pact], 263–64)

In the amassing of absurdities Josiane loses her equilibrium. An onslaught of actions, a compression of memories and nightmares that overrun and disintegrate her. Forced to suffer the events, she finds herself facing an impasse—"jammed into a corner," "entrenched," "wrecked circle," "not a single island." This forces her to be constantly on the move—"wandering." Repetition punctuates the text and reinforces the sense of powerlessness—"tightened," "wandering," "buffeted"—and of terror (nightmares).

In this passage the text turns toward silence on several occasions. In the first paragraph the ellipses break into the narrative, asking the reader to imagine the continuation of the events. In the second paragraph the text clarifies for us that Josiane did have wishes, only to then immediately question their real existence. The despair is such that only silence can convey it.

By determining the obstacles, the political impasses, and the abuses, the writer strives to shake off stagnation. Werewere Liking proposes a renewal of society and the human being through the use of ritual. Disillusioned, other writers deplore the enormity of evil without necessarily believing in a solution. They translate the unrest that inhabits them, reveal the iniquities, evoke the aberrations, and inscribe a perceptiveness in the void that transforms everyday facts in a work that will challenge us and lead us to a better understanding of history and of the world, to the abysses of a political reality distorted by diverse interests, ravaged by brutality, which the author will transgress by the use of the poetic.

Before embarking on the next topic, which deals with the use of madness in writing, we should mention a completely different phenomenon: the social and cultural silences. Across Africa, the formulation of a message, an observation, or a criticism is done indirectly to deal carefully with the interlocutor, thereby avoiding any humiliating situation. The detour requires engaging the imagination. The example of the pot lid illustrates this phenomenon, linking proverb (by means of language), sculpted object (visual representation), and the silence of the speaker (who presents the lid to the one who is creating the problem): "To help resolve marital conflicts, Woyo women use pictographic pot lids to send coded messages to their husbands" (Thompson, "Catalogue Notes," 112). The lid refers to a proverb that prompts a range of interpretations, thus allowing the person who receives it to become sensitive to the problem without losing face. The image, sculpted on an object that is used daily and presented to the individual for whom the message is intended, does not use words and thus avoids any direct confrontation, any exchange of language.

Silence speaks. Carefully placed, it communicates a message: "periods and societies whose literary achievements imply a formidable resource of lexical, grammatical and semantic means, may in fact be founded on underpinnings of inarticulacy and even silence" (Steiner, *On Difficulty and Other Essays,* 69). In many African societies the implicit—indirect statements—is a powerful process that permits getting around the forbidden, providing a space for human acts, promoting the poetic and the subversive. In this fashion, individuals communicate their opinions or feelings without openly infringing the law or wounding another person. Also, silence is used to point out injustices or to question the powers that have taken over.

It creates a space wherein the reader can meditate and wonder about the values imparted. The writer opens a window onto the uncertain without in turn falling into the trap of the totalizing form he condemns.

Madness and Subversion

The above-mentioned political context has had a great many psychological consequences for the individual. During the Algerian War, Frantz Fanon, psychiatrist and writer, was one of the first to denounce the causes of the psychological problems he observed and to connect them to the political situation.

> The truth is that colonialism in its essence was already taking on the aspect of a fertile purveyor for psychiatric hospitals. We have since 1954 in various scientific works drawn the attention of both French and international psychiatrists to the difficulties that arise when seeking to "cure" a native properly, that is to say, when seeking to make him thoroughly a part of a social background of the colonial type.
>
> Because it is a systemic negation of the other person and a furious determination to deny the other person all attributes of humanity, colonialism forces the people it dominates to ask themselves the question constantly: "In reality, who am I?" (*The Wretched of the Earth,* 249–50)

The matter of rifts in identity caused during the colonial period is also raised by Albert Memmi: "Such is the drama of the man-product and victim of colonialism: he almost never manages to coincide with himself" (*Portrait du colonisé* [Portrait of the colonized], 154). Similarly, Édouard Glissant brings to mind the delirium that follows from such a political situation:

> Every colonial society is familiar with this particular expression when an individual is "delirious" about his situation or that of his neighbors, sometimes starting (as if contaminated) exchanges that are beyond any logic but whose crackling is dazzling.
>
> How many can be counted of these wanderers crushing the tragedy of our displacement on the crossroads like this. Their arms slice the air, their screams plant in the heat. They are drunk on their own speed.
>
> We pretend to ignore them: we don't know that we speak the same language as they: the same impossible torment of a truthful production. (*Le discours antillais* [Caribbean discourse],[2] 362)

There is a reality that encourages madness, the impossibility of finding oneself among the imported models: "human beings are *blocked* by their cultural alienation" (ibid., 377). This phenomenon persists during the time of Independence with the spread of similar practices: imprisonment of those individuals who rise up against the established power, consolidation of the military to control the population, corruption on various levels of the social structure, abductions and disappearances of disruptive individuals, wars, and so forth.

In a reflection of this context, many writers of the era of Independence express madness in myriad forms. They use fragmented writing to translate the wavering, the loss, the interference, and the economic and mental chaos surrounding them. In assembling snatches, they mimic the cracks in the existence, the feelings of powerlessness, the abuses, and attempt to depict the alienation that results. In his novel *Mémoire de l'absent* (Memory of the absent one), Nabile Farès describes the effect of marginalization and the psychological problems the narrator suffers at the death of his father, abducted and tortured during the Algerian War.

> They could call my name at the *lycée* or elsewhere, I'd turn deaf, *bewildered,* a thousand miles from the place where my name originated, the *lycée* was built on the other side of Algiers, near the El-Biar Hill, and I no longer recognized my, as if the father's abduction had robbed me of any possibility of understanding my name, syllables or sounds are like that, and so for many years in which I had to be and grow up, I had to *live* above my delirium, in that incomprehension of myself. (30)

The dilemma, inscribed in the text, refers in the first place to a political situation that in Algeria was connected to the long war. In the text the author interprets the mental state of the narrator by surreptitiously omitting a word and producing a narrative hole: "I no longer recognized my, as if," or by spacing out certain words: "I was delirious far far   far   Boundaries where I had to learn to live again" (30). The typography accentuates the state in which the narrator is drifting, that of being absent from oneself and from the world. Thus, by the use of discursive techniques the author inscribes the historical events, the consequences of political acts on humans. In such cases, madness expresses the disarray of the colonized individual who experiences the events and loses his reference points.

Pius Ngandu Nkashama uses madness in his novel *Le pacte de sang* to criticize the excesses propagated by dictatorships and the military. The author reports the innumerable practices developed to punish, subjugate, break down: abduction, torture, rape, disappearance. Corrupt charlatans, unemployed hoodlums, members of factions proliferate and sow the seeds of terror. Moreover, he evokes the consequences of these acts for the population, triggering madness in those who endure the brutalities.

Throughout Josiane's journey to find her friend Sanga, all the events take place around the psychiatric hospital, which at the end burns down with sounds of roaring and the agitation of the confined, who vanish in the flames. It is a place where a number of mutilated women and corpses were kept without the knowledge of the director, Dr. Chikuru. By describing such carnage, the work gives an account of the effects of brutality on humanity and of the human being's capacity for violence.

Inscribing madness at the heart of a narrative is also a powerful way to present events and allow the reader to identify the facts. For example, from the outset of the novel the hallucinations of old Hizambe thrust the reader into the context and depict the atmosphere:

> Don't you hear the machine guns ringing out, spitting fire, sniping in the bush? They're sending suppositories, they say. They're adding sedatives to keep the drowned from being restless in their sleep. Don't you see, Doctor? There they are. They're holding bayonets between their teeth. The blades are shimmering cruelly. You don't know their name? They're Sidji, buzzing hornets, names of a scorpion with venomous spittle and teeth like saws. Sidji, Doctor, a column of scorpions with a fiery bite. Hornets that pierce their stingers into women's genitalia, huge holes, opening up to the ragged petals of roses red with blood. (*Le pacte de sang*, 70)

In possession of many weapons, the Sidji are compared to poison-filled insects. The cruelty is emphasized by the shimmer of the "blades," the noise of the arms, the violence of the images that operates throughout the text like the machine gun so as to threaten the reader as well, sensitize him/her to the hatred that has spread and the chaos that is disseminated throughout the world. What will remain of this military arsenal, of this destruction, of these abusive practices? A void, where the earth in its turn will begin to swallow up the people. The author creates strange images that intensify the violence displayed by using irony and producing various shifts—the bullets become suppositories; the torturers are hornets.

The fractured style that puts forward a form of madness condemns the barbarism and records the loss of humanity in every phrase. The book sets itself up as a tragic premonition of the events that took place a few years after its publication in the Great Lakes region of Africa.

Therefore, while presenting the political and social context in which the work is grounded, authors realize their investment in madness and hallucinations by deploying a particular style, suggesting processes of the fantastic, following the phenomenon of deconstruction between the spaces that movement engenders. They cross the reassuring boundaries that society has established. The disrupted syntax of Farès imitates madness. It inscribes both the suffering and the unrest that isolate, or even destroy, the subject; both that which is illicit and the act of revolt. With recourse to such a process, the work frees itself from a totalizing and orderly system, from conventions and rules—a subversive practice that reveals a special psychological state. Delirium, madness (the power of the "madman" in *The Madman and the Medusa* by Tchicaya U Tam'Si), explore the extent of hidden meanings. By his seemingly strange behavior and by touching on disturbing topics, the character of the madman creates areas that are beyond comprehension. He upsets the customary order of linguistic communication with gestures that interrupt his speech, with the profusion of themes he touches upon, with screams and sudden bursts of laughter.

> It is the refusal of language and its clichés, the abandonment of the phrase, the destruction of the symbol of the word. It is a return to the non-word, or rather to the first, irrational, non-constructed, broken-jointed word. Transgressing the normal functioning of language against which it revolts, the subject finds the original and most expressive word in the scream again, not yet laden with meaning, the anti-signified par excellence. It also finds the primitive act once more, forgotten physical breathing, transposed into the text by the chaotic movement of the writing and by the images that render the physical effort of the vocal expulsion and its effect of relief. (Van den Heuvel, *Parole, mot, silence* [Utterance, word, silence], 59)

Tchicaya uses madness and visions both to depict the psychological effects that result from the abuses of colonialism and to transpose into the written text a visionary state that follows the art of the diviner—the prophecies of the "madman" instill the text with a new poetic power.

This excess, this chaotic expression in a literary work, is a telling subversive act. The accumulation of words and the typography imitate the mental movement and the character's refusal of belonging or acceptance. The acceleration of the verbal delivery, indicated by an avalanche of words, will trouble the reader. This method topples conventions and terrifies by its disorderly aspect. It formulates taboos, individual dreams, and collective fantasies—the immeasurable where everything is possible.

The upheavals of language through sudden unexplained changes are pathways, signs to be deciphered: a passage to verbal tenses that mix past, present, and future, blurring the narrative sequence; unusual punctuation; omission; displacement of meaning; repetition; profusion of the "I" or else the narrator's deletion; use of the vague. Furthermore, through the intermediary of the mad character, the writer escapes censorship, indirectly raising concerns that counter the norms established by society and by the official powers, such as governmental, military, or religious institutions.

In addition, the character of the child who is not yet responsible for his actions and is presumably innocent also allows for speculating on the double significance of words and criticizing an abusive situation from the perspective of innocence. The young boy in Ferdinand Oyono's *Houseboy* looks at the world with the eyes of an adult, not at all those of a child—a sharpened look on the abuses of colonialism. In his diary he meticulously records his everyday life as a servant in a colonial family:

> "You must be serious. Everyone has their position in life. You are a houseboy, my husband is Commandant . . . nothing can be done about it. You are a Christian, aren't you?"
>
> "Yes, Madame, more or less."
>
> "What do you mean 'more or less'?"
>
> "Not very Christian, Madame. Christian because the priest poured water on my head and gave me a European Name."
>
> "I can hardly credit what you are telling me now. The Commandant told me you were a very firm Believer."
>
> "We have to believe the white man's stories—more or less."
>
> "So that's the way it is, is it?"
>
> I had taken her breath away.
>
> "But," she went on, "don't you believe in God any more? Have you gone back to being a pagan?"
>
> "The river does not go back to its spring . . . I think there is a proverb like that in Madame's country too." (66)

Various indications, such as the many ellipses, the observation of the behavior of "Madame," whose "breath" the boy "had taken . . . away," the skill and candor of the "boy," show his ability to bring up with insight and simplicity colonial acts stripped of meaning, while acting naïvely and pretending to realize that his words could turn against him. Behind his comments the voice of the writer appears—the textual setting thus aims at a lucid understanding of colonialism and of the young boy's innocence, playing on the shifts so as to report a reality.

In *Le jeune homme de sable* [The young man of sand], William Sassine uses madness as a narrative technique to build the story. Visionary devices function to reveal events to come and to criticize injustices. Oumarou, the son of Abou, who works for the regime in a high position, revolts against school, against the abusive behavior of his father, who benefits from the system, against the corruption of the government, and against religion. But there's a curse on him, and his actions will turn against the very ones he defends. He will become the victim of a regime that outstrips him, one that he did not choose.

However, despite the inevitable death of characters who seek justice, by inserting the state of madness into which Oumarou sinks, the author uses a literary device that allows him to trace perceptiveness and raise the issue of abuse. Thereby the text achieves its true objective, uncovering the human being's depths, his unconscious, and creating a work whose power is centered on poetic images that draw from magic spaces. It should also be mentioned that Oumarou's madness is structured in keeping with a ritual and thus permits the context to be exorcised, the deadlock to be broken. This passage from one form to another is "deterritorialization"—circular movement. Oumarou is taken to the desert and poisoned, he splits in two, and an internal voice overwhelms him, which sends him to the depths of the anguish that is ripping him apart and to a profound understanding of himself:

- You even thought I was your conscience. No, conscience no longer bothers anyone. I come only when something very serious threatens a people. Then I come, and first I settle into a body, then into other bodies, and together we begin to do away with everything rotten. It's the same with you, Oumarou.
- Don't let me die, then, I beg you. Don't ever leave me again.
- You will not die. I am the only one who can grant you true immortality. Soon we will go back to the city: Banda, Tahirou and many others are waiting for us.
- If I could get up we'd leave right now. Help me get up; I'm still in great pain but if you help me . . .

- No, stay down first. We have millions of years ahead of us. Besides, the body I found is ready . . .
- We'll inhabit it, we'll make it scream in revolt, it won't respect anything, it won't be afraid of anything . . . Like me, it will be treated as an accursed soul . . . as . . . (Sassine, *Le jeune homme de sable,* 216)

The page layout in paragraphs with bullets rather than quotation marks, the ellipses, the overabundant use of the negative, and the entreaties mimic the psychological state of the protagonist, while simulating the presence of a guide to help him find an exit.

The reader notices tugging, gaps, a rift between Oumarou's energy, his heartbreak, his internal torment in the face of an uncontrollable situation, and the effect of distancing with regard to the events that the writing produces. To record the protagonist's feelings, the words approach the verbal. This results in a combination of two distinct forms that clash, deliberately disturbing the reader with the disorder that results.

The writer who represents psychological states and delirium expresses a form of revolt—in denouncing the malaise, the subject speaks without any longer taking boundaries into account—and introduces snags and eruptions that are spaces where memory can emerge. In contact with one another, these fragments, which at first seem incoherent, create unforeseeable openings that the reader must catch.

> Adapted to the singular experience and, in that respect, unpredictable and not necessarily able to be reduced to great forms, Freud says he produces a construction in an exploratory way; which is to say, where literature is concerned, constructing a mobile of narrative pieces that consist of archeological snatches, and to keep the metaphor of the Freudian text: this mobile can merge the isolated elements openly and, in turn capable of provoking the coming to light of new elements, is likely to enter into a more adequate future construction. (Raybaud and Quartier-Frings, "Raconter? (Dialogue)" [Narrating? (Dialogue)], 748–49)

The gathering up of disparate elements is a subterfuge. By suddenly emerging from chaos through verbal delirium, it allows the author not only to take on weighty themes that are sometimes taboo but also to stir up fragments of thought and put them in touch with each other in the text, producing unforeseen, revivifying, and unlimited sparkles—the memory of a society and of an individual's itinerary.

Madness (hallucinations, lack of reason, alienation) in "francophone" African texts reveals a tense political situation that destroys the individual and causes a conflict in him, a loss of identity. Sometimes this person will struggle to be inserted, to have a place, in a restructured society. In other cases, the insanity harks back to the acts of those in power, as we saw in *Le pacte de sang.* One shouldn't forget that in many countries, writers (journalists, novelists, poets, and playwrights) risk their life when they move away from what is lawfully permitted. Thus, the detour is an important survival technique that allows one to be crafty with the law and with power.

In a literary work, a divided, indented, and unstable fabric that imitates madness (such as nightmares, lunacy, imbalance) deconstructs the discourse and goes beyond the spoken word, beyond meaning, in four different ways. First of all, it awakens trauma; secondly, it jostles the reader by dismantling the linguistic order, constraining him or her to reconstruct a meaning from the suggested fragments; thirdly, it foils the customary structures of language and interprets the world, reflecting the fragility of existence where the person can easily vacillate and get lost.

> Articulating madness demands solid formal work from the writer (it is a matter of transcending the unutterable, stating the unspeakable, rationalizing the irrational), and betting on the meaning of experience (he unwinds the thread of madness, shows its logic, and reveals its typical range). The technique serves to reflect on the meaning of life, the meaninglessness of the world. (Plaza, *Écriture et folie* [Writing and madness], 178–79)

Fourth and finally, it deconstructs the categories imposed by society between normal/abnormal, real/unreal, order/disorder. The parallel writers draw between the madman and the visionary (such as the "madman" in *The Madman and the Medusa* by Tchicaya U Tam'Si) suggests the perceptiveness of some individuals who are said to be "mad" and dismantles the marginalization they suffer, inviting us to recognize a connection between delirium and vision, which leads us to an Elsewhere; brings us to a hieratic power, a specific relationship to the hereafter. It shows the capacity of the individual they call mad to see the future, to grasp facts that go beyond what is visible, distinguishable, comprehensible. Inserting madness in these texts from the period of Independence prolongs the approach engendered by circular movement and frees the spirit from fixed demarcations, from notions that are said to be normalizing. For Deleuze and Guattari, schizophrenia is a "deterritorialization" process that produces errancy, a movement beyond what is foreseeable, known, and real:

As Brian Massumi points out, the "schizophrenia" that Deleuze and Guattari seem to promote in *Anti-Oedipus* is not a pathological condition. It is rather a creative process of thinking differently, of "becoming": "Schizophrenia is a breakaway into the unstable equilibrium of continuing self-invention." (Marks, *Gilles Deleuze,* 97)

Cultures, Rites, Divinations

Some writers empower the void to evoke the hieratic in a variety of ways (recording rites practiced by a given society, mystical bursts, wisdom of the character who is thought to be mad, and so forth). At times they refer to ancient practices, reporting on rituals or divination methods—a movement fully directed to the hereafter—as well as a community's secret practices. In her narratives, Werewere Liking turns to ritual, while the art of divination shapes *The Madman and the Medusa* by the novelist Tchicaya U Tam'Si. In *Phantasia,* Abdelwahab Meddeb evokes a mystical course and inserts segments of Sufi texts (Bistami, Hallâj, Ibn Arabî), as well as Taoist, Judaic, Christian, and Muslim perspectives that juxtapose thoughts and periods—a work that will be analyzed in chapter 5. He also sets out fragments of ancient writing whose purpose was to communicate with the hereafter, such as hieroglyphs—segments for which he provides a translation and which call upon the divine:

I was totality when I was alone, / seated on the water, in blindness. / Now, I am Re in his glorious / manifestation, when he rules what he has created. (Meddeb, *Phantasia,* 146)

In this way, some writers inscribe other languages and sacred practices of various cultures into the French language, inserting ancient signs whose primary function was that of establishing and preserving a connection with the Beyond.

It should be remembered that Africa embraces a vast spectrum of beliefs onto which outside ideas have been superimposed. Depending on place and period, diverse practices and religions have become intermingled, among which are the perspectives of Animism, Islam, and Christianity.[3]

On the other hand, it should be kept in mind that, having developed for centuries, ritual and divination both play an important role throughout Africa. They restore balance or clarify obscure phenomena, attempting to target, catalyze, and exorcise problems that come up, skirting impasses, and consolidating community bonds. In a work on the rituals of the Ndembu, Victor Turner makes the following observation:

> Here Ndembu have recourse to divination of sorcery or ancestral wrath to account for misfortune, illness, or death occurring before or during the social drama. Ultimately, rituals of reconciliation may be performed, which, in their verbal and nonverbal symbolism, reassert and reanimate the overarching values shared by all Ndembu, despite conflicts of norms and interests on ground level. (*From Ritual to Theatre,* 75)

Ritual tends to neutralize painful events and uphold a balance, a harmony, within the society. It commits the individual to self-questioning in order to create meaning.

> For a time, however, the *djingo* [a Bassa healing ritual] allowed what had not been experienced to be lived in broad daylight, to express the profound anguish of the group that longed to find a place at the core of a society in the full throes of change. [. . .] The stage, the poetic space (brush, spirits, the heart of unleashed desires) project all the elements of a contemporary tragedy in *tableaux vivants.* This type of Dionysian theater with its rhythms, its wild and frenetic dances, gives free rein to the instincts in order to control them, liberates the vivid Word in order to have it functioning and active, and at last restores each person's integrity and share in the responsibility within a group that bestows the bountiful energy of the ancestors. (Hourantier et al., *Du rituel à la scène chez les Bassa du Cameroun* [From ritual to stage among the Bassa of Cameroon], 20)

Through ritual, the key stages of existence are analyzed and celebrated in order to trace a unity within the self and within the community and to put forward a series of thoughts.

In a literary work, elements of ritual appear via the use of fragments and silences which allow certain mysteries necessary to the rite to proliferate.

> In all major cultural process, from ritual to theatre and the novel, of any complexity of meaning, there are both "sequence and secrets"—to quote Kermode again—"secrets" are those non-sequential bits of creative indeterminacy which get into, and apparently seem to foul up all coherent

> protocols, scripts, texts, whatsoever little hints of the abyss of subjunctivity, that break in and out like *Exu* and threaten the measured movement towards climax on cultural terms. (Turner, *From Ritual to Theatre,* 77–78)

The bits and pieces preserve the foundations of ritual: knowledge is revealed in discontinuity, and the voids created open up onto possibilities to be grasped.

The art of divination functions in a similar way. The methods it employs depend on the region and the problems presented: reading of signs (such as the scattering of objects or traces on sand), dream interpretations, or trance states. It comes close to the nonspoken to determine events and modify them. The individual consults a soothsayer in order to resolve a conflict in which he/she is embroiled or an impasse he/she has encountered. As we saw in the case of ritual, it is a matter of restoring balance and invoking the values of the community. "It is through divination that a harmonious balance can be maintained in which a culture's most cherished values are adapted to the real world of continual flux" (Peek, *African Divination Systems,* 195). It is the diviner's role to unveil the causes of the client's dilemma, to clarify his/her path, and readjust any imbalance. Deciphering signs, decoding enigmatic configurations of objects tossed down after a question has been asked, the diviner puts together the collected bits of information—constructing a puzzle—to figure out what the stumbling block is.

> The ritualization of divination separates it from normal discourse and dispute settlement in order to ensure the necessary shift in cognitive processes. We must now attempt to understand how these alternate ways of knowing and thinking, generated by all this difference making—the symbolism, complex communication, and elaborate ritual—is finally brought together to help the client formulate a specific plan of action. As the manager of this process, the diviner is a translator between worlds as much as between modes of thought. And these communications must be organized as well as translated. (Ibid., 202)

Thus there are various stages. First the client consults a diviner whom he has carefully chosen (some individuals consult outside their community to get an "objective" opinion). The diviner uses a method that helps him read through the problem and see beyond the darkness. He conveys his "vision" to the client and discusses with him what measures can be taken.

In a literary text, the art of divination returns first of all to an ancestral method that has played a central role in upholding social stability, recapturing the values of a community. Secondly, it evokes the vision, the links with the Beyond, the Ancestors, the hereafter, and the insight needed in order to create and disclose a meaning, to probe the person so as to gain a better understanding of him or her and to illuminate the path to be taken. Thirdly, the written work, by putting words (signs) together in a very specific way, also creates voids (enigmas) to be deciphered in order to impart meaning to existence and absurd events. Consequently, to translate the divination processes and rites in a literary work, the author uses the fragment, which, by its brevity, creates a mystery or mimics a frugal, plain, ascetic state.

The fragment is also used to transcribe mystical flights such as those of the Sufis (Muslims), whose writings or sayings (sometimes thoughts reported by a disciple or the community, which emphasizes the importance of orality and the collective) meditate on the Prophet's revelation—the Koran's hadiths composed of short phrases that reproduce the rhythm of breathing. The structure of their thought imposes gaps—a meditative pause—and mysteries as well. The reading of the Koran, like that of other sacred books, is discontinuous, fragmented, made up of ruptures, allusions, detours, silences, and repetitions that are referred to by certain authors: Hampâté Bâ, Cheikh Hamidou Kane, Abdelwahab Meddeb.

As the condensation of a thought that has freed itself of the superfluous, the fragment allows the essential to be captured. It denotes, through the arrangement of words, the importance of silence—memory of the unspeakable, of the Absent One, that the language attempts to grasp but that dissipates as soon as it is verbalized because it cannot be permanently seized. This approach leaves space for the unspeakable—meditations made up of trials and merging entreaties that transport the subject and merge it with the Other. Using language to translate such a trajectory is an artificial means that can only create a rift between experience and speech. Nevertheless, better than any other method, the fragmented style (maxims, brief thoughts, sayings, teachings) preserves mystery, an unutterable aspect:

> If the event is a void or a silence, if the person is dazzling in the darkness, if the writing is the endless pursuit of something that cannot be pursued, one must rid oneself of meaning and of non-meaning so as to reach the absence of place where the question finds no answer, desire finds no completion, the I no subjectivity, and the word no individualization. (Garrigues, *Poétique du fragment* [Poetics of the fragment], 57–58)

The fragmentary erases the subject further to let the Other appear, privileging the metaphor, the mental icon. The power of appearing—in itself such a fragile force—dissolves as soon as it is captured. The perception of such a phenomenon provides no certainty whatsoever.

The writings and/or sayings of sages, prophets, mystics, and diviners thus transcribe the indispensable. They do away with anecdotes and the insipid; and by omitting transitions, the structure of their phrases at first creates countless silences and mysteries upon which to meditate.

For other writers, the void can also be the place for a phenomenological interpretation of existence that considers it a space from which the person and his becoming can emerge (for example, some of the work of V. Y. Mudimbe).

> As Merleau-Ponty has analyzed in *Le visible et l'invisible,* the invisible is not pure nothingness, a negative, but rather that which is immanent to the visible, as "gap," a "winding," and a "dehiscence—bursting open—of the human being." [. . .] the invisible goes back to a plural topological space, always multi-perspectivist and multi-sensitive. It is inclusive, a setting where close relationships and surroundings are defined. A primordial space prior to the space of the idea and the rational, the invisible is the place "of savage perception" that refers to the pre-reflexive strata of the "savage individual" and to what brings them into being, the first experience of "the flesh," the chiasmus of the "seeing and self-seeing, of the sensing-sensitive, and of the touching-touched that is peculiar to the body." This then is precisely the world in its savage state with its mythic time that for Merleau-Ponty was at work in art and proved to be capable of "awakening the entire field of the vertical." [. . .] This means that the sensory is "transcendence" and that the aesthetic world can be thought of as a vertical world immanent to the work [. . .]. That is why the emptiness within the human being, the hollow space in the world, or the blind spot in the passivity of seeing, why all these forms of invisibility refer to the "vertical being" as a "wild unpurified being" where sensitivity's transcendence meets up with the topology of a space on either side of the representation. (Buci-Glucksmann, "Le vertical dans l'immanence" [The vertical in immanence], 247–48)

Other writers, deeply steeped in mysticism, sustain a tight relationship with the void and sublimate this space, drawing creative potential from it while at the same time defining themselves as outside any belief, such as the writer Abdelwahab Meddeb, who will not let himself be pigeonholed. Blurring the spaces, refusing to submit to any definitions, he endows his

Sufi quest with contradictory meanings, eluding the law of the sacred text, distancing himself from any absolute interpretation, and pursuing the aesthetics of nomadism.

In his book *L'espace littéraire* (The literary space), Blanchot mentions the wandering and de-centered characteristic of writing: "The writer belongs to a language that nobody speaks, that is directed at no one, that has no center, and reveals nothing" (21). Since language is not existence, Blanchot traces a parallel between writing and peregrination, displacement, exile—in a foreign country, the writer travels through unknown terrain and unlimited spaces that are indefinable. He may try to understand the world's phenomena by transcribing his thoughts, but these won't let themselves be locked into any one specific interpretation.

> There where I am alone, the day is nothing other than the loss of a temporary stop, intimacy with the outside without a place or any rest. Coming here makes the one who comes belong to dispersal, to the crevice in which the exterior is the intrusion that suffocates, is nudity, the cold to which you continue to be exposed, where space is the vertigo of spreading out. That is when fascination reigns. (28)

The journey is made up of uncertainties, has no truth. "He who digs up the verse line escapes from the human being as a certainty, encounters the absence of the gods, lives in the intimacy of this absence, becomes responsible for it, assumes the risk of it, and endures its favor" (37–38). This view of writing demonstrates that it moves between places and sites, between life and death, between visible and invisible, perpetuating the circular movement and dismantling frontiers.

In some instances the poetic silences that fragmentation inserts are traces of an interpretation of the world, and function as a memory of what "was" at the beginning of Creation, before humanity and the divine were separated. In many texts fragmentation expresses the nostalgia for a lost wholeness, man's anguish in the face of the cosmos, and his schism with the Creator.

In his book *Ambiguous Adventure,* Cheikh Hamidou Kane describes the itinerary of a character named Samba Diallo, who first receives a religious education in a Koranic school before being sent by the Grande Royale (a character in the text) to the school of the whites to master the colonial system of thought. In the novel's second section, Samba Diallo goes to study in Paris and then, when his father calls him back, returns to the land of the

Diallobe, where he will die not long after his arrival. This work contemplates the silence that the spiritual Master and his followers seek and the emptiness that the West engenders. It juxtaposes two irreconcilable systems from which no harmonious solution will be found. Thus, to render the battle and the protagonist's mystic quest, the text is filled with silences that simultaneously evoke a philosophical approach, a spiritual quest, and a series of deadlocks. Various ways of articulating the void are presented: the alienation produced by colonialism in Africa; the "authenticity" embodied by "the Madman," who holds fast to fixed and restrictive values; the unfolding of an entirely different site that opens out onto a hieratic reflection. The former two lead to absurd forms of emptiness, while the third produces not only a philosophical contemplation but also a quest whose verbal register, visual descriptions, proverbs, and arrangement of the unspoken attempt to render the spiritual journey: "Thierno had jumped up as if he had stepped on one of the white-hot paving stones of the gehenna promised to evil-doers" (Kane, *Ambiguous Adventure,* 3). Samba preaches against life, as he expresses his religious inclinations: "'Men of God, you are warned,' Samba Diallo took up the theme again. 'One dies lucidly, for death is violence in triumph, negation imposing itself. From now on, may death be familiar to your spirits . . .'" (13). The unspoken is suggested by the many ellipses, by the dialogues interrupted by descriptions, by the use of terms suggesting silence, by the mention of immobility. And Samba's conversation in a cemetery with the spirit of the Vieille Rella nurtures a relationship with invisible, mysterious powers. Proverbs are inserted to illustrate in writing the concepts of the protagonist and his mystical trajectory as faithfully as possible, and the narrator has recourse to speech that is composed of images. Strangely, Samba's murder by "the Madman" will allow the character-hero to find the peace he seeks as he unites with the Absent One. In the final chapter, which is divided among several voices, Samba reaches eternity and fusion with the Unspeakable:

> "Where are you? I no longer see you. There is only that turgescence which rises up in me, as the new water does in the river in flood." [. . .]
>
> "Be attentive—for, see, you are reborn to being. There is no more light, there is no more weight, the darkness is no more. Feel how antagonisms do not exist." (164)

The text unfolds discursive strategies both on the level of the language used and on the level of the story told, breaking the framework and indicating the quest by means of methods that create silence. At the end, the story "takes off" in imitation of the flight of the protagonist—his upward surge. Irreconcilable voids clash, tearing at Samba, who will find peace only in death. The story ends when the main character disappears, as if any mystical text can only culminate in the abandonment of language.

The texts of Amadou Hampâté Bâ, drawn from Peul initiation narratives, show a spiritual approach specific not only to a culture but also to the writer, a great expert in the oral tradition and in the Islam of West Africa[4]—a region through which he traveled extensively, collecting countless tales that he transcribed, annotated, and published. However, he was careful to show only what could be explained, scrupulously respectful of the secrets of a given community. The tales evoke stages of initiation and are thus filled with symbols and mysteries that call for patience and perspicacity. Their meanings are provided only in part, inviting the disciple—and thereby the reader—to follow an internal journey, to seek meaning within him- or herself that will lead to multiple interpretations—as a reflection of the enigmas of our existence.

Bâ's story *Kaïdara,* of which the third version, in prose, was published in 1978, contains a great deal of silence. Three characters, Hammadi, Hamtoudo, and Dembourou, travel for twenty-one years in search of Kaïdara, the god of gold and knowledge:

> They embark on a journey into a "subterranean" world, that is to say, the world of meanings hidden behind the appearance of things, the world of symbols where everything is meaningful, where everything speaks to those who know how to listen. During their journey they meet up with events or animals, each one of which is a symbol to be deciphered. Thus there are eleven stages to cross before arriving at the heart of the "land of Kaïdara," the center from which the forces of life flow. (*Kaïdara,* 87)

Only Hammadi survives and succeeds in acquiring true Knowledge, since he is not motivated by power and profit. At the appropriate time, he receives clues containing an entire Peul cosmology to guide him. Many mysteries are scattered throughout the text, creating a magical effect and a mysterious atmosphere. Animals appear and disappear "by magic" (17), talking and singing, suggesting leads to be decoded that often have several meanings and thus require Hammadi to use his imagination, patience, and skills.

The hero is educated as he travels through unfamiliar regions and finds an inner strength that sharpens his outlook on life. Along the way, Hammadi collects a string of advice including that of the old man, thus assembling the foundations of initiation based on wisdom and insightfulness. He goes through a number of natural trials, meets up with twelve symbols, each of which has an "auspicious" and a "harmful" aspect that will be explained well after he returns home, thereby prolonging the anticipations that are one of the requirements of such a journey.

Therefore, the silences here reflect the teachings of a community, the foundations of Peul initiation, as well as the dimension of a spiritual journey on which nothing is permanently acquired. Furthermore, the wise person will always seek to learn more: "He will never think he possesses complete knowledge. He will always see himself as ignorant and continue to be a student for all time. He will be consistent enough to respect the truth of others and aware enough to recognize his mistakes" (73). He works inside the discontinuous, the unlimited realm—his quest is infinite because the unspeakable (Kaïdara) is elusive, constantly changing shape: "He was the supernatural being Kaïdara, Kaïdara who changes shape at will without having a permanent one" (36). Or this: "The throne on which Kaïdara was seated turned continuously and Kaïdara was the great sun. No one was able to describe his shape" (36). It should be added that, according to the text, silence protects: "If observation is a quality, knowing how to keep silent protects one from disaster" (17). Silence is also a reminder that looking and listening—availability and perception—are the bases for a quest toward the Elsewhere and for the knowledge with which to manage the events of existence resourcefully.

Writing that brings in rituals, divination processes, or else a mystical flight uses a discursive arrangement to overcome the limitations of the verbal and preserve the feeling of a vision or an indescribable fusion. The linguistic project is built across structural voids that provide a space for the Absent One. Through the writing, a hieratic gesture is also outlined that for centuries has been pursuing the first objective of writing, that of communicating with the hereafter. Whether atheistic or not, fragmented literature holds the traces of a first itinerary within its structure, within its chasm, in remembrance of the sacred, to which writing was consecrated when it first appeared.

The unspoken that a writer, a language specialist, carefully scatters throughout a "francophone" work conveys important signs. Doing away with a framework to deal with various thoughts momentarily inscribes the rift, the unspoken, between the fragments. The incursion of clichés, worn-out words, or, in contrast, completely unusual ones; the changes in register; the intertextuality; or the appearance of untranslated foreign languages disrupts the reading process, fractures the enunciative development, and obscures communication. Skillfully gathered points of view that contradict or rule each other out enrich each other and take the complexity of the subject into account. By going beyond the predictable, by breaking conventions, by having experiences and cultures exchange ideas, the work reveals the world and captures a form of freedom, while responding to questions and satisfying queries that have long been held in suspense. Sometimes the void delineates reactions to history, to political events, or demonstrates a withdrawal. The voids that are traced by the use of an emotional, violent, cynical language, by the blurring of voices (the reader no longer knowing who speaks and who acts), articulate the crying out and express an overthrow, anguish, and chaos. Sometimes the void is the place of a mystical quest.

Elements originating in history, in the psyche, in culture, intermingle, making categories useless, providing the silence with an enigmatic and elusive dimension. And even as one deciphers the motives of such a silence, it will elude any definitive grip, evade any rigid interpretation, so it can be understood in what is possible and changing. Meddeb inscribes silence in his textual fabric by inserting a great many bits and pieces. He records the void in the face of political acts (bombings, explosions, deaths) that in some places are part of everyday life. But he also invests the unspoken with other meanings so as to reproduce the rhythm of the breath in the reading of the Koran and a search for emptiness in order to create.

Words are threadbare, illusory, and the writer will put strategies in place to find a way around the lacunae and the obstacles, refusing to disclose everything, retaining mystery, while at the same time rebelling against the reader's expectations.

> Verbal powerlessness, inscribed in speech whose creator is a language "specialist" par excellence, is an avowal of the greatest importance. [. . .] This textual void is obviously a *sign* in the same way that the *word* is: we know that silence "speaks," that its "eloquence" plays a crucial role in communication, and that it can be just as "terrifying" as the scream. (Van den Heuvel, *Parole, mot, silence,* 67)

Silence is a powerful space in which everything is possible and where any number of situations are shaped and come undone. Still, one needs to know how to understand it. Similar to the metonymy that suggests a totality, the blank space evokes something larger, a secret labeled with a few signs to be furtively noticed without ever offering any certainties. Consequently, it requires the reader's active participation so that he or she can find a meaning in the text and give it a plausible interpretation.

George Steiner thinks of the unspoken as a space in which the subject can create his identity, can structure and organize himself by speaking to himself or moving toward the Other. "One does not need Kierkegaard to remind one that where a secret has been dislodged and published, a kind of malign emptiness remains" (*On Difficulty and Other Essays,* 59). Thus, he shows that silence has a function that hasn't always been evaluated or recognized. It allows for human deepening and is a place where the subject gives meaning to his journey and finds a balance by keeping a secret, talking to himself, and devoting himself to silence.

> [A]cross deepening planes of silence and near-autism, which made possible the descent into the self of St. John of the Cross, of Pascal, even of so modern a listener as Amiel? There are crazily-shaped, almost monstrous creatures who survive in the great deeps of the sea. Brought to the surface, they burst or shiver into inert powder. (59)

By choosing to keep quiet, the writer sets the limits of language and counts on the value he has given to the void. It will be the site of an abyss where a multitude of enigmatic signs are hiding. The unspoken preserves the power of the ambiguous. Carefully placed, it defers the described action or the development of the thought and transcribes the unfinished—a place where, by accommodating multiple meanings, movement has been made possible. From this space, from these thousands of pieces, emerges the identity of the subject who suggests to the interlocutor a double itinerary—anxious/pleasurable, empty/full, dark/luminous—in which he can be mirrored.

3 Verbal Flow between Orality and Writing

Widening the Spectrum

THE USE OF ORALITY by writers of the Maghreb and sub-Saharan Africa is frequently explained by the presence of clear-cut oral components: the mother tongue is not necessarily a written language, and the various cultures use large numbers of proverbs, tales, riddles that are transmitted by the mother, for instance, or by an artist whose vocation is the spoken word. Driss Chraibi, Assia Djebar, Nabile Farès, Werewere Liking, Abdelwahab Meddeb, V. Y. Mudimbe, and Tchicaya U Tam'Si, among many others, borrow forms from the oral art. What exactly is the power of the verbal that the written text attempts to portray and rediscover? What does the author want to capture through the written word? Why does he or she seek methods that, rooted in orality, lose some of their characteristics in a written context?

On the one hand, the writer reverts to techniques from distant worlds where cultures were established in which the imaginary unfurled. On the other hand, while suggesting the methods of the oral artist, the writer transforms them by conveying other meanings via the written text. The oral method evoked in a literary work relinquishes many aspects specific to that art, including vocal resonance, breath, gestures and movements of the speaker, and the spontaneity that enlivens the hundreds of verses the oral artist performs. We shall see below how texts by Catherine N'Diaye, V. Y. Mudimbe, and Aminata Sow Fall borrow forms from orality, inscribing sound play and verbal techniques in their texts while at the same time creating a disparity, a distance, from that art by modifying it.

While this study will focus primarily on forms elaborated by the "griot" in order to analyze these texts, there are many other facets of orality. Although an ancient form, it has never become rigid and has always remained in motion. In the article "Résurgence de l'oralité dans le roman maghrébin" (Resurgence of orality in the Maghrebian novel), Antoine Raybaud insists on the variety and complexity of this art. It is the memory of a society, changing as it adapts to history and motivating the imagination. It is subversive, too: "Words of social places and positions without status, outside of the official circuit, possibly even clandestine, [. . .]—against the domain of the established social, political, religious powers" (90). He cites the numerous forms (both oral and written) that have crossed and influenced each other in the Maghreb, from the tales of *A Thousand and One Nights* to heroic poetry (religious, warlike), love poetry, mystic poetry, and Bedouin epics (Beni Hilal), not forgetting the profusion of tales (with figures of ogres, animals, and spirits) that circulate. This list is a reminder that the space is traversed by countless events (conquests, displacements, exchanges) in which a multitude of stories, artfully unfolded, are juxtaposed and intermingled. Consequently, for Raybaud, the relationship between orality and writing is perceived "in terms of a dynamic and possibly turbulent interaction" (89).

The writer Abdelwahab Meddeb will refer to forms of orality such as the embedding of narratives (interruption, repetition, detour) or the composition of themes and variations. In *Face à l'islam* he states:

> I vividly remember those family evenings when a storyteller would lend her voice and her imagination to the *Thousand and One Nights*. Those were moments of true happiness. The storyteller, an old illiterate woman who was part of the circle of the family clientele, would alternate the places where she stayed, going from home to home. Although illiterate, these women communicated to us a whole imagination as well as codes and systems of signs. In them I recognized the link with the distant past: as storytellers they were text producers. (23)

This art (particularly the tale) disobeys the norms and the law. Meddeb sees it as a way to manage the evil within humans, to face up to it, thereby allowing children to "create their own space to internalize the law and learn to free themselves from it by the practice of transgression, the temptation of provoking punishment, the apprenticeship in guilt and overcoming it" (27). This popular art uses everyday speech expressions, dialects, sometimes coded lively phrases that belong to a specific social group.

A multitude of genres, forms, and approaches make up this art, which is constantly enriched, not only by populations, cultures, and imaginations coming in contact with each other, but also by closely maintained links with written forms (whether these be sign inscriptions or texts as we know them). And to this day the art of orality continues to be modified and to respond to a need. One finds it also in the way that everyday interactions are handled through a number of exchanges based on a theatricalization of often highly codified communications, such as greetings, expressions of gratitude, or negotiations as they are practiced in West Africa. Orality can also be a subversion or a reversal in order to better tolerate the forces of power that are in place, or else an opening onto magic, the mysteries of religious ceremonies, initiations, and rites. It invites one to contemplation, to enjoyment through the elaboration of ingenious verbal jousts—an expression of having a hold on the everyday by giving it form so that it becomes a performance, a spectacle, a demonstration of skill, granting power through the wonder that is produced.

Nevertheless, the present study will be limited to certain aspects of orality, namely those that lend themselves to an analysis of the selected texts, and is therefore far from exhaustive. It quite simply seeks to present certain characteristics to show that orality is grounded in an ancient form that has changed constantly over time by adapting both to individuals and to history. For a long time it was considered to be an inferior art, since it was thought by the West, in the wake of colonization, to lack the support of written forms. However, since then it has been demonstrated, and repeatedly so, that the written work generally accompanied orality in a variety of forms:

> There is no single culture without a system, however rudimentary in our view, of conservation and communication of certain messages. The support of this common memory and the material of coded communication are essential for group cohesion, collective identity and permanence, and for contact with other societies. (Battestini, *African Writing and Text,* 23)

This position is clearly opposed to that of linguists and the literary types who think that writing is a more sophisticated form that appeared after the oral art—an idea that perpetuates the point of view established by the colonial system.

Let us first go back to the elements of the oral art in order to understand what terms characterize it, who uses it, and what its principal forms are.

There are a great many designations by which to refer to the oral artist, such as *meddah* in Algeria, *izibongo* (praise poet) in South Africa, or *gewel* among the Wolof of Senegal. In some languages several terms may exist to designate the art, which attests to its great complexity. The often used term *griot,* which probably comes from *gewel,* appeared during the period of colonialism.

The profession demands a rigorous training period in order to report on the past, on the genealogies that link the individual to the Ancestors, preserve the memory of a people, and convey important historical events. The oral artist learns to perform at significant life events such as weddings, funerals, and other celebrations. He commemorates life's important stages, helps to resolve conflicts and bring peace so as to maintain a certain calm, and he familiarizes himself with the communities within which he moves. He often plays several roles and belongs to a "caste":[1]

> In traditional Africa the functions of artisans are not professions in the modern and economic sense of the term, but correspond to what is known as "castes." [. . .]
>
> The "casted ones," which include not only the blacksmiths, cobblers, weavers, lumberjacks, potters, etc. but also the *dieli* (public performers, normally known as "griots") who are called *nyamakala,* that is to say "antidotes to the *nyama*" or "masters of the *nyama,*" with *nyama* being the mysterious power that, to some degree, dwells in all that is alive. Their ability to transform matter in order to create new forms is considered to be a projection, a reproduction of the supreme God's creative role. They are meant to maintain occult relations with the elements of nature that correspond to their respective functions: mineral, vegetable, fire, etc. In every special branch of *nyamakala* a specific initiatory training linked to the secrets of that function is transmitted from father to son, from teacher to student. (Bâ, *La poignée de poussière* [The handful of dust], 7–8n)

Because of his use of the spoken word, society grants the oral artist a unique relationship with the invisible forces and entrusts him with a special role.

Some griots play an instrument or have musical accompaniment. The open setting of a public square or the indoor hall has an effect on the way the work is received, as does the body language or pantomime that allows an otherwise obscure situation to be clarified. The ceremonial dress can be astonishing, spellbinding, make the motions more fluid, and in some cases its patterns and colors impart additional information. Orality is a complex assemblage of word, music, and dance. In addition, it is also a production of ingenious inventions used to respond to unexpected comments from an audience and to delay the story's progress.

In her work on the griots of Senegal, Isabelle Leymarie observes that because he belongs to a "caste," the oral artist has an inferior status that he does not necessarily have a hold on (although society's rapid changes must be taken into account). Undervalued as well as acclaimed, he knows how to take advantage of the immeasurable value of the spoken word to fill his discourse with indirect comments aimed at unsettling those who proffer discourteous remarks in his direction. The spoken word allows him to articulate disparities (his own and those of others) and at the same time to negotiate a space in which problems are exorcised. Bassirou Dieng makes the following observations:

> Depository-transmitters are guardians of a form of knowledge that the ethics of a society places above the practical and everyday knowledge conveyed by the family. [. . .]
>
> The "oral word" integrates the rhythm in its very structure. Among other things, it plays a sociologically integrating role: the oral communication space is a theater where the community is glorified, and the past and future are experienced in a socio-dramatic present thanks to the "power" of the word. ("L'épopée dynastique ouest-africaine" [The dynastic West African epic], 24)

To create maximum effect, the oral artist follows a highly orchestrated system, often beginning by thanking his sponsor or master, and evoking the grandeur of the Absent One or of the invisible forces so as to receive favors—inspiration—from the world beyond. Then he will normally situate himself within a lineage of artists, recalling the value of the spoken word and the importance of what is to be said, preparing his audience to fully appreciate the words he will be sharing with them. Referring to the text of *Sundiata: An Epic of Old Mali* as retold by Djibril Tamsir Niane, we find traces of these processes, which will be found again later in some literary works of Independence:

> We are vessels of speech, we are the repositories which harbor secrets many centuries old. The art of eloquence has no secrets for us; without us the names of kings would vanish into oblivion, we are the memory of mankind; by the spoken word we bring to life the deeds and exploits of kings for younger generations.
>
> I derive my knowledge from my father Djeli Kedian, who also got it from his father; history holds no mystery for us; we teach to the vulgar just as much as we want to teach them, for it is we who keep the keys to the twelve doors of Mali. [. . .]
>
> I teach kings the history of their ancestors so that the lives of the an-

> cients might serve them as an example, for the world is old, but the future springs from the past.
>
> My word is pure and free of all untruth; it is the word of my father; it is the word of my father's father. (1)

This passage reminds us that the word is not acquired by accident but according to a strict discipline, carefully transmitted from generation to generation by those who possess the knowledge.

For the Lebanese poet Adonis, orality forges the marvelous by uniting clarity and beauty, committing itself to going beyond the historic narrative, retracing the past of a people through a celebratory use of the verbal. It presents contradictory feelings: sorrow and joy, courage and fear, life and death, illuminating the itinerary of the individual, and inspiring him to know himself better:

> This poetry is the first incarnation of our language, in which we state what we are and with which we clear paths for ourselves through the darkness of the unknown. From then on it doesn't constitute just our spiritual memory but also our physical memory, and the original source of our imagination. (Adonis, *Introduction à la poétique arabe* [Introduction to Arabic poetics], 39–40)

Orality participates in the formation of individual and community identity, relaying a metaphysical value, a whole body of wisdom, so that the everyday can be skillfully managed, and is at times prophetic. It plays a vital role and provides various approaches that use indirect routes so as not to hurt anyone explicitly or impede any exchanges, and philosophies that seek to propagate a balance and exorcise evil in order to settle problems that might otherwise provoke detrimental, uncontrollable reactions and destabilize the existence of an entire society. The oral art, which is extremely sophisticated, consists of a vast array of techniques and has contributed to the creation of highly diversified genres of different lengths.

Let us go back to those forms found in written texts to better understand the transformations that derive from them, pursuing the themes this study has been developing with regard to circular movements.

Repetition is a device of oral art which allows the public to better grasp the subject at hand and emphasizes specific facts by insisting on the importance of an unusual event. At the same time, it functions as a pause and involves the listener so that he will take part in the development of the story as he recognizes certain phrases. It clarifies the recitation, regulates the flow that goes back to what has already been said, and allows the public to better understand the plot.

> Repetition opens the way to the argument in the academic (and thus fruitful) sense of the term. A discreet, hidden courtesy, it offers the listener—who always thinks of the perfect retort too late—time for reflection, time for verbalization to the one who is not necessarily quick to respond.
>
> Consequently, instead of producing weariness by being futile and distracting the listener, repetition "gives weight to the words"; it reduces the gap between reality and language, things and willpower, vague attempts and action.
>
> Repetition is the production of a hammering-away that is needed when one knows that language will always be unable to fully translate reality, or to fully make the integrity that weighs on this reality come through. (N'Diaye, *Gens de sable* [Sand people], 110–11)

Repetition is also stating the same thing in another way by using a different tone, a new body language, delaying the narrative for a moment to call upon music or a melodic refrain. Pierre Garrigues thinks of the power of repetition in these terms:

> In *Entretien infini* Blanchot accentuates the way phrases have of wearing-out to the point where he suggests the possibility that repeating the same thing is done to state otherness: "Saying the same thing twice, not out of concern for the identical but by refusing identity, as if the same phrase by being reproduced and moved about were developing on its own and according to the features peculiar to the space created by the move, rather than according to the organization outside the rhetoric development."
>
> Thus, repetition is indispensable to the movement, to the rhythm of the fragmented space: more or less innocent, more or less forgetful, between cry and harping on the cry [. . .]. (*Poétique du fragment,* 121)

Repetition is reassuring. It provides the opportunity for deepening the engaged reflection, for pondering further before moving on to something else, possibly offering time for finding different dimensions. "Emmanuel Lévinas insists on the notion of the 'echo' and on the complexity that it puts forth" (ibid., 122). And Édouard Glissant sees in it the possibility of having a thought ripen that would give birth to a new creation: "I think that in our world repetition is one of the forms of knowledge; it is by repeating that we begin to see the little speck of something new appearing" (*Introduction à une poétique du divers,* 33).

In a written literary text, repetition plays with the various aspects already mentioned and forces the reader to grasp the meaning.

Language games and distortions intensify the narrative. They turn norms upside down, demolish the borderlines of what is lawful, and cause laughter, true verbal pageantry. Onomatopoeia accentuates a description with acoustic mimicry and brightens up the story. Drawing out syllables or modifying words causes an expressive magnification that makes the recounted event comical. Voluntary stuttering simulates stumbling. The deformation obscures the term in order to adapt it to a new situation, giving it new energy. By imitating the sounds in nature, the pounding of the rain on a metal roof, the wind in the trees, or the whistling of a machine, the narrative gives another dimension to narrated facts and frees the word from the way it is commonly used. This dislocation, this displacement, celebrates excess, resembling a carnival, and participates in going beyond the ordinary. To some extent **puns** fulfill the same function, since they reverse the usual order and encourage us to catch the meaning hidden inside a disorderly setting that disobeys propriety and norms. These methods, like the use of **metaphor** and **symbol,** disregard the scope of the verbal and open up unlimited spaces in which the listener's imagination and experience will provide the words with meaning. "Jurjâni explains what it is that spurs us to admire metaphoric language when he says: 'Human nature is such that when something appears from an unusual place, emerges from a strange source, it will generate all the more surprise and fascination in the mind'" (Adonis, *Introduction à la poétique arabe,* 60). As for symbols, they are often used in divination, since they are in contact with the hereafter and thus contain things that cannot be spoken.

Digression imitates the labyrinthine path and keeps suspense going by delaying the story. It intensifies the thread and increases its complexity. The use of **irony** allows for the discovery of new meaning that lies beneath what is being said, within the depths of a displaced significance. There is more to what has been told. These methods spill over the parameters of language and make the speaker discover spheres that go beyond words. A clever juggler, the poet knows how to play with many different verbal techniques and thereby keep his audience awake. As he does so, he skirts the restrictive and limited use of the spoken word, and gives meaning to the world. Through his stories he develops a philosophy, accompanying the individual through the stages of existence, celebrating birth, rites of passage, and supporting the person in the face of death. In written work these insertions attempt to rediscover the word's power and spontaneity, as well as its almost sacred value.

Through the centuries, orality has developed different genres, including epic, myth, tale, song, riddle, and proverb. The length varies widely from one form to another, but they all belong to a collective body of knowledge. The **epic** suggests and idealizes the past. It describes the extraordinary journey of a great figure who succeeds in saving a community; the griot uses it to present specific values:

> More than accuracy, it is the preservation of an idealized past that serves as the model for which the griots strive. "'The epic' that praises noble sentiments such as bravery, nationalism, honor, and glory," Seydou Camara notes, "is a genre that identifies a society." The story's heroes are often depicted in the process of unraveling a crisis. In contrast to the historian who is expected to be impartial, griots in their narratives tend to exalt the virtues of the protagonists and defend the honor of their people. (Leymarie, *Les griots wolof du Sénégal* [The Wolof griots of Senegal], 93–94)

The world of the epic is generally immutable and inaccessible to ordinary mortals; the supernatural intervenes, playing a decisive role: "The epic world of the absolute past is by its very nature inaccessible to personal experience and is not open to any individual opinions and judgments" (Bakhtin, *Esthétique et théorie du roman* [Aesthetics and theory of the novel], 452). It recounts historic events that are both magnified and glorified, while the psychological characteristics of the individuals remain undeveloped. Glissant considers it a fixed form that conceals an uneasiness:

> The epic—perhaps I said this the last time—is what is exclaimed when the community, not yet sure of its identity, by tradition needs that cry for reassurance in the face of a threat. It has always been thought that the epic is the exultation of a victory, but I believe that the epic is the redemptive song of defeat or of uncertain victory. (*Introduction à une poétique du divers,* 36)

Nevertheless, in depicting an idealized world the epic offers models that impel humans to surpass themselves, and sets itself up as a source of inspiration.

The **proverb** is geared toward brevity and a compression of images. It is an anonymous collective utterance that represents a community's values and observations. It is ancient wisdom that contains a hidden, displaced meaning. Its succinct form is lightweight, symmetrical, and made up of metaphors and metonyms, which are easy to memorize. Rhyme, assonance, alliteration, and anaphors characterize its musical sound. The proverb suggests a precise message to the listener, calling on ancestral knowledge, mixing past and present. The narrator seeks indirectly to convey a message, a piece of advice, in order to alter a situation. It's a detour that becomes didactic and aims at using a compact, dense, and stable image that involves the visual. It offers knowledge by which to overcome sorrow, misery, and conflict.

On the other hand, the proverb is an opening, since it appears to resolve a disagreement, to stabilize a chaotic situation, to find a way out by solving the problem discreetly. It harbors a truth that may not necessarily have been taken into account. At the same time, the proverb is closure, a closed system: "The proverb is a small, quasi-closed, inflexible system whose function is to fight against the erosion of the word" (Khatibi, *La blessure du nom propre* [The wounded noun], 34). It remains vague and, to be effective, must not only be deciphered but also understood in order to generate the desired adjustments.

Proverbs correspond to the variety of difficulties that humans confront. To facilitate the memorization of proverbs, different techniques have been invented, such as proverb strings. Objects are placed on a thin cord, and each one is a reminder of a specific proverb—a mnemonic device that links the object-sign to the verbal. The cord functions precisely like the sculpted cover of a pot—suggesting a specific and carefully chosen proverb in order to change an unhealthy situation—which is presented during a meal to the person in question to sensitize him or her indirectly to the problem (s)he presumably caused. Thus, the proverb may rely on a pictorial or sculpted image to transmit its message and propose a transformation. Additionally, there is the technique of referring to the human body, whose individual parts correspond to specific phrases:

> In order to remember proverbs, some people use a mnemonic device, expressed in accordance with various parts of the body. There is nothing surprising in this economy of language. Dressing the body with a symbolic, coded space is a common practice in (Moroccan) popular culture: medicine, divination, or bewitchment. (Ibid., 25)

The **riddle** is a game that calls for reflection and is frequently intended to provoke laughter. A concise observation of the world, it offers a critique disguised beneath a jovial and festive appearance. In some cases, just like the song and the proverb, it can only be spoken in a particular situation, for instance during a ritual, or only in the presence of men or initiated individuals. Thus, rules dictate the use of these forms of expression, since they involve the word, which, in an inappropriate context, may have harmful consequences—the unforeseeable power of the spoken whose fleeting aspect is misleading.

The riddle contains a single response that the interlocutor must try to find by digging through his store of knowledge and deciphering the data hidden in the question:

> In the Riddle the individual is no longer in touch with the universe: there is one man questioning another man in such a way that the question forces the other one to arrive at a form of knowing. One of them possesses the knowledge, is the individual who knows, the expert, the *wise man;* thus the other is faced with a partner who, by his question, leads him to put his powers and his life at stake so that he, too, comes to possess the same knowledge and proves himself to be wise. (Jolles, *Formes simples* [Simple forms], 105)

The riddle is used a great deal in secret societies where it is concerned with making a specific piece of knowledge emerge, or a clarification, a clairvoyance, based on a silent reasoning that allows the gamut of possibilities to be considered. This art requires the individual to be initiated into the process in order to reveal the single and often unexpected solution.[2]

As for the **song,** it touches more on emotions and unites music with the word: the ethereal. It involves rhythm, melody, as well as voice, which comes forth from the depths of the body and conveys vibrations that penetrate the person. Vocal tone emits the joys and anxieties of daily life, mirroring the feelings that inhabit the individual and society. For example, it marks the time for collective labor in fields or workshops, while expressing both restrictions and moments of happiness. Song is liberating, criticizing difficulties and suggesting solutions, a path that the musical composition conceals.

The **myth** explains the origin of a phenomenon such as the beginning of the world and depicts an inner quest. Man seeks to understand the universe and give it meaning. He tells himself a story based on an observation of the world which he has heard, interrogated, and whose coherence he seeks. Just like the epic and the proverb, the myth is timeless and implies the marvelous, the magical, and the supernatural. The myth sublimates human actions and presents fabulous beings and heroes. On the edge of two worlds—the here and the elsewhere—it originates in a distant, elusive muddle and goes beyond what is lawful. Its goal is to astonish, amaze, bewitch, calling on invisible forces and linking humanity with the divine, often one of the functions of oral literature. But it also marks closure and restricts the world to an interpretation so that it can begin to have a meaning. In addition, Glissant sees myth as an alienating form that closes again when it links the human being to a totalizing system that hurls a truth at him, thus provoking intolerance:

> Among the myths that have traced a path toward the awareness of history, founding myths had the role of consecrating the presence of a community on its land, by binding that presence to a Genesis via a legitimate lineage and continuity. That is what gives it its atavistic character.
>
> The founding myth is dimly reassuring on the unfailing continuity of this lineage from a Genesis onward, and then authorizes the community in question to consider the land it inhabits, having become territory, as *absolutely* its own. (*Traité du tout-monde,* 196)

Yet, by creating extraordinary stories it has managed to make humanity dream.

As for the **fable,** it fills people with wonderment and, at certain times, can lighten the burden of existence:

> In the legend the aim is to record, that is to document a historical experience or some stage of a people's cultural growth. The aim of the explanatory tale is to educate by providing the origins or backgrounds to a familiar or accepted phenomenon or habit. And in the fable the narrator basically aims to entertain by exposing the audience to the aesthetic delights of the tale and leaving them free to derive whatever message they see fit. (Okpewho, *African Oral Literature,* 221)

According to Glissant, it is a free form that welcomes variety, welcomes what changes and does not go back to a lineage. It plays with the unfamiliar, the marvelous, motivating the imaginary, clearing a path for itself between places, between the here and the elsewhere.

The various forms of orality are rarely demarcated. Depending on the regions of the continent, they may include other genres, such as genealogy or praise songs, that are often fitted inside other forms as they intersect. For example, genealogies, praise songs, proverbs, and songs regularly appear in the epic. Their popular characteristics link them together. All of them illustrate the teachings of a community or the origin of a feeling or an experience, and communicate with the unspeakable, transgressing the ordinary, deepening interactions and human feats. The griot's art embraces many methods, inserting elements that come to be added to a culture, Islam for instance, thereby creating close links between this religion and its ancestral art, problematizing demarcations once again.

> Fiona McLaughlin points out (1997) that in Senegal, marabouts often speak to a crowd in public through the intermediary of a *guewel.* In fact, the muezzins, who call people to prayer, are often of *guewel* origin. Today there is a new form of Islamic popular music marked by praise for marabouts. McLaughlin argues that when popular singers of *guewel* sing such songs, they undertake a shift from the griot-noble relationship to the *taalibe* (Islamic pupil)–marabout relationship. Although the relationship changes, McLaughlin notes that the form of the praise song does not change. It becomes, instead, a praise to god, via the marabout. McLaughlin concludes that by attaching the form of the *guewel*'s praise song to the Sufi tradition, popular singers have created a new genre that enables them to straddle creatively the boundary between the roles of the *guewel* and *taalibe.* (Hale, *Griots and Griottes,* 318)

Oral art is wide-ranging and circulates. In serving the community, it reflects the elements that traverse it. Moreover, since the griot sometimes travels hundreds of kilometers to attend celebrations where he has been invited to perform, he is steeped in multiple practices and develops a whole range of methods that will not be locked into a single form or philosophy: this is what gives oral art all its power.

Let us now return to writing to analyze the use of orality in a few texts. We will examine others in greater detail in subsequent chapters on Werewere Liking and Tchicaya U Tam'Si.[3]

In the "Ouverture" of *Gens de sable,* by Catherine N'Diaye, the author-narrator introduces herself in a manner that resembles the griot's practice of addressing his public before beginning his story:

> The patronymic, the legal, affective designation, the indexing of the subject is substantial.

> My name is Cathy N'Diaye. For anyone who has some knowledge of the Sahel, Senegal is the origin of the name. I go there as often as I can but that is only every now and then. (7)

But although this introduction is reminiscent of the griot's familiar practice, Cathy N'Diaye shortens her lineage considerably. For example, comparing the opening of *Sundiata* as retold by Niane, mentioned above, we see that in her text N'Diaye only gives us her name and place of origin. Thus, right at the beginning of the story something is lost because there is no mention of a genealogy, which, with her being so far from her original community, would hardly make sense. In addition, she stresses the scarcity of contact with her people by using the expression "every now and then," while the griot is in permanent contact with his community. The presence of this form sketches links with the past while adding changes at the same time.

In Mudimbe's *Before the Birth of the Moon,* the narrative inserts fragments of songs at a discotheque. They translate the feelings of the (female) protagonist and disclose events to come:

> Don't judge them by their swords or thrones:
> All notables, of any rank, still have
> a coarse and carnal eye
> the same raw look of the leering beast . . .
> . . . .
> Far from the tree's trunk, away in the brush
> grows the rare shoot, alone of its kind.
> And you recognize your kindred
> by the pure light in their eyes . . .
>
> (24)

These song insertions are a reminder of orality and give us important information. Short phrases, some of which function like proverbs, provide us with details of the place—"the brush." The vocabulary is reminiscent of the epic—"swords," "thrones"—and the proverb because of the brevity of the phrases and the didactic condensation of images. Terms appear that have to do with sight—"look," "light in their eyes"—the opposition between the pure light and the leering look. The author uses the imperative, anaphors, and poetic images. But in the heart of a text, these song references, where the reader must imagine the music and the atmosphere, function like fragments and impose silences. They are compressed, allusive fragments containing information that for a long time will remain obscure and that the reader won't grasp until the end of the story. In addition, there is a discrepancy, a gap between the nightclub setting ("visibly impassioned and at the same time spent by this invasion of music which entangles her in a sea of cigarette smoke and the stale smell of alcohol," 23) and the premonitory import of the lyrics, presenting a contrast between the body language of the female character, a prostitute, and the philosophical content of the song. These disparities create mysteries that will be elucidated as the text progresses. On the other hand, there is distance between the music suggested and the song the community or the griot sings during a celebration:

> The role of the urban oral artist is therefore reduced almost entirely to entertainment for people who simply want to be relieved after a hard day's or week's work and who care somewhat less for what the artists say in their songs than for the music which accompanies them. (Okpewho, *African Oral Literature,* 41)

Mudimbe plays on two stages: one is the urban setting—the discotheque where the music prevails—while the other is the ancestral value of the word uttered by a poet, fine connoisseur of language who, in the context of this tale, imparts the impending events to the reader.

In the same novel, a radio excerpt of the president's speech illustrates another reference to orality, while at the same time it differs from the art of the griot:

> Absentmindedly, he turned the radio on. They were replaying the speech delivered by the Chief of State the night before.
>
> > . . . Let us never forget that those who hold a public mandate are the target of all the people. It is upon the discipline which you will impose upon yourselves, upon the example which you will set, that the prestige of the Nation and the authority of the State depend. It is difficult to require our population to submit to the law if those who make the law are the first to trample it under their feet. (Mudimbe, *Before the Birth of the Moon,* 98–99)

With radio, visual display is lost: body and movements are absent, as is the finery of the griot, who would often appear in public by the side of the chief or the leader in order to speak for him. There is also a temporal gap between the broadcast and the time the speech was actually given; it was "delivered . . . the night before." The power of the verbal, the oral, creates the narrative while corroding it at the same time. This speech (which in the past would have been pronounced by the griot) of the Chief of State, whose word is all-powerful because of the rank he holds, criticizes the behavior of some of those who work for the government. In the specific context of the story, the text alludes to the Minister, who, incidentally, is the one who picked the radio program while absentmindedly playing with the knob and, besides, isn't really listening to "this morality lesson" (99). A breach sets in at the heart of the text between this speech inserted into the story and the acts committed in the novel, between the wisdom of the words, paralleling the clairvoyance that the griot is committed to present, and the Minister's inability to listen. Words conveyed via an apparatus airing the speech given the previous night by the Chief of State fall on deaf ears, reminders of a complex oral art condemning corrupt politicians in a textual structure but without the ability to achieve any transformation.

Thus, the silence as to genealogy in Catherine N'Diaye's text shows us that values have changed and that lineage no longer suggests the roots of a given individual. In *Before the Birth of the Moon,* which takes place in what was formerly Zaïre, orality and the placing of voice (insertion of characteristics specific to the verbal, to communication by means of typography, of descriptions that evoke a cry, a song) are used to link the novel to the oral art, all the while shedding a critical light on the country's political situation. By the same token, they fragment the text, inscribing a rift with the ancestral value of the word, describing a malaise that eats away at the characters.

During a roundtable devoted to the mainstays of francophone works,[4] Djibril Tamsir Niane gave a presentation on his text *Sundiata: An Epic of Old Mali,* recalling the immeasurable value of the knowledge transmitted by griots, based on a meticulous underlying organization and rigorous teaching, disseminating essential principles for maintaining cohesion within a community, establishing taboos, and encouraging approaches that help to avoid irreversible conflicts. He feels that certain current problems could be avoided by enhancing the wisdom that this art contains.

In her writing, the Senegalese author Aminata Sow Fall takes a similar position. Her novel *Le jujubier du patriarche* accentuates the knowledge conveyed by the oral art, which, by glorifying certain characters, impresses the reader and recommends ways to live life, giving meaning to existence and motivating a hieratic quest:

> She also understood that Naarou's claim was consistent with her personality and with the mystical relationship she had with the epic. The song: a love, a passion that would never leave her and whose flame—not

destructive, fortunately—might shine above her grave when she was to join Dioumana in the bed of the Natangué River. (89)

Meanwhile, the text distinguishes the griots, who possess incomparable knowledge and are able to guide a society, from those who have not acquired the necessary knowledge and are motivated by profit and swindling:

> She was a griotte of the new era—without the mission, the vocation, or the talent of the people of her caste; her sole objective: her money god, the money of sycophantic behavior, lies, intimidation and additional covert dealings of which other griots scornfully accused her [. . .]. (79)

Pursuing a social and political dimension in her written work, Fall also condemns the inequalities that have emerged and that allow those with a social position to arrogate certain rights:

> Yet, over time, "blood had been mixed" at the highest level of the hierarchy without resulting in any true union because the exchange was unequal: noble men allowed themselves romantic escapades outside the perimeters of their caste, while others could only chase women within the boundaries of their territory. (23)

As a result, the work pursues displacement. Naarou, who has been fascinated by the art of the griot Naani since her childhood, asks his son to let her sing the epic during a pilgrimage to Babyselli, which she ends up doing. This permits someone outside the "caste" to perform like the griot. This is also a transition from the male to the female and from the oral to the written. The text alludes to the voice by using the term "song" (164), "lament" (164), and to methods of the oral art by using repetition, the poetic, the marvelous, by using proverbs or inserting silences, not only by the breaks and jumps between the images drawn but also by the countless mysteries that it preserves within the text.

> The equilibrium of our world rests on the shoulders of the woman, the marabout, and the griot . . . My God, if they were to reveal all the secrets they possess, the world would explode! It would break like a bowl thrown from a mountain top . . . Of course, it would break into a thousand pieces because of surprises revealed by the light that shines into corners, which should remain eternally in the dark for the sake of society's peace and stability . . . (148–49)

The work highlights an art that for the author holds enormous power developed over centuries, sets out a highly sophisticated system, and acts as a guide by setting itself up as memory for an entire people. The presence of the oral enriches the text, indicating a social, cultural, and aesthetic dimension, providing pathways that link up with ancient methods and metaphysical foundations, tracing limits not to be disregarded, and yet calling on the imaginary. Nevertheless, as noted before, the changes made to the griot's art in his absence can in no way create the same effects. The text cannot be a substitute for his person. However, it can be a reminder of the contribution of his power and the possible social modifications to be made in order to meet present needs and to see the griot endure.

Obviously, the griot's art has undergone numerous changes and doesn't necessarily have the same function it had in the past. The organization of a society changes, and cities regulate populations differently when people are crowded together in the daily struggle for survival. But scattered, dispersed, and fragmented, the foundations of this art survive, and clever tricks are used to preserve practices that, even in a veiled way, try to stand up to the feeling of powerlessness in which a growing number of individuals find themselves trapped. In Algeria, large groups of youth left to their own devices are turning to language games to gain influence on the political and social context. Watchful, hoping to see a change before long, they meet on street corners where they display astounding humor, their weapon to counteract stagnation and the violence they have endured. In Senegal, marabouts are of increasing importance for a whole generation of the unemployed, and, as McLaughlin mentioned above, the former are turning to the art of the griot to help guide them.

As far as writers are concerned, this chapter shows that they are working with the word in a manner that differs from the griot or the storyteller. Tonality, body, and expressive movements are missing:

> The masks and other artwork taken from Africa by colonial-era collectors often seem to have lost their power when exhibited in museums today. In the same way, the printed words of griots seem to have lost the power they had when sung or uttered in performance. Words on the printed page, like masks in a display case, cannot convey the atmosphere of the event at which they were expressed. If it is difficult for us to grasp fully the nuances of African systems of prosody from the printed text, it is even harder to comprehend the power that lies behind the mask of words created by griots and griottes. One reason for that difficulty is that these words are so often spoken or sung in a synergistic blend of voice and another medium [. . .]. (Hale, *Griots and Griottes,* 145)

Nevertheless, there are methods that circulate within writing and result in inventions that appear frequently during the period of Independence. These writers, who go about things differently from those of the preceding generation, are no longer attached to a culture. They draw their knowledge from languages and arts, thus creating an eclectic assemblage—verbalizing and visualizing the text.

> The phenomena of creolization at work in our world concern not only the various eras that communities go through, whether in contact or not, but also the interchange of written and spoken languages. Beyond these languages, the imaginary (or imaginaries) of humanity could inspire languages, or archipelagos of languages, which would be equal to the infinite variety in our relationships. (Glissant, *Traité du tout-monde,* 112)

They draw from the scope of the world, dismantling distinctive roots, borrowing and modifying ancient techniques—such as repetition—that ask us to meditate on words, language play, and irony so as to criticize better; they go back to forms like the riddle, proverb, song, and elements of the epic to illuminate the human journey while, at the same time, reconnecting it to the past.

Bakhtin shows that the novel is a form that is particularly well suited to heterogeneity, since it represents an open and unlimited system, which allows for the inscribing of pluri-lingualism, multiculturalism, and intertextuality and thereby responds to the needs of the present. By creating contradictions, the story asks to be questioned. Interpretation is multifarious and highlights the ambivalence of the language, which, having been misused by various groups (colonial administration, dictatorships, the enticements of globalization, and so forth), can no longer have absolute power.

> The novel is in contact with the elementary forces of the present, which prevents the genre from becoming rigid. The novelist orbits around all that is not yet finished. He may appear in the field of the imagination in any of the writer's attitudes, evoke realistic moments of his life or allude to these, join in the conversations of his characters, openly enter into the debate with his literary enemies, and so on. It is not merely the appearance of the author's character in the arena of the representation that counts, but also the fact that the real, formal, and first author (the author of the author's image) is involved in a new relationship with the representation of the world he has devised: they have the same temporal and axiological dimensions, the discourse of the author representing is on the same level as the represented discourse of the character and can form (better yet:

can't help but form) conversational relationships and hybrid combinations. (Bakhtin, *Esthétique et théorie du roman,* 461–62)

The novel combines genres (myth, psychological analysis, the epistolary, memory, fable, proverb), styles (intertextuality, local linguistic features, jargon), and languages. Postcolonial writers collect methods from diverse cultures, interweaving practices that are sometimes ancient, sometimes recent, recording, describing, and developing the complexity of humans, their thoughts, their flaws, and criticizing the violence and abuses they have suffered. They depict an environment in which countless approaches come in contact, an environment that attests to melding and combining. This, in turn, has consequences for oral transmission.

Examining African literary texts, we find orality present in the use of proverbs, citations, dialogues, indications of gesture and voice; in references to the epic, the myth, the fabulous, and the collective; in the use of repetition, digression, onomatopoeia; in the presence of image (metaphor, symbol) and music (rhyme, repetition, alliteration, assonance). It links the person back to the past while it inserts changes, as we saw in *Gens de sable, Before the Birth of the Moon,* and *Le jujubier du patriarche.* By recapturing oral techniques, the novelist evokes the power of the word and its capacity to subvert what is lawful, to open out onto magic in order to exorcise reality and thus activate deterritorialization. At the same time, through its structure the written text "encloses," "contains," "captures" the verbal and, in a sense, removes its substance, its spontaneous and vivid essence. The resulting void, from which emerges and in which ferments and vibrates the first cry and the word with its multiplicity of sonorous combinations, this void will have indirectly expressed the sacred, the unutterable. At the same time, the separation between human beings and the Divine is drawn from the void created. In many cases, narrative writing no longer affirms absolute values and immutable givens, but depicts the fragility, disillusionment, exchange, permeability, fluctuation, and uncertainty of life; it refers to the innumerable tricks and practices that have developed, clearing infinite paths that sometimes overlap, sometimes disperse in fragmentation, in an attempt to reproduce what develops throughout the world on a daily basis, to the last and tiniest tremor found in the deepest part of our being.

1

2

3

4

5

6

7

8

9

10

11

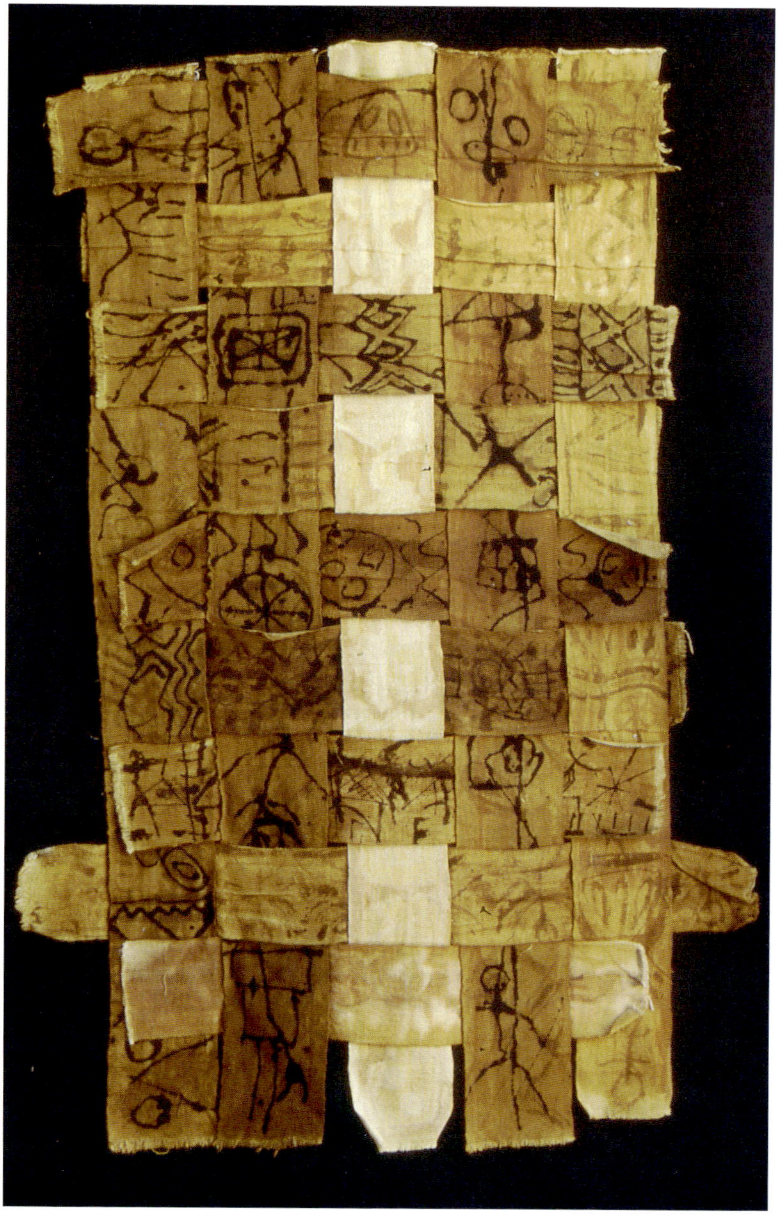

13

14

15

16

4 Aesthetic Flow between Visual and Written Art

Multiplying the Sites

A NUMBER OF "FRANCOPHONE" African writers, such as Abdelkébir Khatibi, Werewere Liking, Abdelwahab Meddeb, Nabile Farès, Jean-Baptiste Tati-Loutard, V. Y. Mudimbe, and Assia Djebar, refer to the image (drawings, geometric patterns, or painting) in their texts. What is the significance of this coming and going, this close relationship between writing and image? Why does writing turn toward the visual? Can it not stand on its own merits? What does it gain by moving into other fields, by incorporating painting into the narrative, for instance, or by constructing a plot on the model of a tattoo or a picture, by evoking an image to translate a specific idea? What does the visual art transmit that the written word does not express, or that the spoken word overshadows, drives away, or even invalidates by the use of words?

Conversely, there are numerous painters in the Maghreb and in sub-Saharan Africa who turn toward writing, who insert elements of calligraphy into their paintings or include signs they find on objects (rugs, jewelry, pottery) or on the human body (tattoos, scarifications). Why do painters borrow forms from writing, use signs even though they may transform them? How can their use of the signifier lead to something such as recall, movement, contamination, and the combination of the signified?

Abdelkébir Khatibi mentions these links in a work devoted to Ahmed Cherkaoui:

> Thus an unsteady balance takes shape that resembles a calligraphy of signs. But what should be contemplated is how the standard of a composition makes it to the word. "Writing and drawing," Klee said, "are essentially

> identical." How else can we think about painting? (*Cherkaoui, la passion du signe*, 18)

To try tackling such a problem, we must consider the cultural context and go back to the source of writing and of the plastic arts, follow their itinerary, their transformations, ramifications, and their intertwining with other arts. Their evolution responds to necessities, questions left unresolved, intercultural combinations, exchanges, and inventions that go way back in time and have been transferred from one form to another:

> What rouses our attention is the migration of a sign (or a symbol) to another, no matter how minuscule (a dot for instance), and then gradually the quite ample shift of graphemes, that unprecedented repertoire of objects that can go from a rock carving to a calligraphy, for example, via rug, tattoo, wickerwork, or head-scarf design. (Khatibi, *La blessure du nom propre*, 61)

And in its migration the signs end up by evoking disparate and distant elements—an assemblage of segments which the plastic and literary arts endowed and which they enjoy using and organizing.

From the time it first appeared, writing has been connected to the sacred: it records the modalities of a ritual, the relationships with the beyond, and calls out to the invisible powers, sometimes to the Ancestors. It stems from signs that are the expression of a vision communicating with a hereafter. Their course is all the more difficult to determine in that they do not necessarily correspond to a particular word. Markings or incisions on objects or on the human body are a means by which to crystallize thought. In Africa, this process supposedly appeared as a way for a griot and for closed societies to jog their memories. For instance, the Luba who live in the southeast of the Democratic Republic of Congo had cleverly devised a mnemonic system based on the sacred objects that surrounded the king. Fragments of the past were engraved on pieces of wood known as *lukasa*, on stools, spears, axes, arrow holders, beakers, and divination objects. These inscriptions spring from an unutterable knowledge that only a few initiates can decode. The messages recount events, respond to questions that have long been left unanswered, and describe the trajectory of a chief or a king.

> For Luba, staffs and stools are historical documents whose hierarchical compositions of two- and three-dimensional forms are intended to be mnemonic texts. Verbal exegeses are derived from them that not only reaffirm relationships between visual and verbal arts, but lend insight into

> the ways that individual holders of power view their roles and validate their social positions in Luba political hierarchies. (Roberts and Roberts, *Memory,* 152)

It is not a question of deciphering an alphabet but rather of comprehending signs skillfully set into a wooden surface, beads positioned on slabs, markings inscribed onto objects, symbols of survival. Complex parallels can be made between inscriptions on the human body (scarifications), sacred works in the service of the community, and objects of divination. This migration of signs that safeguard memory extends to innumerable civilizations located well beyond Central Africa. The mnemonic supports and techniques differ from one population to another, but the similarities reveal parallels, at first sight surprising, between regions that are sometimes very far apart, from the Maghreb to sub-Saharan Africa and far beyond.

The Arab graph links a variety of African regions and joins the pictorial stroke with the written word. Tradition has it that it appeared in Arabia at the very beginning of Islam when Mohammed received the divine revelation and transcribed the sacred words of the angel Gabriel, thereby suddenly learning to write. Opinions vary as to the sources and influences that contributed to the development of this writing. Today, its complexity incites a myriad of questions, as Khatibi describes:

> The origin of writing may be explained—or it may be a matter for reverie and meditation.
>
> From the outset the Muslim finds himself mysteriously confused. For while Arabic script is definitely revealed in the Qur'ãn as a miracle, we also know—from the other side of the looking-glass, so to speak—that it existed as the successor to Nabato-Aramaic, and therefore to Phoenician, beginning with the first letter *alif.* [. . .]
>
> According to Abû Al-Abbas Ahmed al-Bhûni, letters arose from the light on the pen that inscribed the Grand Destiny on the Sacred Table. Allah had ordained that therein should be recorded the deeds of all creatures, till the Last Judgment. After wandering through the universe, the light became transformed into the letter *alif,* from which developed all the others.
>
> In another variation of the myth, Allah created the angels according to the name and number of the letters, so that they should glorify him with an infinite recitation of the Qur'ãn. (Khatibi and Sijelmassi, *The Splendor of Islamic Calligraphy,* 21)

Some historians link the Arab graph to signs and symbols that the Nabataeans, nomads from Arabia, had used for centuries.

Whatever the origin of Arabic calligraphy, on a canvas it generates a variety of connotations. It refers to Islam, to a language, and to a mystique. It is abstract, playing with lines, plenums, and voids. Calligraphy connects sign, word, and writing. It grounds the word, while engaging gesture and gaze, combining several arts. It is the expression of a vision. Closely resembling drawing, it reproduces sounds, while it is related to music by its undulating movement. In addition, it traces a labyrinthine course reminiscent of the medinas of the Maghreb. Even if the letters that the painter has altered no longer contain any meaning whatsoever, they evoke a mystery as well as a language, a culture, communicating trails, indications, playing at one and the same time on the gestural movement that painting requires and also with letters and language.

In an article entitled "La trace, le signe" (Trace, sign), Abdelwahab Meddeb contemplates the significance of the trace in Arab culture. "The word trace (*athar*) becomes a technical term defined in its relation to inscription and deletion. It throws light on the context where the initiate experiences the obliteration of his identity and the investiture of otherness" (28). This observation stimulates the elaboration of an extension between inscription/deletion and between memory/time—the work (text, image) setting itself up as memory in opposition to oblivion. Meddeb continues his thought by turning toward the ideas of Ibn Arabî on the relationship between "Calame" (inscription) and "Table" (prop):

> Know that the Preserved Table, likened to the universal Soul, is the first created being. It is a primary being that has acquired its dignity as a being owing to a cause that is none other than Calame (Pen), identified with the Intellect, which is the first being created ex nihilo, without reason or model, under the aegis of the One named *al-Badî'*, the Inventor. Calame/Intellect is the very first created being. God caused him to become by an exhalation from the One named *al-Badî'* (the Inventor), when the world had not been created, when it was nothingness, bathing in a dense cloud ("*amâ*").
>
> It is in the joining of the Calame/Intellect and the Table/Universal Soul that the entire creative process is established. Thus creation is comparable to an act of writing, as it uses the tools of writing. (29)

Furthermore, the first letter of the Arabic alphabet, *alif* (ا), to which the letters that follow yield, refers by its shape to the pen that produces the line. This vertical letter, linking earth with heaven, calls upon the divine through its yearning, inaugurating the designation "god" in Arabic: الله, Allah.

To continue with Ibn Arabî, between the Calame and the Table he sees the metaphor of love which engenders creation, bringing the passive and active poles together. The art of the line that is inscription (memory) is connected to the elaboration of a mystique that itself closely unites letter and image: writing and painting that handle pen or brush on the—deserted—expanse of the page or the canvas to turn away from the insignificant void.

> This agreement between the aesthetic and the metaphysical sheds light on the position that calligraphy reserves for itself in the topic (characteristic) of the arts in Islamic civilization. Its hegemony is certainly not built on the desertification of the other artistic areas. On the contrary, one should understand the other artistic activities, especially the pictorial ones, from an iconology to be conceived of according to the same metaphysical principles.
>
> This would clarify a large part of the art of the miniature, which links letter and image, and renders gesture, the body movement that traces or colors the image, subordinate to the posture of the calligrapher. Besides, the illuminator and calligrapher often were one and the same person. (30)

To return to African artists, we notice that some of them—Mustapha Boujemaoui, Wosene Kosrof, or Tayeb Saddiki—cite fragments of the Koran, use calligraphy and transform it, thereby adapting it to the pictorial material.

Other artists, such as Farid Belkahia, Ahmed Cherkaoui, Abdoulaye Konaté, or Rachid Koraïchi, inscribe signs that go back to ancient languages or evoke enigmatic forms, linking with a distant, deeply buried past. The Moroccan artist Farid Belkahia inserts writing fragments into his works (Iblissian, Smaq, Tifinagh). He interweaves methods, calling upon music and script, upon the rhythms and signs that were the foundation of writing.

> Numerous motifs used by Farid Belkahia were inspired by the heritage of the tattoo and the signs/symbols that decorate traditional (popular) art objects, which is also because, being pre-calligraphic, these elements refer to a whole problematic of the sign—and of the pleasure of the sign—that modern art has brought to us from the depths of the collective

> consciousness. (Maraini, "L'important, c'est d'être bien dans sa peau" [The important thing is to be comfortable in one's own skin], 40)

The skin on which he paints is reminiscent of the parchments, the sacred scrolls. The shape of the works (oval, disk, triangle), the colors (red, black, ochre, white), link up with the mnemonic techniques that we find in various regions of sub-Saharan Africa (red may symbolize energy, a possibility of transformation; black can stand for knowledge) and are fragments of processes, of rites that crisscross each other and are linked to an unconscious, which is rooted in a complex expanse. The artist constructs signs, thereby emphasizing the power of the written work, while draining them of their signification. He/she dislocates their meaning to retreat from language and lead us toward a world of shapes and colors that demonstrates the illusion of the verbal. Signs are adrift, scattered, deconstructed; they guide us beyond language, lead us astray as well, all the while simulating a sacred gesture. Thus, the sign takes on its pictorial, aesthetic value once more and extricates itself from language to find silence again and induce vision.

The painter Ahmed Cherkaoui (1934–67) banks on the double Moroccan heritage: the writing in the Koran, the patterns of tattoos, rugs, and various objects. He traces connections, links concepts, providing the sign with a sacred depth. The sign goes far back in time and is the result of intermingling cultures, of convergences. Through the centuries signs have been modified, and on their way have run into different methods, into other techniques and forms. Cherkaoui's canvases bring to mind both Arab calligraphy and pre-Islamic signs, and even suggest Egyptian cartouches:

> In these compositions he has recourse to a process well-known to art history, the inscription of some writing inside a *cartouche,* that is to say, inside an ovoid or rectangular space that allows for a part of it to be solitary while rendering its content sacred. We know that in Egyptian hieroglyphs the names of gods were thus set apart. (Maraini, *Écrits sur l'art* [Writings on art], 155–56)

In both cases they link up with a mystical quest, working the trace, drawing from an imaginary built on a cultural *métissage* that left its mark on Morocco. Geometric patterns, tattoos, Koranic boards, labyrinths, masks, shields: Cherkaoui's painting makes the processes converge and suggests the talisman composed of a multitude of fragments, juxtaposing bits of knowledge.

The Tunisian painter Gouider Triki makes large numbers of ancient signs emerge from his canvas. Prehistoric animals, fish, tools, vertebrates, mix together, vibrate at the contact with one another, moving toward the magic and thereby forming a secret writing that calls out to the gods.

Boujema Lakhdar, another Moroccan artist, draws his signs from magic (arranging letters that coincide with numbers), from the occult (the eye that reminds us of Egyptian hieroglyphs), and he engraves, cuts, paints, on wood, fabric, or other materials, creating three-dimensional works: chairs, tables whose shapes are lengthened and changed.

A great many artists use signs. The Algerian Mahdjoub Ben Bella is equally interested in Arab graphs, which he arranges on his canvases in such a way as to make them illegible. He thereby draws links between writing and pictorial forms while staying away from language. His compatriot Rachid Koraïchi has civilizations and writing enter into dialogue—a mystical play of dancing shapes. The Malian Abdoulaye Konaté introduces masks as well as signs of Mali into his paintings and graphic installations. His fellow citizen Modibo Franky Diallo works with signs—traces of transformed ancient processes that outline a new direction. Pathways and intersections in which the artist draws upon a past, all the while expressing an individual specificity, playing with the flat surface of a canvas and with luminous depth. The Senegalese painter Abdoulaye Ndoye refers to writing systems but has drained them of all meaning by not referring to a specific language. On a henna-painted surface (a technique reminiscent of parchment) he traces lines that look like writing. This arrangement of markings that have been freed of the verbal rejects linguistic, national, and religious frontiers. The assemblage hints at sacred texts—which could be the Torah, Bible, Koran, as well as Tibetan or Hindu texts, unrestricted by absolute and exclusive characteristics. The parallel between the visual arts and scripted systems emphasizes ancient connections and the contribution of the sacred, while it removes itself from the uncompromising values of a language.

From the Maghreb to Central Africa, including Côte d'Ivoire, Nigeria, Sudan, and Cameroon, many painters juxtapose several different heritages. Souleymane Keita, who is Senegalese, makes reference to the Dogon signs of Mali, to calligraphy, and to modern art, thereby converging systems. The Ivorian Nguessan Kra brings together ancient letters and fragmented geometric forms, while recalling the custom of writing in the sand.

These artists bring back forms of knowledge with complex origins. They are relying on the richness of the intertwinings, turning toward the present, linking up with the trajectory of modern art, while at the same time making unique use of ancient symbols.

> Just as we speak of bilingualism, we will speak of bi-pictorialism as the combination of two codes. Don't be surprised, for instance, to see it work between cubism and Arab calligraphy; or between signs of an ancestral visual memory (tattooing, hieroglyphs, talismans, magic numbers . . .) and abstract painting of the West. (Khatibi, "Croisement de regards" [Looks crossing], 20)

Another example that illustrates these combinations is the use of the *adinkra* signs of the Ashanti of Ghana, which proliferated throughout the past century, moving away from their earliest role. *Adinkra* signs originally appeared on the fabric worn by a king or a chief during a mourning period and referred to specific proverbs. Thanks to their plastic and symbolic dimension, they circulated across the world and have been used by stylists, designers, and artists, such as the Ghanaian painter Kofi Antoubam or the Togolese Okué Adobé.[1]

Painting opens up linguistic borders and bestows a collective knowledge that goes far back in time, while calling upon techniques drawn from numerous sources and delineating correspondences.

What is important here is the quest for a trace of knowledge, of a revelation, of a movement rooted in the past, a past dating from well before Islam and moving beyond current borders. This quest shows itself across countless cultures through the use of calligraphy and the geometric abstraction that can be found in rugs, fabrics, ceramics, and on the body and is a language whose significance has sometimes been lost. It circulates in spite of the opacity it generates, from the *arrières-pays* (the hinterlands), as Yves Bonnefoy puts it, that inhabit us and that the artist conveys, thus linking us to worlds gone by, resuscitating knowledge we once had: "Artistic memory is a palimpsest. Every period of reflection upon oneself and one's roots works around the area of this fertile and archaic memory. Painters discover it in the crucible of their imagination" (Maraini, "Au rendez-vous de l'histoire, la peinture" [Painting meeting history], 28). In this text Toni Maraini speaks about a "non-apparent," a "veiled" history still in gestation, which "follows its own path underground" only to reappear unexpectedly, joltingly, suddenly pouring out, made up of multiple experiences.

> Artists are here the symbolic heirs of the universal anthropologic patrimony whose very powerful imagery this century has put into circulation through contacts and reproductions. But even more so in the sense of

> becoming conscious of the past, of a past that cannot be ignored since it prepares its own evolution anyway [. . .]. (27)

Writing is a complex system that was born from the sign. It has changed to adapt to human needs, surrounding conditions, and shifts, and has been through many transformations. Sometimes it originates from a realistic image present in the world and is a mnemonic process close to the pictorial or the sculptural (hieroglyph); sometimes it takes on an abstract appearance (Arab calligraphy). Signs in a myriad of shapes have existed forever and use various techniques: inscriptions in the sand, marks used to brand animals, patterns tattooed on the body that provide historic information or that appeal to the favor of the Beyond. These signs lead to the forms of writing that we know and that firmly fix languages. Signs formulate a configuration of the world's experience. On the side of the signified, they allow thoughts to be secured, to be transmitted to future generations, and to organize everyday life. On the side of the signifier, they contain a force that painters are trying to find again: a graphic composition that is both powerful and simple and evokes a sense of harmony, balance, and magic. Signifier and signified draw their forms from ancient cultures, going back to signs that have allowed thought to be crystallized and to communicate with invisible forces—expressing a metaphysics and a view of the world.

By referring to the signs that gave birth to the writing forms we know, artists remind us that the objective of the latter was to communicate with the hereafter. Signs have a hieratic value, a sacred power, and convey a mystery. The artist combines them with his painting medium, transforms them, and adapts them to the new support. He links himself to the past, to signs drawn from the world, in order to communicate thoughts that live within us and have led us to where we are now.

These alliances (painting-writing, gesture-rhythm) also reveal another important characteristic: in contrast to the arts in the West, the arts in Africa have always been closely connected. A kind of weaving so as to represent the entirety of experience, the complexity of human beings, and to translate their manifold facets:

> Okediji (1988) describes the painting of an altar dedicated to the Yoruba deity Oluorogbo. He explains the rigorous sequentiality of the dramaturgy. [. . .] The painters are women who act, dance and sing a traditional act. But over and above the reference to history, the actresses mime their present aspirations and solutions, sacred or profane. The original ancient

> text is *mis en abyme,* i.e. encased in other more contemporary narratives which it enhances, thus proving its essential role. A simulated sacred diegesis founds the mimesis, which in turn magnifies and justifies the first. [. . .] This form of dramaturgy is not new, but Okediji sees in it a tradition exclusive of Ile-Ife, once the mythological and historic capital of the Yoruba world. Wall paintings of temples and altars are in fact attested in all Africa and the association of pictographic (or other) writing with place and local rite is common. (Battestini, *African Writing and Text,* 222–23)

As for African literature written in French, numerous authors refer to signs, to methods of transcription (tattoos, tablets, hieroglyphs), that go back to the sources of writing. Some writers cite a painting or drawing, and thus create a void for the reader, who must find the link between the text and the canvas mentioned, connect the elements, decode the leaps, the pieces, to interweave the many practices.

There is no denying that language is incapable of expressing "everything" and runs up against limitations. Striving to represent the human experience, it is always located beyond and adjacent to what is elusive by nature. The trials of the word are all the greater for African authors who by borrowing the French language relinquish their mother tongue. In the Maghreb, Arabic is circulated within the framework of Islam through the Koran but is not necessarily used in daily life. As for regional dialects, which are often mother tongues, they have only recently been transcribed. Under colonialism, the French language fulfilled the double function of both the written and the spoken. Using it might eventually provide access to a worldwide dialogue and to written works being more readily published and distributed. However, appropriating this language in a literary setting can create obstacles, as Khatibi has described:

> I have suggested—and Kateb stated it very clearly—that the Arab writer who uses French is caught in a chiasmus, a chiasmus between alienation and inalienability (in every sense of both these terms): this writer doesn't write in his own language, he writes his proper name in a changed form, he cannot own anything (if a language can even be appropriated), he owns neither his mother tongue which is not written, nor the written Arabic which is alienated and replaced, nor that other learned language that tells him to lose himself in it. Unfathomable suffering when the writer doesn't assume this erratic identity in *a clarity of thought that lives on this chiasmus, on this schism.* (*Maghreb pluriel,* 201)

The use of French causes a laceration that requires shrewdness in order to overcome the deficiencies of an external language that does not contain the sound fluctuations of the forsaken dialect: its formulas, its metaphors—its soul. An entire music, rhythm, and breath are destroyed, or even abandoned:

> Now, as Moncef Chelli reminds us, classical Arabic grammar itself uses other concepts (such as) *as-sawãmit* (the silent and mute ones) for consonants; *al-harakat* (the movements) for the vowels and diacritic marks. This linguistic thought of movement, stasis, and silence, which belongs to a different logic, a different metaphysics of the sign, demands to be approached in its element of theorizing and categorizing. (Ibid., 182)

Thus, as this study has suggested, the works of the postcolonial period play with blanks, diglossias, gaps, approximations, and juxtapositions in order to come closer to the subject's experience—procedures that via the detour attempt to formulate the convoluted and equivocal and give shape to the multicultural experience. The linguistic expressions of the mother tongue are indirectly evoked through innuendos, allusions, and analogies that nourish the text from underneath, and the reader must be on his/her guard to grasp the references, since the fabric is riddled with blank spaces.

By placing him- or herself outside language, the author momentarily escapes from words that lug a past around and frees him/herself from a verbal system. At the same time, he provides the power of the trans-aesthetic, of the interdisciplinary, and pursues a familiar *métissage.* The author skirts the lacunae of the adopted language that cannot necessarily express certain (geographic, cultural) characteristics and examines other arts, delving into rhythms and images.

Furthermore, words are worn and illusory, and the writer puts strategies in place by which to avoid redundancies, clichés, and refuses to reveal everything, thus preserving mystery. Insertions interrupt the narrative and decentralize the structure by opening up onto other means of organization.

There are other reasons that must be taken into consideration as well. In Abdelwahab Meddeb's *Phantasia* the references to paintings by Malevitch, Mondrian, and Rothko indicate a path toward abstract art in order to explicate the quest, the narrator's thrust. Modern art promotes abstraction, and in Islam the letter replaces the icon. The figure is not forbidden but plays a limited role. Meddeb explains the function of the image in Islam, where figurative representation is discouraged as a way of motivating the creation of a mental image in every human being. However, in his article "L'image et l'invisible, Ibn Arabî/Jean de la Croix" [Image and the invisible, Ibn Arabî/St. John of the Cross], he explicates the complexity of this problematic by citing Ibn Arabî's position on figurative and abstract art. Meddeb refers to two terms that are perceived to be in opposition: *tashbîh,* which he translates as "anthropomorphism (or figurative)" and *tanzîh,* translated as "abstraction (or transcendence)."

> *Tashbîh* and *tanzîh* are two opposing terms. If *tashbîh* implies connection, *tanzîh* suggests separation. If the one plays on similitude and resemblance, the other establishes distance and disparity. [. . .] What makes our duel of opposites, *tashbîh/tanzîh,* work is the way in which each of them covers the distance that separates. *Tashbîh* proceeds towards a movement of connection that cancels distance, while *tanzîh* removes the *thing* that separates in order to establish God in darkness, unknowable, impenetrable. ("L'image et l'invisible," 29–30)

Meddeb adopts the position of Ibn Arabî on the importance of bringing together allegedly opposing positions, noting that these two terms are not contradictory but rather they complement and clarify one another. One cannot do without the other—an abstraction needs a boundary:

> According to Ibn Arabî, absolute abstraction (*tanzîh motlaq*) cannot be formulated. No word, whether revealed or not, can achieve such a project. The abstraction (transcendence), the *tanzîh* that corresponds to the infinite and the indefinite cannot obtain any form other than by accepting boundaries, outlines (*hadd*). (31)

The result would be that "the only possible knowledge of God that would support any representation of Him consists of espousing a movement oscillating between *tanzîh* and *tashbîh,* between transcendence and anthropomorphism, between abstraction and the figurative" (32). Ibn Arabî seeks to combine *tanzîh* and *tashbîh* in the imaginary by moving from one form to another, avoiding any absolutes. So in referring to modern painting, Meddeb follows this approach and elaborates the theme of the void and the plenum, the visible and the invisible. By means of the pictorial, a new structure, an energetic potential based on combinations and mergers, crisscrosses his novel *Phantasia.* The mention of Malevitch's white canvas provokes a deep silence by the insertion of both another art and by the painting itself, which opens up onto what is possible: "Absence gleams within a white square that you fill by using your imagination" (*Phantasia,* 39). This representation allows everyone to develop his or her own interpretation and images.

Steeped in Arabic and therefore in the calligraphy that forms an abstract image, the "francophone" writers of the Maghreb rediscover a similar path in modern painting. On the other hand, writers feel the need to supply silence in order to communicate. By relying on an image or inserting pictorial references in their account, authors interrupt the story. Mentioning a visual image in a literary context defers the narrative's unfolding. The painting is something unstated that makes you see, makes you think inside the span of the gaze, preserving its mystery and power. This vision sends you to a hereafter, to metaphysics: "Because the rift of the human being is unnamable and the (still divine) Idea unattainable, the visual form attests to traces in a specific game of codes via a metalinguistic detour" (Buci-Glucksmann, "Le vertical dans l'immanence," 250). And this brings us to the thinking of Merleau-Ponty, who links vision to painting because it generates looking: "the painter, whoever he may be, practices a magical theory of vision *while he is painting*" (*L'oeil et l'esprit* [Eye and mind], 27–28). For Merleau-Ponty, painting involves the body and the gaze. The artist translates his perception by way of his spirit and his unwonted movement through the world. He makes us see the invisible, the unutterable, and offers us a vision by the use of colors and the placement of lines.

To recap, authors play with numerous elements: mother tongues (dialects); written and nonspoken languages, such as Arabic by way of the Koran; signs (tattoos, traces, scarifications, fabric patterns) that are part of everyday life; urban structures (medinas). These are what make the framework and shatter the narration with many quick glances that refer simultaneously to the myriad ways of conveyance, exchange, organization, and distribution. Writers bring together various devices, while not hesitating to include different ways of constructing a story in keeping with a musical or pictorial composition, with melodious segments or with colors and shapes. In turning toward the visual and toward silences, this literature links people in spite of themselves, while communicating ancient concepts that have always provided the human journey with a meaning.

Mémoire de l'absent, a novel by Nabile Farès, illustrates these observations. The author incorporates in the text drawings that fulfill several roles, some of which the narrator explains as he traces a parallel between writing and drawing, agreeing with Klee's thought, mentioned above, that writing and drawing are essentially the same: "and Hamid's brother approached me and looked over my shoulder to see what I was busy writing or drawing: I was happy [. . .] to see that Hamid's brother was able to read or understand what I was drawing [. . .]" (*Mémoire de l'absent,* 106). The drawing is read like a text. This close link to writing is also suggested by the style of the drawing, which is reminiscent of cave art, ancestral markings, as well as signs, patterns, lines picked up from rugs, pottery, and ornaments that have circulated throughout Africa. These drawings go back to other worlds, linking the present with the past, acknowledging the various influences that have left their mark on Algeria, including those of black Africa—a position for which the narrator himself argues throughout the text.

Mémoire de l'absent empowers the fragment, the split, mimesis of memory's movement made up of snatches, and it records the history of colonialism (abductions, tortures, psychological brutalities). But, more than anything else it is a search for silence so as to defy nothingness, the void that has assailed the narrator, to come within reach of an opening. The lines of the drawing cause hope to emerge: "the moment is right, instead of the impossible emptiness of his death, lines, assemblages, and the tensions of our world, are materializing" (226). Thus the lines come together with distant worlds, vast spaces, imbuing the events with meaning.

The inserted drawings symbolize power. The patterns' simplicity attempts to grasp the quintessence, getting rid of what is superfluous. Beyond language, they allow the narrator to surmount obstructions and wounds caused by history; they translate the fundamental elements of what is being, renewing contact with the world:

> [He] held his pencil bending over slightly toward the right and began to draw, there, in front of me, deep inside me, in me [. . .] and, I felt as in that earlier *Jidda* time that one day I would be able to speak again, [. . .] not just to the part farthest away from me, but on the surface, toward the surface, toward others, the other humans, those from whom I am literally cut off, detached, ever since *you're no longer* [. . .]. (110)

They allow him to escape from the power of words, of a language—French—that has removed the mother (mother tongue). And they refer to children's drawings that "tell" beyond language of what is haunting and distressing.

Especially significant is the drawing with which the work concludes:

The two characters with African masks are closing off the river (which, according to the narrator, symbolizes the mystery) as they would close a book; they lift the obstacle (barriers) and allow free access to where people coexist with other people and with themselves. The resolution of the puzzle (recognition of oneself and of the elements that create the collective unconscious, with its African impregnation) opens onto the world's space, overcoming history's wrongs and the injuries encountered on the individual path. The drawing engages the eye. It suggests a solution, moving away from the spoken, only to link up again with the signs that produced writing and have become established in a vast network of cultural exchanges, reconnecting human beings and arts beyond any borders and eras.

In his short story "Un pari d'artiste" (An artist's bet), Jean-Baptiste Tati-Loutard also links the arts, painting in this case, and writing:

> It happened more than once that the brush would fall from his hands; he then understood that it was pointless to insist, that he was being tortured by the blank page, the writer's block of which authors so often speak. For him it was the blank canvas watching him like an eye that had been consumed by opacity. (*Chroniques congolaises,* 84)

The story describes the itinerary of a character named Jacques Pomolo, who suddenly decides to leave his job as a typist to devote himself completely to his passion for painting. Thus the text endorses painting as an art that puts meaning back into the character's existence, and traces a parallel between the arts.

In his novel *Between Tides,* V. Y. Mudimbe refers to art repeatedly, especially to the painting of the Italian Renaissance. The protagonist, Pierre Landu, is tormented by the contradictions in his life that tear at him, and particularly by his role as an African priest. This role is based on a highly hierarchical

Western structure and is closely related to the colonial past as well as to an imperialist system. He then decides to join the underground resistance movement and, as a Marxist, struggles for a political change. This commitment leads him to perpetrate horrible acts which he is unable to justify and to which, in any case, he shuts his eyes. He then marries a woman whom he later deserts to go back to the church, once again fleeing from his commitments. Mudimbe paints a merciless picture of a person whose gestures and actions make his life absurd. Nevertheless, as he draws a caricature from the vicissitudes of the character's life, he poses crucial questions about the role of the Catholic Church and of Marxism in Africa and about the rifts caused by the introduction of foreign models that are often ill-suited to the continent's needs while compelling people to deny values that are inherent to their culture.

> The truth is that my seminary education exiled me bit by bit from my own people. The Occident was the norm, Europe the universal reference. The theological tradition of the Latin Church, Thomism, the orthodox Roman Catholicism of the Council of Trent, all protected by capitalistic sociopolitical institutions, prepared me well to despise people and their beliefs. (89–90)

What is the role of visual art in this context, and more specifically art of the Italian Renaissance, which appears so frequently in the work? What does it bring to the text? Is it merely an accessory to highlight the situation in which Landu finds himself, or does it contribute to new conceptions that turn the existing structure upside down? If that is the case, what then are the ideas that the pictorial suggests?

First of all, by referring to Italian Renaissance art depicting Christian scenes, the writer shows that other positions appear beneath the actual presentation—the Renaissance artist frequently subverted the institutional framework in order to point out numerous problems and social inequalities of the period.

> Once at the Academy of Venice, I stood for some time before Gentile Bellini's *Procession of the Relics.* "What's so unusual about it?" asked a Dutch colleague, Piet van Steel.
>
> "It's a Bellini and it speaks to me of the proletariat," I said, "the revolution." Did that shock him? I don't know. Crazy as it sounds, I was telling the truth. I don't know why that blatantly lugubrious procession across the piazza should symbolize a classless society for me. (15)

In a covert way the artist promotes values in which Landu believes or which keep him from being trapped in restrictive dogmas. Bernini's depiction of Saint Theresa of Avila, which suggests her ecstasy, is a sensual work in which her whole body welcomes the mystic song that calls her and expresses her love of Christ.

> The voluptuous sensuality Bernini so scandalously depicted in this statue was a revelation, helping me to accept my own desires and to love the *pensée* of the great mystic of Avila—which lectures in Asceticism and Mysticism had so badly misinterpreted at the Angelicum. The professor, a Dominican dry as a fishbone, destroyed the mystique masterfully, explaining it by psychology, psychoanalysis, and even parapsychology. (57)

The artists mentioned in *Between Tides* offer an entirely different view of the world, marking off the problems and unifying body and spirit. By turning to the Renaissance artist, the text shows that even though he worked under a very controlled system, was employed by great patrons of the arts, and was called upon to work for the Church, he managed to convey other, cleverly disguised approaches. This transfer is ingenious and suggests other possibilities; avoiding the imposed rules, art turns itself into an example both for Landu and for the narrative text.

On the other hand, not unlike Catholicism, which was established in Africa through colonialism and reflects a specific ideology, the French language is tainted by a number of prejudices. By existing outside of language, painting achieves a more complex dimension of the world: "In the unreal but realistic light of a Caravaggio. A finished composition against a dark background, so that a diffuse life, between light and shadow, surges forth. A masterpiece . . ." (137). Just as the art of the griot has an extraordinary power because what is essential is stated indirectly via proverbs, metaphors, and silences, the painter works through the image in a similar way. For the writer, pictorial art has access to other truths that language, being depleted, cannot reach: "I was in agony; my mind clutched at psalms. To sift out the meaning and learn the words again" (38). In a different passage: "And for all that big talk, I'm a liar. I must start again" (114); and, "Weary, I choose the lulling fluency of official institutions, the falsehood of catchwords" (154).

For Landu, language expresses clichés, and the scriptures have propagated coercive precepts. By posing innumerable questions around the role of the Church in Africa, the text forces the reader to recognize the problems. By turning to other art forms, Italian Renaissance painting in this case, the text provides models—although they are imbued with a specific culture and dominating religion—that are able to generate or express different ways/voices and impose new perspectives in spite of the taboos. Via the pictorial, the text points to tensions while seeking solutions that are built on a combination of thoughts, arts, and cultural systems. As he remains caught in dichotomies, Landu is engulfed by nothingness. Going beyond the verbal, the text in turn subverts the context and the norms provided, and suggests taking another look at the history of colonialism.

In addition, terms linked with sight reappear throughout the work and quite often lead to disgust or emptiness:

> Whenever my eyes turn to the earthen wall of the barracks and pause at my lucky crucifix, hidden in the withes, I feel like making a monstrous face. [. . .] But the reaction is automatic, and is always followed by a rising gorge, a foul new horror. (7)

One must be able to see in order to grasp existence, and Landu, who always flees from any distinct difficulty, isn't always capable of doing that. Still, the text provides the reader with keys, with pathways to lead him out of dead ends, calling upon the visual arts to achieve this, and showing new perspectives.

Not only has the writer Abdelkébir Khatibi written extensively on art (calligraphy, contemporary Moroccan painting, tattooing), but his novels also incorporate patterns and images that have circulated in Morocco throughout the centuries. The writer arranges some texts around a tattoo or an architectural structure, inserting signs, shapes to be grasped and revealed, in the work itself.

An autobiographical novel retracing the narrator's experience from childhood to adulthood, *La mémoire tatouée* (The tattooed memory) is constructed on the model of the medina in which the child grew up, by means of fragmented writing that reproduces its dead ends, labyrinths, and intersections. The text says of this architectural structure: "the street holds me so close that the medina and its allegories echo in the labyrinth of my sentences" (42). He also suggests this model by using words that keep returning throughout the text: "entanglement," "labyrinth," "bifurcation," "maze," "dead end," "zigzag." The medina protects against the invader by its structural complexity: "But a rift common to the colonized and the colonizer, since the medina would resist with its maze" (44). By reproducing this "maze-like" structure, Khatibi's writing forces the reader to pass through a space that isn't readily accessible and that, through leaps and fragments, records the unstated in the image of the medina: "child, when you go flying, bare-footed, through the maze of the streets, be sure you know your way. Know what you won't dare do, be careful of what's unformulated!" (48). For the author, this labyrinthine structure also illustrates Morocco's history; it consists of countless tangles.

> Where do Moroccans come from? What is their origin? When did their prehistory begin? [. . .] The more the periods succeed one another, the greater the space between them, the more the traces multiply. A true labyrinth that, by complicating our journeys in space, hides the secret of time, the secret of our immemorial origin. (Khatibi, "Paradigmes de civilisation," 73)

In this same essay, speaking of Morocco's contemporary art (he gives the painter Ahmed Cherkaoui as an example), Khatibi describes the intertwinings:

> [E]xtremely heterogeneous, a magic bric-a-brac that captures mysterious connections, images from the Islamic light or a pagan past, inscrutable and undecipherable signs, the forgotten language of the past and its riddles. An intersemiotic culture, in tattoos, mural decoration, on the ceilings of common homes, inside the folds of a talisman—whether for good or evil purposes—all kinds of signs bearing improvisations, naïve and absurd and sometimes dazzling imagery, that in some way line memory, which is enchanted with this heritage. (80)

Khatibi's writing follows a similar course, by the use of signs, translating a double memory, that of his childhood and that of the Moroccan community, interwoven with a complex collection of methods.

La mémoire tatouée is also organized around the model of the tattoo: patterns traced on the body that refer to desire. In another essay, Khatibi states:

> [T]attooing is a form of writing made of dots (the name that Arabs sometimes use to refer to it), which one assumes obeys a form of knowledge, a competence, a desire, a movement of signs occasionally inscribed on the body, at times migrating into other spaces, signs whose original symbol is often lost to us [. . .]. (*La blessure du nom propre,* 64)

Memory is tattooed like the female body, and it depicts the past, through bits and pieces, traces, like the tattoos on the bodies of many Moroccan women.

> The same fascination takes hold of me whenever I encounter a tattooed Bedouin woman. When she opens her ancestral hand, I link my enthrallment to the myth. All calligraphy removes the death of my desire, and tattooing has the exceptional privilege of preserving me. Not a single port of call amid the chaos, just the power of a disentangled impulse, a graph swift as the wink of an eye. (*La mémoire tatouée,* 11–12)

Tattooing retransmits signs and connects to the past. It conveys a knowledge that has grown obscure with time, and by removing evil—"has the exceptional privilege of preserving me"—it protects. Since signs migrate from one place to another, from an object to a body, the tattoo's pattern records the maze-like structure found in the medina's configuration: "Which woman, with a slow, brightly henna-painted hand, would have given us the mystery of the labyrinth?" (ibid., 74). Tattoos "illuminate" certain parts of the body just as the text "illuminates" certain fragments of life. Through these insertions in the French language the writer records ancient signs that go beyond language, referring to other methods and arts, empowering silence, the unspeakable, the mystery, all that can never be evoked through words.

> There is another reason for our interest in tattoos: this has to do with the taboo imposed upon them by the great monotheistic religions as if, with a single palimpsest line, divine writing wanted to erase all previous writing, especially writing traced on the body. [. . .] It is for that very reason that we must go back to the repressed archi-writings, which haven't stopped inhabiting us. (*La blessure du nom propre,* 66)

In conclusion, writing and visual image fit together perfectly and cannot easily be separated.

> How can one think of a *visual art* as submissive to the mechanisms of the word / how can one think of a *text* as submissive to the mechanisms of *vision*? Everywhere isolated-connected at some point and, by necessity, by a common dynamics; otherwise, where do we begin to establish our grasp of the universe, no matter how minuscule? (Paris, *Lisible/Visible* [Readable/visible], 166)

Let us return one last time to Toni Maraini, who contemplates the presence of the sign in painting:

> Fetish and magic spell, the sign is reassuring: it "signifies" . . . it gives meaning to the unarticulated; pretence or presence, it feeds symbolic thinking. We need it as a way to exorcise the annihilation of memory: countless are the painters who leave signs here and there along their way. (*Écrits sur l'art,* 68)

Writing, in turn, seeks painting—vision—the image to express what words can't manage to say and to attain a sacred quality as well as an equilibrium. It goes back to another characteristic mentioned by Khatibi, which the African artist knows so well: the drama of exile that so often is the result of moving around to survive or create and that brings together methods and cultures: "An encounter between different outlooks, between civilizations, between writing forms, between desires (from the letter to its drawing, from the drawing of its drawing), such is the place of the other (the foreigner) that is suggested to us. From one place to another, the topography of exile" (Khatibi and Sijelmassi, *L'art calligraphique de l'Islam,*[2] 226). And exile juxtaposes perspectives, leads to syncretism, which the artist translates through aesthetic combinations, moves to other locations, other arts, while at the same time delineating freedom, wholeness.

Since time immemorial, signs and writing systems have been linked throughout Africa, and poets and painters have sought the image. These signs circulate from one art to the other, from the sign to the written, from the pictorial to the poetic and vice versa, combining methods, creating works in which cultures and arts mingle. Trans-aesthetics breaks through demarcations and offers a perception of the world. And by evoking other arts, the artist or the writer engages with the other in dialogue. At first the artist or writer establishes a void, a blank to be interpreted (the presence of another art is to be grasped), playing with the combinations—the unexpected—the multitude of possibilities.

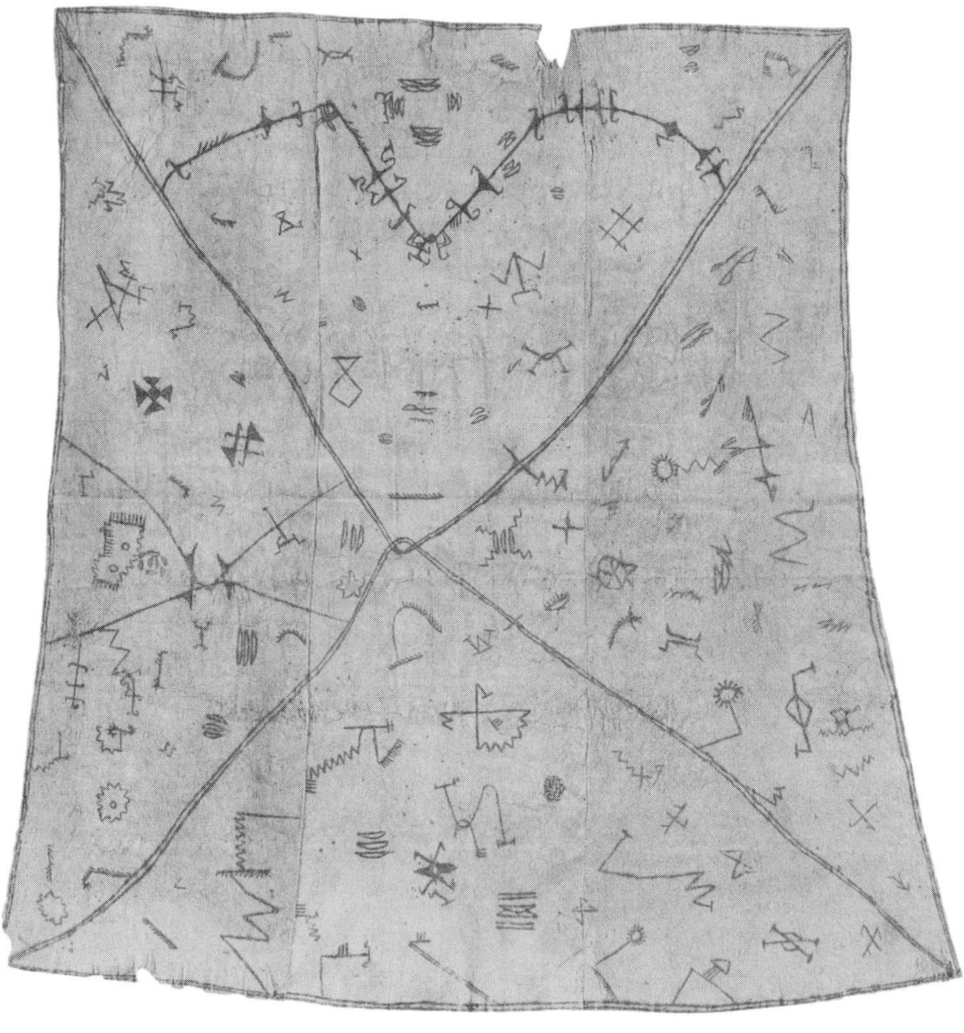

PART TWO

Voyages and Voices of the Unspoken

السماء

5 Abdelwahab Meddeb

Phantasia, or the Crossing of References, Discord, and the Heterogeneous

Abdelwahab Meddeb, a Tunisian writer born in Tunis in 1946, lives in Paris, where he teaches at the University of Paris–X. He has published two novels: *Talismano* (1979) and *Phantasia* (1986); one short story: *Aya dans les villes* (1999); three volumes of poetry: *Tombeau d'Ibn Arabî* (1997), *Les 99 stations de Yale* (1995), and *Matière des oiseaux* (2001) (Max Jacob Prize); one play: *La gazelle et l'enfant* (1992); four essays: *Blanches traverses du passé* (1997), *La maladie de l'islam* (2002) (*Malady of Islam,* 2003) (François Mauriac Prize), *Face à l'islam* (2004), and *L'exil occidental* (2005). He has written many articles on painting, film, politics, and literature which have appeared in *Libération, La revue d'études palestiniennes, Intersignes, Levant, Pleine marge, Les cahiers du cinéma,* and in catalogues of the Institut du Monde Arabe. In 1995 he founded and edited the journal *Dédale,* aimed at creating a dialogue between cultures, religions, eras, and places. He hosts a program known as *Cultures d'Islam* on the radio show France Culture.

Meddeb has also translated mystical Sufi texts by Bistami (1989) and Sohrawardi (1993) from Arabic to French. Passionate about pictorial art, he rediscovers in modern art the value of the abstract image advocated by Islam and invests his writing with trans-aesthetics in order to evoke the unutterable, thus joining Klee in his approach to the plastic arts.

As a thought of opening, his writings cross borders in search of meeting points. Interweaving cultures and arts, the author looks into the way that concepts circulate: "I place myself between languages, cultures, territories, continents, and genres. I would like to rediscover the complete book that medieval polygraphy encountered, that of Ibn Arabî or Dante. The latter's poetic work is at once philosophical, political, and religious" (quoted in Husin and Person, *Abdelwahab Meddeb,* 25).

At a time known for its divisions, exclusions, and profound ignorance of Islam, the Tunisian writer Abdelwahab Meddeb[1] condemns intolerance and fanaticism wherever they exist and refuses to be defined by an exclusive and inflexible stance. Located between places, motivated by exile and errancy, he joins the Andalusian mystic Ibn Arabî in his need for displacement, for openness, for otherness, by insisting on a better understanding of the complexity of Islam, and of Sufism in particular. He elucidates its approach in countless articles and by translating texts of the great mystics Bistami and Sohrawardi, distancing himself from any sort of intransigence and withdrawal.

In his writing he brings together a multitude of reflections and methods to record the intercultural and interdisciplinary combinations that interest him, and he keeps his distance from the dichotomies established during colonialism:

> The architectural model provides me with the decisive argument that substantiates the structure of my work, not in some arbitrary quest of someone besieged, nor inside that dichotomy between East and West, between North and South, between Islam and Europe, but rather at the crossroads, the shifting, the movement, the mutation of forms and idioms. (Ibid., 30)

While looking for interconnections, he moves between here and elsewhere; between different art forms, finding in modern painting, for example, a graphic elaboration akin to Islam; between past and present, upholding traditions in order to connect with modernity. He abolishes schisms, barriers, draws unexpected parallels, and dismantles partitions.

In order to evoke this idea drawn from the world at large with its many ramifications and its inexhaustible sudden manifestations, the writer uses the model of the Maghreb medina, its twists and turns, its dead ends, and its never-ending branches. And while he refers to other languages, he writes in French, for reasons he explains both in his work and in various interviews: "The choice of French is an easy way out. In that language it is possible to sustain the strategy of writing in the most advanced manner while invoking what is ancient" (ibid., 19). Somewhat later in the same interview he offers the following explanation:

> The literature that Arabs produce is currently written in many languages: not just in Arabic and French, but in Hebrew as well, in Italian, German, Spanish, and English; and the boundaries of literary currents are no longer determined by the differences between the languages used by the writer. This porosity of borders (even the most carefully guarded ones), which has always existed, is rapidly changing today, thus confirming Goethe's insight that wanted the writer to be the vigilant critic of the group to which he belongs and have his work spill across national frontiers in its criteria and sources so that he could participate in the foundation of a *Weltliteratur,* a *Weltkultur.* (22)

Arabic is not discarded but nourishes the text from different angles: "the beneficial effects of a language that for you is no longer alive, Arabic, a liturgical and instinctual language that, by its absence, sustains the creative imagination, which you convey in the Frankish language of that moment" (Meddeb, *Phantasia,* 66).[2] If during the colonial period French in the Maghreb was grafted onto Arabic, a language learned at the Koranic school, and onto the spoken mother tongue (dialect) in order to try to replace them, the writer makes them reappear in the French he uses, which is enriched by insertions and references. They appear in the rhythm that stems from the arrangement of Koranic phrases, infusing the imaginary (the structure of *A Thousand and One Nights* where Scheherazade tells countless stories full of digressions and bifurcations),[3] presenting Arabic terms that have no French translation and are inserted into the narrative,[4] or resorting to an approximate translation. Thus the author has other languages circulate within the French text, particularly those associated with the sacred and with childhood.

Published in 1986, the novel *Phantasia* values the mystical Sufi path, promotes the void—which in this text is also the creative space—in order to be attentive to what is fermenting inside, to create: "For days on end I seek, my senses sharpened. I prowl around the form that hides from me as long as I am hunting for it. When I grow desperate and decide to let it go, the object of my search takes hold of me. Dwelling in the void will not have lessened my receptivity" (163). The power of the work comes from the spaces between creation and void, from the tensions that lead from word to uncertainty, and its emergence gives birth to the text: "One ceases to exist if one doesn't fluctuate between veil and vision, impediment and realization, contraction and expansion" (99)—a labor that rests on the strength of the uncertain.

Sentences move rapidly from one subject to the next, fleshing out a construction in snippets to transcribe the inner experience and the pathway of thought, depending on the journey's movement. The reader roams all over Paris, its cafés and restaurants, its parks and monuments, and its various quarters. He/she follows the wanderings of an "I" who splits in two, inside whom reflections mingle, coming from imperceptible voices that put forward any number of political, historical, and religious observations. The plot reproduces the movement of the character passing both through the city and on an inner quest:

> If the character, the novelist's creation, is already no longer the person [. . .]. He will have to move about like a ghost through a novel that juxtaposes inside visions with outside landscapes. Sometimes in the first person, sometimes addressed by either the informal or the formal "you,"[5] my character is a phantom with many facets. (139)

The narrator runs through various ideas that alternately complement and oppose each other.

Drawing from the breadth of the world, the novel allows for genres to be brought together (by combining poetry, essays, autobiography), for languages and writing systems to be linked (by inserting text fragments in Sumerian, hieroglyphic, Chinese, Hebrew, and Arabic writing), for extended horizons (Jews, Christians, Muslims, Taoists) as well as eras (Middle Ages, the Renaissance, Modernity) to enter into dialogue, for arts to be combined (by turning to pictorial and musical references). These transitions from one text to another, from one form to another (from letter to image), from one language to another, invite the reader to travel to unknown lands and break the discursive linearity, the thread of the action. This juxtaposition of sentences that build an image and then abandon it leaves one in suspense, hanging in the void, and inscribes the uncompleted, the indefinable into the fabric of the text, brushing aside any kind of certainty. Such leaps make the writing more dynamic, demanding the reader to actively participate, requiring an alert presence so that the overlapping of images may be grasped and the narrative given meaning.

The narrator in quest of a mystical direction sometimes meets up with Aya, who brings him closer to the Absent One. The metro symbolizes the underworld—publicity posters, artificial light, where smells and trash become entangled. This descent is a necessary link, not only for the development of the subject (as in *Orphée-Dafric* by Werewere Liking, which I discuss in the following chapter) but also for the organization of the literary project, which implies movement from one site to another—passing from light to darkness, from word to silence, from presence to absence, from fullness to void, from unity to explosion. In Islam, various spheres govern the hereafter and describe the stages of the human being, the levels he must attain in order to complete his voyage and fully unite with the Absent One. The narrator stays in close touch with "hell" to attain the third heaven, the place of Venus and Joseph,[6] and thanks to the clear-sightedness of the latter, he harmonizes eroticism and art, order and chaos, violence and moderation. The reader is made to realize that the various juxtaposed elements question, neutralize, and complete each other.

In chapter 5 the narrator goes down a metro entrance and embarks upon a Dante-like journey, suggesting that darkness is needed for writing. The subject then goes on to a description of his father and grandfather, and of the family home. Subsequently he goes back to the metro to present images of hell, the horrors of the world, and murderous acts. He uses techniques from musical improvisation, of melodies taken up again, abandoned, transposed, and from the art of counterpoint. A parallel can also be drawn with the nomad's journey across the desert, where places that are visited regularly (here through the themes evoked) are sometimes abandoned definitively and sometimes revisited later on.

While strolling around, the subject looks for the unexpected. The moments when he stops are moments of pause, of reflection, before pursuing the movement of displacement (wandering through the city, through museums, into metro entrances) where places are revisited, themes picked up again—a process that interweaves the elements he encounters according to the rhythm of walking when a free, alert, and moving body is ready to take in the elements it sees, to be immersed in the emotions that emerge from the spaces traveled. This process, which makes the body become wholly immersed in the context in which it moves, in the spectacle (theatricality) of the everyday, is an invitation to observe new approaches, to participate in unexpected interactions all across Paris, to fit into the movement that emanates from them and is made up of perpetual *métissage.*

The following study shows, first of all, how the text, as it circulates, is fragmented and reproduces the trace. It then analyzes the question of the circulatory movement between places and art forms, dwelling on the value of the visual image that so often appears in the work. Finally, it examines the function of the composite whole that, in eliminating borders, crisscrosses ideologies and sets itself up as baroque—at the crucible of imaginative worlds.

Fragmentation

Phantasia consists of ten untitled chapters. Sentences follow each other without being arranged in paragraphs, and themes change surreptitiously. As mentioned above, by passing abruptly from topic to topic, and by inserting quotations from other thinkers (Bistami, Ibn Arabî), by mentioning other arts, especially painting, that lie beyond the realm of words, by referring to other eras and juxtaposing places (Paris, Tunisia, Italy, sub-Saharan Africa), the author fractures the text. The intermingling of genres and the intertwining of other forms of writing upset the coherence and create a road that consists of bifurcations, radiating lines, and intersections.

The fragmented narrator makes himself part of the world and finds fulfillment between places, actually enjoying the disorder that is brought about:

> You *mix up* notes taken later from reminiscences and memories. You *jumble up* techniques. You *rip up* your own sketches and turn them into a *collage* with *polyglot bits and pieces.* You do not disdain *digression.* You don't dismiss the idea in the name of sensation. You make genres *meet by chance.* To sort out the clutter you refine the art of *editing. Thread by thread* you *knot the chain* of the narrative. (164, italics mine)

The act of writing passes here through a process of cross-pollination, dismantling and reorganizing, like the weaver who fastens the threads and draws upon both the individual and the collective (signs, symbols . . .) imagination. Rearranging segments of knowledge and thoughts, this montage opens up onto the unknown and is to be seen on the model of the trace. The trace marks the work through the dissemination of sense—snatches of signs scattered over the full expanse of the text—and by the work of the narrator who is digging through memory: the collective memory of archaic traditions; the individual memory of a personal past, such as childhood, where elements emerge fragmented and changed. As he moves through the world's concepts and immerses himself in them, the narrator becomes a mosaic.

> For me, the project of living, feeling, thinking, writing is located in a new space that extends beyond any tradition, which has a decisive effect on

> me through the sparse elements of the trace. Thus my western and eastern references acquire the dignity of the trace and it is as such that they are recorded, that they run the risk of being erased or superimposed, of overlapping or being printed one on top of the other until they are distorted: in short, they are at the center of this adventure seeking a form yet to come that will surpass everything, both the oriental origin and the acquired occidental elements. (Meddeb, *Face à l'islam,* 56–57)

This elaboration is presented as trickery, circumventing the dogmatic and intractable aspect that fidelity to a principle or a value might entail. The writer invites us to travel across methods, roam beyond borders, collect the encountered signs and snatches of information, to decipher them and meditate upon them to grasp the suggested itinerary. The desert is present via signs that have been carefully concealed there, that demand to be read in keeping with the practice of making traces in the sand for survival, and here right on the page so that the suggested itinerary can be understood.

> The question of trace begins from the origin and foundation of Arab culture. It is a paradigm in pre-Islamic poetry. It honors the opening of the ode. The scenography of the desert organizes itself around it. Between the inscription of the sign and its deletion it forms an intermediary indicator. In the desert's ecology the sign has an ephemeral destiny. As soon as it is written it is erased again so that only its trace might possibly remain. [. . .] The metonymic relationship between sign and trace functions wonderfully in the founding poetry and launches the desert as a myth in writing. (Meddeb, "La trace, le signe," 28)

The juxtaposition of ideas produces the unexpected, a part remains elusive, inexplicable, and uncontrollable; the reader of a trace works with forms that hide out and hold mysteries. Consequently, disorder is inevitable: "Be aware that the construction that prescribes the vision of the world does not eliminate its chaos" (*Phantasia,* 28).

To reproduce the trace, the writer uses stylistic methods such as ellipses, deletions that create numerous mysteries that the reader must catch. Compression is assured because of the absence of articles and prepositions ("Nerves on tenterhooks, visions chase each other, mad speed," 11), because of the omission of verbs ("Nothing upright anymore," 109). Some sentences consist of just a single word or two: "Trust in beauty, which is feminine. *Be patient.* Dig deep into your anxiety" (16, italics mine). Others leave the reader hanging by using a construction that is left unfinished: "When the body is immobilized in the lava that boils within him" (11).

Meddeb doesn't use direct discourse and omits quotation marks and hyphens. The narrator conveys his thoughts without simulating communication, eliminating the illusion of reproducing a realistic context: "She opens the door for you like a sleepwalker, wrapped in her sheet. Give me shelter, I want to sleep. Yes, you can borrow my sofa" (73). The writing intentionally turns its back on certain conventions—erases certain characteristics.

The switch from the first- to the second-person singular pronoun, from I to you, also contributes to breaking the narrative sequence. This transition calls out directly to the reader, encouraging him/her to become involved. At the same time, the narrator is split in two, divided, and the two parts question one another. By talking to himself, the subject is shaped, is created:

> [W]e speak to ourselves in answer to a limitless variety of external or somatic stimuli (hope, fear, self-castigation, self-encouragement); we speak to ourselves in order not to speak to others [. . .]; we speak to ourselves to anchor our own presentness, to ground the threatened or elusive sense of self [. . .]; we speak to ourselves to store the acquisitions of experience, to hoard and make inventory [. . .]. (Steiner, *On Difficulty and Other Essays,* 64)

It is a course of action that allows the narrator to confront his double and go more deeply into himself: "Man changes. His doubles are fickle" (208). At the same time, the use of the second-person pronoun is directed at the listener, a technique that requires the reader's attention, inviting him or her to participate in the narrator's quest—the goal of meeting the Absent One. By developing his or her own imagination, the reader will in turn become a creator (the trace demands that the reader supply the missing elements). Thus the writer blurs the boundaries between reading and writing.

The context provides a multitude of complementary pieces of information that call upon various readers depending on the themes raised, readers who are not the same from one passage to another, complicating the reading:

> He [Freud] turned away from the sort of belonging that upsets an individual's balance as soon as the power relationship urges his will to placate its hatred, at the risk of a hegemony that will necessarily turn against *you* the day *you* are to harvest the fruits of misery that *you* have sown. *You* should

> remember that man wavers between oblivion and memory, between forgiveness and rancor. (135, italics mine)

Here, the "you" is directed at those who claim origin through the use of violence at the expense of others, causing unforeseen reactions. In other cases the "you" calls on those who know Arabic: "If I'm not teaching you anything in reminding you that in Arabic *Aya,* آية, indicates the verb, signals inside the unity of the verse, you should know that in Japanese *Aya,* 綾, addresses the complexity of the weft, threads crossing, precious fabric, soft material" (198). Thus, the text is directed at a variety of readers.

As for verbal tenses, the author frequently uses the imperative and the indicative, avoiding deictics and shifters. Time is compressed: "Past and future are converted in the present" (27). Sometimes the present is the expression of a return to the past (memory), of a projection toward the future (expectancy), and of attentiveness to what is (vision): "Expectation creates the future. Memory garners the past. Attentiveness controls the passage from one 'ecstasy' to another, in the break of the strain that reflects the always exploded present" (Garelli, *Rythmes et mondes* [Rhythms and worlds], 452–53). The narrator directs a given thought by relying on his wanderings through Paris, the primary place where his reflections are anchored. Trusting the moment, the past conspires with the present, memories and meditations enrich Paris, endowing it with a throng of places, eras, forms of writing, eluding the linear notion of time: "You disturb the exchange when you deal with past and future in the present. The moment is not accountable" (27).

Stereotypes are introduced here and there: "On the screen, before my eyes just back from somewhere else, a pursuit in the avenues of New York, limousines, moccasins polished to shine, yellow cabs, gangsters with dark glasses, unflappable cops, chewing gum, handcuffs, firearms" (31). This method inserts a commonplace, worn-out image that functions as a rift, simulating a scene from a violent action film ("pursuit," "gangsters," "handcuffs," "firearms") in bright colors ("yellow"). A dislocation that breaks the narrator's train of thought with a stereotype saturated with predictable gestures, seen over and over again on the television screen. "Artistic writing, resolutely removed from common speech, appropriates the cliché to expose it as an *object* from elsewhere, paraded around" (Van den Heuvel, *Parole, mot, silence,* 58). This abrupt change vulcanizes the utterance, suddenly passing from a subjective thought to a commonplace—an interstice that provides a pause, an empty space, for the same old cliché has been stripped of meaning.

The techniques Meddeb uses to break up his writing—we have mentioned omissions in the middle of a sentence, interruptions between sentences, abrupt changes of pronouns, insertion of clichés, unexpected transitions between cultures, languages, religions—subvert the usual order, dispensing fractures that sometimes bring energy to the text, sometimes mystery. Shuffling forms of knowledge and art, the author outlines the journey of his narrator as a quest located at the crossroads of cultures where it occupies the interstitial space.

We must add that the Koranic text, constructed like a trace on which the narrator meditates, functions as an archetype for *Phantasia*. The sentences follow a similar structure, linking segments of varying lengths, dismantling the rifts, the illusion of a coherent and immediately perceptible whole. The unutterable can only be known through the fragment, and *Phantasia* is dedicated to silence so that it can listen to the Absent One, reproducing in snatches the scenography of the desert (the place where the sacred text was born) and of traces:

> The [Koranic] text is interrupted and lets in fragments that, through their irruption, divide the drama and disseminate its meaning. Hence the discrepancies, doors opening onto innovations. The Koran is an inspired book, a voice that conveys a part of the Table. The Prophet receives it through the intermediary of the angel on the stage of the imagination. Caravans cross the desert. And legends move around from tribe to tribe and country to country. (59)

The fragmented style gives access to multiple viewpoints, to the other with his/her differences, and presents the full gamut of inventions, of tricks that have nourished and enriched imaginations.

Movement between Places

The title *Phantasia* guides the reader toward Italy by the transformation of the word's final letter (*fantasia/fantaisie*) and the presence of painting and architecture (Mantegna, Pontorno, Primaticcio, Bernini, Cavallini, Bramante, Michelangelo). In his analysis of Meddeb's novel *Talismano,* Khatibi explains the inclusion of this Italian space, showing us that it allows the author to keep his distance from the dichotomies created by the historic colonial context:

> We should point out that the title of the book, *Talismano,* is Italian, a word that comes from the Arabic *tilasm* and the Greek *telesma.* This is not a haphazard designation. In fact, Italian words are scattered throughout the text. Italian is the language of pure pleasure here, language of paradise and hedonistic play, far removed from the violent contradiction of French and Arabic. Whether he uses Italian expressions and words, whether he describes Italian cities, arts, and landscapes, the author is immersed in bliss. (*Maghreb pluriel,* 188–89)

The title *Phantasia* refers both to the creative imagination (fantasy, phantasm, hallucination) and to the fantasia, the Arab equestrian celebration that is the art of the flamboyant and the fluid, of costumes, gunshots, and of what's striking, where lightheartedness and violence, excessiveness and brilliance mix. The horse comes up repeatedly in the text, symbolizing elegance and soaring flight: "There's a TV screen in my head broadcasting a fantasia on the barren steppe, nimble race of horses galloping on the loose soil" (136). This evocation by the narrator at the metro exit explains the book's title and suggests several themes: the desertlike location (aridity), symbol of emptiness, much coveted to bring out the writing from the "desert" of the blank page, which is the space of the quest, elegance and soaring flight of horses, of the words themselves.

The indications and repeated uses of terms that are sometimes placed in an unusual context—the desert subtly put inside Paris—draw connections between places which at first seem surprising. Such connections are present from the first chapter on, in which the childhood garden, consisting of "orange trees, pomegranate trees, jasmine and roses" is superimposed on the Luxembourg Garden. By means of the narrator's wanderings across Paris and strolls suggested to the reader, the customs, scents, and distinct features of other places intermingle: "sand," "light," "intense shadow," "perfume," "noise," "labyrinth," "recitation," "prayer." Parallels abound, connecting spaces and human beings: "The pale sun reminds me of the only snowy day of my African childhood, a Friday without school, when the white earth had swallowed the call to prayer" (15–16). Leaps erase differences and juxtapose the Maghreb (Tunisia, to be more precise, the country where the narrator grew up) and Paris, his chosen city.

The "desert" is often present in Paris in an unusual way: "The [Luxembourg] park is deserted" (15). Or: "On the other side of the pit, a deserted street, cars go by at the speed of light" (50). Walking in the Bauer development: "In the deserted depot Indian colors are dancing to the sound of some sort of black music" (165). Coming upon a souk in the same place: "You spread it [a rug] out on the ground and sit down on its pure colors that typify the desert, when going down the Atlas Mountains" (168).

The multiple meanings of the desert suggest ways of reading: an abyss where humans sometimes come to ruin, the meaninglessness of wars and violence: "Of a desert that I find in Europe, too, before making it into the metaphor of history, when with each disaster the desertification of the world reoccurs, the desert of Europe, I said, with all its prerogatives, the reign of the void, the alternation of sand and stone" (Meddeb, "Tous les déserts du monde," 16). The desert of existence but also, in the written work, the desert of the text where the reader must trace a meaning in order not to lose his or her way. Desert and silence suggest immensity, barrenness, the nomadic life, death. The topography of the desert in *Phantasia* mirrors the wandering and emptiness, the mystical path, the quest, that will lead in part to revelation, to the Absent One, to meaning, and in part to creation, to writing: "it is advisable to adapt to the vocation that prompts you to embark upon writing, a discipline that forces you to asceticism" (164). And, to repeat what has already been suggested, the desert refers to an expanse in which the snippets of scattered and concealed indices are essential in order to find one's way.

Other spaces are mentioned. Sub-Saharan Africa plays a crucial role, examined in the first chapter by the valorization of the trance and of forms the author refers to as "archaic." It is also present in the mention of Egypt and the insertion of hieroglyphics. The text weaves in Japan and China, too, through the use of their writing, and the Near East through the presence of Sumerian, Arabic, and Hebrew script.

By investigating the many approaches that exist throughout the world, the narrator assumes a composite identity, seeing exile not as a loss to be overcome but as a rupture to be utilized. The speaker purposely thrusts himself into moments of emptiness, to be conquered through the encounter with what is dissimilar and the questioning of conventional values. He escapes from the predetermined and finds himself to be different when he comes upon what is new to him. He resituates himself by discarding established ideas in order to welcome the syncretism produced in the text through the use of verbal ruptures. This rupture motivates the quest, while at the same time introducing vertigo. Leaving the Maghreb, going across

Italy to head farther north, the narrator abandons familiar gestures and habits and faces loneliness, emptiness, nightmares, and the anxieties that pursue him. But once he has overcome the ordeal, exile sets him free: "The stranger who lets go of values and steals the foolish certainty away from what are truths" (53). Exiled, relinquishing his dialect and Arabic, the narrator favors French, abandoning expressions of his mother tongue that are untranslatable. The text indirectly alludes to this. The absence of these expressions creates "holes," things unsaid to be flushed out. In its depths, silence shields a number of elements that lose neither their power nor their mystery when deciphered, since it offers no certainty whatsoever.

> In our inability to clearly formulate it, we have recourse to a metaphor: silence often resembles the *sleep* of discourse resting, but a silence that one senses to be laden with energy at rest. It's as if, by keeping silent, the word is placing itself in a state of expectancy. Source of new energy, immobility then suggests the potential of what can be spoken since one knows that silence is capable of anything, of generating the most unexpected word, the word one fears and the word one desires: silence can say *anything*. (Van den Heuvel, *Parole, mot, silence*, 77–78)

Ideas remain unexpressed, just as elements of the pattern that creates trace disappear. Nevertheless, the vestiges allow for a restitution of the missing marks, just as what is spoken helps one grasp the meaning of the silences. It is by determining the range of possibilities that the reader will join the quest, running in turn through an array of meanings that come from various places, as in an initiation.

Exile produces the heterogeneous, creating a dizzying energy one must learn to control to overcome tensions, to eliminate rifts, and to enjoy opposites: "Exile elicits the intermixing of ethnicities and languages. Only an education sure of its worth is capable of welcoming the cosmopolitan effervescence" (67).

> To the extent that mankind lives on the edge of the in-between where the lines of demarcation that divide worlds remain blurred, to the extent that the *situs* of humans is moved at the mercy of peregrinations and moods and that nostalgia becomes a way of survival, one may come to the conclusion that in this new situation any way of being refers to an elusive hereafter. (Shayegan, "L'entre-deux dans la littérature d'aujourd'hui" [The in-between in today's literature], 296)

The exile's condition divests the individual of attachments and thrusts him toward emptiness, a place of opportunity, of dialogue. Split between cultures and ways of thinking, he puts himself on a new path.

Circulating between Aesthetic Forms: Input of the Visual Image

First of all, let us go back to some of the elements mentioned in chapter 4, above, on the function of the visual image where the close connections between writing and painting and the possible reasons for their interlacing were examined.

To begin with, there is no way that language can evoke all things: some part of existence remains inexpressible. The image that lies beyond language (French, in this case) discards the colonial past it carries and the constraints it conveys, breaking through linguistic barriers. On the other hand, the plurality of languages has generated countless conflicts, as the narrator in *Phantasia* observes, and removing himself from the divisions created, he goes toward the third heaven where art resides: "The separation of languages instigates war. The discord between peoples is sharpened when territories are divided according to the languages they speak" (82).

Secondly, the writer rejects the split that is commonly practiced in the West between different art forms. In his book *Iconology: Image, Text, Ideology,* W. J. T. Mitchell analyzes the debate between Western writers and painters, each side claiming the superiority of its own art form. The painters of the Renaissance felt that painting, by being disconnected from any use of language, allowed them to convey a message more clearly and efficiently, because it went beyond linguistic associations and the abstract and arbitrary aspect of such a tool (the terms by which to indicate the same object differ from one language to another). Banking on that very characteristic, the poets responded, putting forward the idea of the value of such a discrepancy for transmitting emotions, human feelings. They suggested the advantage of using a tool that sets itself apart from existence so as to describe it better. Whatever the outcome of the debate, it is interesting to note that through the centuries the arts have been involved in a discussion about the superiority of their own artistic form, a discussion that indicates their interrelationship. Meddeb follows an entirely different notion, which links the arts across Africa in order to gather a maximum of forces. He interweaves writing, painting, music, architecture, and cinema, drawing parallels to support his narration.

Thirdly, by passing from one art to another, the writer as nomad travels between cultures and artistic expressions, reproducing elements of the scene of exile, and rubbing shoulders with what is other and different: "Every individual is fascinated with the outlook of the other" (88). In Islam the journey is coupled with knowledge:

> Displacement and exile are also at the basis of Islam since the Prophet Mohammed and his companions were forced to leave Mecca and seek refuge in Medina to save the budding religion.
>
> Furthermore, Muslims saw the journey as a source of knowledge; in this regard, one of the Prophet's hadiths recommends that one seek knowledge "even in China." (Memmes, *Littérature maghrébine de langue française* [Maghreb literature written in French], 191)

For the writer, the journey is a way of accumulating other locales within oneself, of practicing otherness, of opening oneself up to other concepts.

Fourthly, modern art connects with the value of the abstract image in Islam. Islam limits depiction of the figure to discourage idolatry and motivate the creation of a mental image. Calligraphy is used to embellish the walls of mosques, thus connecting word, writing, and abstract image.

> The originality of this written form, which in some respects has no equal, is created by the architecture and rhythm of the letters: here we recognize the force of the "arabesque" as a plastic form.
>
> Calligraphy can be seen as a reading and a writing in the second degree. It obeys a geometry of the spirit that is created in the opening of a space between the statement contained in a phrase and its realization as a work of art. (Khatibi and Sijelmassi, *The Splendor of Islamic Calligraphy,* 6)

And thus: "Calligraphy reveals the plastic scenography of a text: that of a letter turned into image, caught in the physical act of creating a line which is animated and led onwards by an inner rhythm" (6). In *Phantasia,* Meddeb mentions such painters as Matisse, Malevitch, Rothko, Kandinsky, Mondrian, Klee, tracing convergences between cultures—between the West and Islam, especially the Sufi path: "I read Kandinsky, Matisse. I see Mondrians and Malevitches. I listen to Bram van Velde. Their thoughts and images, which become fixed inside forms or refuse them, kindle resonances with my Sufi intuitions" (87–88). Drawing connections, the author endows his words with numerous meanings. He dismantles schisms, exclusive and totalizing interpretations, by bringing to the fore correspondences between seemingly divergent systems, by developing intertwinements between thinkers, such as Sufi and Christian mystics, and between Islam and modern Western art. He places himself in the opening, instructing his reader on the complexity of different forms of knowledge that have developed through the centuries and are often connected, such as Judaism, Christianity, and Islam. He links Sufi practices with Taoism without eroding or sweeping aside their differences.

Mondrian, Rothko, Malevitch, Kandinsky, and Klee all study the question of emptiness and the invisible. We are familiar with Klee's pictorial objectives through his theories and his *Journal.* He sees painting as the best way to translate a metaphysical trajectory, for it involves looking and it "penetrates" things: "All paths meet in the eye, at a juncture from where they are converted into Form to end up in the synthesis of exterior gaze and inner vision" (Klee, *Théorie de l'art moderne,* 46). And: "Art goes through *things,* it goes beyond the real as well as the imagination" (42). The plastic arts allow him to make "a secret vision visible," as he puts it. As mentioned in chapter 4, this idea was pursued by Merleau-Ponty in his essay *L'oeil et l'esprit,* which suggests that painting has the power to be visionary. Meddeb agrees: "Painting enters the visionary stage where prophets erected their fictions" (87). "Behind color hides a vision. The canvas is an iconostasis. It conceals what is not to be presented, not to be pronounced" (93). The pictorial is invoked to translate the mystical quest. Abstract art rids itself of what is superfluous, trifling, it frees itself from the representation of nature and human beings to suggest their internal structure, their light: "I link modern painting to my mystical impregnation. I recognize its echo in Islam, in China. [. . .] Traditions meet up" (39).

By referring to the visual image, Meddeb clarifies his approach, providing the Western reader with a familiar example. On the other hand, by choosing painters who practice vision he shows the importance of pictorial art and its function, and highlights the limitations of language in describing the unutterable. He joins Klee in assigning a specific power to painting and in seeking to approach the indescribable:

> We cannot say what it [this hieratic power] is, but we can approach its source to a greater or lesser extent.
>
> In any case, we need to reveal that power, show it in all its functions just as it shows itself in us. (Klee, *Théorie de l'art moderne,* 57)

Klee chose painting but always evoked writing, inserting into his compositions countless signs that are reminiscent of written script at its birth:

"*Writing and drawing* are identical *in* their essence" (ibid., 58). Meddeb invests in writing, while turning toward the visual image, to show they are inseparable.

By referring to the white canvas by Malevitch and the works of Rothko, Kandinsky, and Mondrian, the writer turns away from language to be open to silence, to the void where form and color materialize and make magic. It is that hieratic power that signs and some writing forms, such as Arabic calligraphy, express:

> Writing as such continued to be an art that was important in a very special way, where technical skill and magic mingled, with a large share of hieratic wisdom that would soon be part of the aesthetic experience associated with knowledge and ritual. (Jabra, "Calligraphie et art moderne dans le monde arabe" [Calligraphy and modern art in the Arab world], 25)

Arab calligraphy has remained a particular art whose initial function was to reveal the divine word. By abandoning Arabic and thus calligraphy, Meddeb replaces them with art forms that are involved in a quest for the void and the unutterable.

Here and there he inserts calligraphy that links drawing and the written, such as the ideogram that likewise appears in the text. In chapter 2, a segment of Sumerian writing is inserted in the fabric (26):

This language, which has disappeared and become indecipherable by the reader, is transformed into a drawing on the page: dancing marks, a ballet of signs, a play of lines that cross, electrify each other, and separate. The relationship between curves, straight and oblique lines, creates an intense internal dynamic from which a synergy emerges that makes the narrative sparkle. A little later, one sentence seems to describe the Sumerian assemblage and corresponds to the work of writing for which the author is looking:

> I construct figures and banish them from the events of which they are the motive. And I place them on the stage in their capacity as sign. I subvert history as narrative and suggest precognition. Whether far away or near, I move forward into the sacrilegious. Do you think that the present text, a definite incantation, is under the control of a bygone inspiration? (27)

The Sumerian writing is to be decoded through a visual approach—the art of deciphering signs, lines scattered on a surface verging on the art of divination and the reading of a trace.

The ideograms that appear a few pages further on (32) offer an entirely different picture but follow the same approach:

王 天 土 手

They invite a thrust toward the sky, a search for stillness in the configuration of lines that impart elegance, subtlety, and undulation. Arab calligraphy, which is strewn throughout the work and translated by the author, is presented as visual image and language. The lines mimic the fluid, flowing, ephemeral aspect of existence (36):

سبحاني ما اعظم شأني

The pen slides across the surface of a sheet of paper in a undulating, flexible, rounded movement that sometimes takes flight to pierce the sky, sometimes bounces back, tumbles down, and brushes the earth.

All these writing forms are converted into images that, through the juxtaposition of lines, perform a dancing language of gestures that invites us to dream, to run through existence in a movement of flight, and to decipher signs that present themselves as abstract images. By moving from one site to another, the author energizes the narrative and juxtaposes methods. He emphasizes both their similarities and their differences, showing where they converge and where they radiate outward to other spaces.

In this chapter, which develops reflections on writing and art, Meddeb mentions a Byzantine virgin, Pontormo's *Deposition,* Mantegna's *Sebastian,* modern art, Primaticcio's *Danae,* and a work by Picasso. The various canvases are connected to the written by means of the erotic: the parallel between a poem by Abu Nuwas and a painting by Primaticcio, and then by Picasso. In the middle of the chapter, the reader finds a process of articulation that constructs the segment and links it to the whole of the book via the character's wandering, passing through death as depicted in the European painting of Pontormo or Mantegna, to freedom from suffering and the joy of the ethereal forms found in abstract art.

African art appears several times, for not only does it lie at the foundation of modern art, which has drawn its approach and its representation of the world from it—the handling of abstract forms—seeking to capture the essence of existence, of a feeling, of human beings, but it has also managed to exorcise death, communicate the power of the sacred, of magic, and impart a relationship with the hieratic:

> Between the rite that keeps death at bay and the fascination with power sublimated by the supremacy of gods and kings, Black art depletes primitivism, which doesn't embody the beginning phase in its spiritual adventure, disruptive to formal evolution, but insists on the magic that permanently inhabits mankind, no matter what its science. (153)

This approach is the foundation of the author's design, for it provides ingenious methods that sustain a relationship between here and elsewhere, enhancing what is unutterable, undetermined, and surprising.

Phantasia is also based on a Sufi cosmogony, an ancient order that divides the heavens into several arcanas. Meddeb briefly mentions the first two but deals primarily with the third one (referred to above), that of art and love. In an article entitled "Épiphanie et jouissance" (Epiphany and pleasure), he presents the philosophy of the Andalusian mystic Ibn Arabî on the subject of man's relationship to woman in Islam. Woman, born from man, presumably left a part missing inside him.

> And since the place in man from where woman was removed is filled with a longing for her, his affection for woman is what the big one feels for the small. In addition, women are the site where the form of perfection is created; and their love is thus an obligation as well as an imitation of the Prophet. ("Épiphanie et jouissance," 137–38)

Script, originating in the visual image (hieroglyphics), pleads with us to conceive of a similar loss—in this case that of the pictorial image in writing. "In remembrance of the hieroglyph, the ideogram, what is it that the calligrapher's eye flaunts when faced with his alphabet if not the loss of the image, the letter's mourning? From the sacred to the saintly, the letter pursues the lost image that the graph still preserves" (20). As a result, to gain access to the unutterable, some writers attempt to make up for this visual loss by reinserting it into their written work.

By specifying the importance of painting and giving it a vital role in the text, *Phantasia* empowers a greater silence. The text goes beyond language, explicates the narrator's quest, tracing a parallel between cultures and illuminating the Islamic context, which prizes abstraction and reminds us that the written is connected to the image.

By referring to innumerable paintings and including hieroglyphic and Sumerian fragments, the text provides the reader with pictorial patterns and designs. Indeed, the author goes so far as to tell the reader that his written text is constructed like a painting: "Like a painting, my writing leaves likeness behind to better mimic feeling and achieve the analogy with music and tragedy" (87). By arranging fragments and taking up certain themes throughout the work, the text works in strokes and lines, suggesting pathways that are in no way confined to one interpretation. Meddeb invites us to see beyond words and language and to become submerged by the void so we can find vision again.

And ancient writing forms, abstract painting, and African art connect to other worlds—they clarify. They seek to attain the Elsewhere, to grasp its meaning, disregarding words when they become confining ("I escape from the prison of words," 88), guiding us to other arts—in a state of flux, in the unspecified, in what is different.

The Composite

The assembling of fragments gathers forms of knowledge, imitates the working of the mind as it moves from one subject to another, reproduces the character's peregrinations through the world's systems, and delineates the narrator's withdrawal (exile): "Between silence and pause, the verse states the discontinuity that removes me from the world" (24). On the one hand, Meddeb sketches the chaos that emerges from the clash of opposing concepts, tracing dispersal and the dissolution of reliable values: "The quintessence is dressed in all kinds of finery. Adhering to this or that dogma grants you a frail belief, soon contradicted by the rivaling verb" (57). On the other hand, he elaborates an aesthetics that imitates explosion, the clash of positions that occasionally meet up in violence and discord in such a way that at times the rhythm reproduces the movement of a trance to exorcise a given situation. Through repetition and the amassing of bits and pieces, the writing inscribes the structure of ritual: the ordering of things, melodies that unite rhythm and breathing, recording the body's vibration. The poetic work functions as an offering then, exorcising the historic and individual past, exploring the multiple empty spaces in order to prevail over the abyss.

The question of excess, trance, and vision is developed in chapter 4 of *Phantasia.* The section begins with the transcribing of a dream that brings together a number of images and mimes excess and immoderation: "Between sleep and wakefulness, dream alternates with vision. I no longer know which factory produces what I see. I fall asleep in the arms of a strapping jinn with an animal's coat and face" (74). This leads to an astonishingly violent carnival-like scene that personifies the forces of nature and ends with the slaughter of a white horse—the presence of sacrifice. A conglomerate of disparate elements, a composite jinn ("animal's face," "tail," "stag's antlers"), gives this creature maximal strength, a wink at the forcefulness of the fragments on which the text is built. Juxtaposed to this are monsters with huge sex organs, a palanquin, a Chinese princess, and other surprising elements. The jinn suggests magic, a figure drawn from the tales the narrator's mother told him. His excessive adornments ("massive gold rings," "heavy jewelry," 74), his helter-skelter movements accompanied by music and dance ("A frenetic dance stirs the kingdom of the jinns. Arms and legs flail. A couple of black jinns beat on steel rattlesnakes, Basque tambourines," 74), simulate trance ("frenzied dance," "gyration," "circle around," 74), a longed-for state that frees the body from its weight and disregards the real, to attain "fanâ" (annihilation), an important component of Sufism. The text reproduces the fury, excess, and chaotic forces needed to surpass the everyday.

> During my childhood I used to know the stage where the Dionysian ritual took place; it was a theater frequented by women where trances were performed in celebration of saints, a remnant of the cult of Dionysus as revealed in Euripides' tragedy *The Bacchae;* in some sects the theatrical trance is the product of an undertaking akin to that of Vodun: in the case of the Maghreb, Islam adapts to the influence of the shamanism of sub-Saharan Africa, passed on by the Black communities that moved northwards, toward White Africa during the centuries when slavery was thriving [. . .]. (*Face à l'islam,* 35)

The rhythm of the words as they follow each other in rapid succession, the themes described, the sudden transition of images, remove the imposed limits. By recording the described dream, the author traces a parallel with the written work whose construction follows the processes of the unconscious—as thoughts wander beyond the real, beyond borders, beyond eras. After the dream, the narrator visits the Beaubourg museum, and so moves on to painting, which evokes excess via a different kind of vision, that suggested by the visual artist. The chapter ends with the differences between the coupling of a stallion to a broodmare and two tortoises: parallels to the labor of writing, where words sometimes unite and fly off (horses), sometimes get stuck in sluggishness (tortoises); where words reproduce the movement of the search that sometimes ends in clarity, sometimes in a state fraught with confusion.

Thus it is a carefully orchestrated whole that refers here to a trance session led by an initiate in which disorder is sought in order to be surpassed. In *Face à l'islam,* Meddeb explains the reasons why he turns to "archaic" processes to move freely within all created forms:

> I embraced the love for the archaic because of excessive modernity, I found myself exceeding secularist, rationalist, and positivist reduction. [. . .] And as a poet, a man of immoderation, of excess and adventure, I embraced the transmutation of values [. . .]. (38)

The text advances a dynamic by means of this composite structure, while skirting the possible danger of a sterile clash, thus demonstrating the importance of exorcising the conflictual forces that are inherent to humans and tear them apart. Aware of the presence of inevitable violence, the author transgresses taboos by transcribing a dream, by articulating repressed content, or by remembering murderous scenes that are wreaking havoc throughout the world and endangering democracy in Europe: "Ambivalent Europe that unhinged intelligence by running the risk of leading the mind onto a path of the most radical destruction" (109–10).

The author also discusses a different form of violence: madness, which according to him is a twofold force. *Phantasia* recalls the madness that seized Van Gogh and caused him to become involved in a battle with himself that gradually destroyed him. But the text also speaks of the perceptiveness that madness is able to communicate, just as exile can: "It [madness] also provides the beatific vision and dooms the seer to non-action. [. . .] The Great Absent One moves within the eloquence of an obscure vision. Dispossessed of his consciousness, his sighs emit the sounds of the mystery" (100).

By exacerbating the violence through the use of a fragmentary, volcanized style, the writer subjugates, wards off, the outburst and exploits the disorder he generates in a different manner:

> I like to find myself lost in the chaos of concurrent forms of order, claiming the imperative of being: *be*, and the thing prostrates before me, perfect in its revealed orders, and then, fleeing, it fades away like the end of a laugh striking the horizon, a cascade of words, echoing mirages that break down depending on the way the water falls, torment that carries me off toward drowning. And I turn around the evasive axis. And I who court loss, I grab onto it so as not to be destroyed. Numerous images are inscribed on the body, fictitious surface on which things are printed and erased. Letters distort other letters. Divergence threatens. Representation is ruined. (13)

Physical frailty and strength caught in the movement of roaming that calls for opposites to be united, where nothing is fixed, stable, or eternal. An apparition vanishes, just as letters are superimposed on parchment, only to be dissolved in the end. The state of dissolution—"fade away," "break down," "carries off," "evasive," "erased," "distort"—refers to the trance that is also suggested by a gyrating motion ("turn around") that allows for an escape from any form of control.

We should remember, too, that *Phantasia* deals with silence in order to distinguish the buried voice—"I write as an interior voice dictates me to write" (16)—and thereby invokes the value of the unspoken: the space of negotiation, of sharing, of the possible. This intoxicating quest for emptiness is an opening: "And the *tao* is a way of being on the path that subjugates emptiness without populating it with gods" (68). And again: "Even though this isn't obvious, I am of Muslim ancestry. And you? I am not a believer" (194). Courting the posture of the mystic, the text seeks the Absent One by using fragments, moving around between positions (see chap. 2 above) without necessarily perceiving a God there. It subverts communication through silence and an arrangement of images.

In her analysis of two works by Salman Rushdie, Annie Montaut speaks about the quest for an Elsewhere that does not in any way rest on the divine and that we find in Meddeb's work: "polyphony (a way of the subject's movement that is also a pluralizing of the voice) as the place of transcendence: 'that is what takes the place of the sacred,' the world without god doesn't imply a world without transcendence" ("Des *Enfants de minuit* au *Dernier soupir du Maure* [From *Midnight's Children* to *The Moor's Last Sigh*], 319).

Countless shrouded trails appear strewn through the text to guide the reading while offering clarifications:

The world is a book. Be its reader. Interpret it the way you decode dreams. Give things their primary meaning. Confront tropes. Don't take them literally. Come back to the substance of what they adorn. Seize what lies concealed in the folds of the verses and signs that are inscribed on the face of the world. (200)

In order to sustain a certain clarity, explanations are supplied, connections are made, thus providing the tools needed to grasp the author's objective. The novel's title, polyphony (the participation of other voices, other horizons), trans-aesthetics (mentioning paintings, the power of the image), connections (places, religions, ideas), explanations, repetitions, and reformulations mark and elucidate the work.

In some way the writing expresses suffering, by referring to the fragmented experience of events and to meditations. The past, no longer accessible except through memory or imagination, settles down and becomes nostalgic: "In my western exile I remember the arak whose fragrance assails me. Nostalgic, I go back to my prison. I hear the voice saying: *Islam was born in exile, it will end in exile*" (71). Thus, in order to disregard suffering, the novel is a pilgrimage toward it—in Greek the word *nostos* means "return" and *algos* means "suffering"[7]—and pays homage to the past while focusing on the present via the project of recording thoughts from other horizons in the West: "In order to steal the ground from under the murderous eye of the troublemakers that occupy the political territories of Islam, it would be appropriate to work at bringing it into Europe. That would embellish [Islam] with a dignity marked by the aura of the universal" (118).

The craftiness consists of having created a novel that inserts traces of ancient elements, remote signs that established writing and still inhabit it, cultivating an interior space where religions are in dialogue through images, metaphors, and signs that carry vanished worlds, unusual inventions, all interweaving philosophies and arts.

The intersecting of forms; the play of apparitions and evaporations, of lights and shadows; the effervescence of desire, change, and excess allude to baroque art. The baroque expresses the tension that emanates from diffracted desires and calls for fantasy. It entangles the arts, blurring demarcations, and attempts to balance religious and secular positions—a propensity of the narrator, who is positioned between places.

This evolution reached its high point in *métissage*. Through its vertiginous styles, languages and cultures hurtled the baroque will. [. . .] From then on what it expressed in the world was the proliferating contact of diversified natures. It grasped, or rather gave-on-and-with, this movement of the world. No longer a reaction, it was the outcome of every aesthetic, or every philosophy. Consequently, it asserted not just an art or a style but went beyond this to produce a being-in-the-world. (Glissant, *Poetics of Relation,* 78)

The narrator holds fast to the baroque through contrasting settings (the passage from darkness to luminosity), through the use of a specific language ("darkness," "shines," "fleeing," "boiling" "vibrant," "fires," "tatters," "chasing," "fading," "volcano," "hazy," "blurring," "cavern," "luminous," "evaporate," "eclipse"), through the mention of Bernini and Pontormo, and through explanatory comments ("by delighting to the point of despair in the multitude of orders buried in all things," 12; or "a baroque way of giving up the ghost and being reborn while listening to the water flow," 22).

The narrator follows this ephemeral movement of emergence and disappearance in keeping with the visual process, reproducing the elusive characteristic of the quest toward the unspeakable. The mental icon surfaces only to immediately withdraw: "Inspect the image as it rests before it evaporates again" (11). This baroque thrust conveys a constantly transforming notion of the world in contact with what is diverse and changing. The narrator is firmly rooted in the wandering movement. In his state of flux his reference points commit him to dash toward the unknown: "To grant that what exists changes while it endures does not come close to an absolute. What does endure in the changing or the change or the exchange, is first of all perhaps the propensity or the audacity to change" (Glissant, *Traité du tout-monde,* 26).

Thus, a large number of methods are brought into play, at odds with a totalizing view, illusory, a variety of voices speaking to one another through polyphony, through juxtaposed languages and writing forms, through linked themes that reflect the vagabond condition of thinking, through trans-aesthetic references that cross verbal borders in search of an indescribable essence. The creation of voids reflects the terrifying abyss inside us and, at the same time, promotes our hearing the inner voice, which allows a work to be produced. A crucial space that demands the openness and availability of the reader-spectator and the skill of the writer in order to break through the commonplace, the trivial, exploring excess and verbal possibilities to exorcise the laceration, while preserving the significance of the unspoken, deliberately suggested, carefully veiled. In adhering to the baroque, the author turns the conventional upside down; by joining a mystical quest and visual, musical, and architectural arts, he defies the limitations of the verbal and, by way of the poetic and the image, maintains the hieratic and the sacred.

> Thus, we must puncture the screen of illusion to see what lies behind it, consider the written *mot* in its totality as a *parole*[8] emerging from a single voice, seek the place where the subject is located by exercising its linguistic activity. Obviously, it is impossible to fully discover and explore that place, the source of the *parole*. Such knowledge would rob the poetic utterance of its *secret,* the very condition of its "literariness," and its *meaning,* which must by necessity be ambiguous. That is why this place is hidden. One can only approach it, make its contours emerge.
>
> [. . .] Thanks to artistic writing, which transposes the unspeakable reality to the level of fiction and to indirect discourse, appearing as a substitute for everyday *parole,* the subject blossoms by slowly establishing its identity and offering its interlocutor the opportunity to find his or her own. (Van den Heuvel, *Parole, mot, silence,* 276)

By way of traces, fragments, and assemblages, Meddeb moves between cultures, occupying the interstitial space, connecting the invisible threads woven across the centuries throughout the world. Movement, intertwinements, shifts, and circular flow sustain the interstitial lair, where a threatening, baroque silence is stirring that ties in with the "tout-monde" ("whole world").

6 Werewere Liking

It Shall Be of Jasper and Coral, Song-Novel, and *Orphée-Dafric,* Ritual-Novel—Interconnecting Art Forms

Werewere Liking was born in Bondé, in the Bassa region of Cameroon, in 1950, and settled in Côte d'Ivoire on the outskirts of Abidjan, where in 1983 she founded an artists' community and cultural center, later known as the Village Ki-Yi. All arts—theater, music, painting, sculpture, dance—are brought together here.

Coming from a family of musicians, Werewere Liking studied theater in Paris, became interested in painting around 1968, and then began to exhibit her work. She has published a volume of poetry, *On ne raisonne pas le venin* (Venom can't be reasoned with) (1977), and several song-novels: *Orphée-Dafric* (1981), *Elle sera de jaspe et de corail* (1983) (*It Shall Be of Jasper and Coral,* 2000), *L'amour-cent-vies* (1988) (*Love-across-a-Hundred-Lives,* 2000), and *La mémoire amputée* (2004) (*The Amputated Memory,* 2007) (Noma Award for Publishing in Africa). She has done extensive research on the Bassa, and, with her passion for rituals and her knowledge of their techniques, she has written several ritual-plays for the stage: *La puissance de Um* (The power of Um) (1979); *Une nouvelle terre* (A new land), followed by *Sommeil d'injuste* (Sleep of the unjust) (1980); *Les mains veulent dire* (Hands imply), followed by *La rougeole arc-en-ciel* (Rainbow measles) (1987).

The arts—gesture, dialogue, song, music, masks—come together in her works in order to communicate a polyphony of human emotions, using ritual to transform society. Imbued with pan-Africanism, Werewere Liking, in her play *Un Touareg s'est marié à une Pygmée* (A Tuareg married a Pygmy) (1992), addresses all of Africa: "I am preoccupied with Africa, her contradictions, her conscious and unconscious aspirations, her failures, her flaws [. . .]. I don't know whether an artist like myself can get along without politics. Politics drives everything and the artist must follow it to redirect our fate" (Tagne, "Werewere Liking," 195).

In her writing, Werewere Liking blends theater, poetry, visual art, and music, subscribing to the syncretic process of African art which calls upon a multiplicity of forces through the composite.

> At first I wrote poems that I put to music [. . .]. Then I stopped adding music [. . .].
>
> Still, I had the impression that I wasn't fully expressing myself . . . At the same time that I was writing I was also painting. Now, painting provokes an *a posteriori* reflection. It is an invitation to contemplation and so I wrote things that had to make connections between poetry and painting. (Magnier, "À la rencontre de . . . Werewere Liking" [Meeting . . . Werewere Liking], 17)

She works a segment, creating countless silences, combining genres: myth, novel, poem, essay. She inserts theatrical features and elements of orality, while also turning toward other arts to express herself more completely: "And it is only by blending different genres that it seems possible for me to attain different levels of language, different emotional qualities, and to approach different levels of consciousness from where one can experience everything . . . " (ibid., 18).

She refers to ancient practices, especially to the Bassa rituals of Cameroon, which she knows intimately and which she links to the expression of current preoccupations and desires. She makes this clear in an interview:

> We are inspired by traditional ritual communication devices and techniques. My theater and my other work draw from this same source. But oral literature influences only the form of these works that, generally, rely on all the genres at once. As for the themes, they tend to be modern and commonplace. (Tagne, "Werewere Liking," 195)

Thus, various methods crisscross the written work and the use of French, traveling through centuries, cultures, arts, and inscribing the work with characteristics of song and visual imagery; of processes that come from

Greek, Egyptian, and Cameroonian myths; of ancient rites. The result is a fragmented compilation from which numerous silences emerge.

In chapter 2 I mentioned that ritual and divination have been used for centuries and that it is their function to maintain harmony by settling the problems that arise within a community. They remind the society of its values, exorcise anxieties, and connect humans to the cosmos. Ritual celebrates life's stages (circumcision, birth, mourning), marking the passage from one period to another, preparing the individual to overcome difficult times. It puts the person in touch with sacred forces, while guiding him toward a more thorough inner examination, as John Conteh-Morgan shows in his study of the role of Bassa ritual among the Ngué in Cameroon in his analysis of Werewere Liking's *Une nouvelle terre:*

> An astringent ethic of self-investigation and awareness (in a strong psychoanalytic sense) is then at the heart of the Ngué. It is this imperative that explains the outburst of recrimination, of public confessions and collective stock-taking that are encouraged during its performance. By plumbing the depths of their psyche, by lapsing into ecstasy (a process facilitated by the intoxicating rhythms of drum music, the language of repetition and incantation), the participants in the ceremony release repressed desires. A result of this process, it is believed, is greater self-knowledge, an experience of cosmic harmony and the emergence of a revitalized community. ("Myth, Ritual Performance and the Search for a New Theatre in Francophone Africa," 224)

With a worried look at Africa's situation, Werewere Liking finds viable solutions in the renewal of ancestral practices which she transcribes throughout her written works by the use of repetition, verbal sounds, and rhyme. For example, words come back as incantations echoing songs used in ritual. And her protagonists, while expressing the apathy and feelings of lethargy in which they are bogged down, examine their own lives and attempt to rise above impasses as they wander through the various stages of a quest for Knowledge in order to rid themselves of the state of torpor that paralyzes them and to come to know themselves better.

It Shall Be of Jasper and Coral, a song-novel published in 1983, associates words with music suggested by the rhythm, sounds, alliterations and assonances, reminiscent of the Mvet, an epic, sung or preceded by songs, which sets the immortals against mortals yearning for the secret of immortality. "These are battles between the divine race and the men of *Oku,* who are attracted by the immortality of the first, which constitute the epic tales from which the epic literature known as *Mvet* came forth" (Belinga, [*L'épopée camerounaise*] *Mvet, Moneblum ou l'homme bleu* [The Cameroonian epic, Mvet, Moneblum, or the blue man], 25). Consequently, "[t]he Mvet initiation is an initiation into the Mysteries" (15).

In addition, the staging of the dialogues of the characters Babou and Grozi, who hold forth on the scope of their existence and help each other elude the absurd, is reminiscent of Beckett's *Waiting for Godot*. Their interactions, gestures, facial expressions, and fervor resemble those of Vladimir and Estragon, whose exchanges explore the breakdown of meaning and weave a thread running through various psychological states. Word play and discursive inventions suggest a perceptiveness and earnestness that disregard the everyday.

Added to the words of the protagonists are the thoughts of a woman whose name is never mentioned and the voice of Black-Night, a character who evokes the past, the lost paradise, and proposes deliverance. The text addresses various reflections on the prospects for Lunaï, a town marked by colonialism, poverty, inequality, and corruption. The woman dreams of better times and tries to keep a journal, suggesting steps to be taken to defy evil. However, her writing project is constantly interrupted by Babou, who incarnates "Black-Emotion," while Grozi represents "White-Intellect." The narrator criticizes the attitudes of each, reporting on people's failures as well as on the everyday obstacles they encounter. The fragmented form juxtaposes skepticism (Babou) and transcendent drives (Grozi). Numerous repetitions punctuate the narrative and thereby echo oral performance and ritual practices, reproachful of stagnation, injustices, and weakness. Despite the inertia of Lunaï and despite the incessant interruptions the woman confronts in keeping her logbook, only nine pages of which have been written so far, as she listens to the world the narrator suggests an equilibrium. In spite of her entrenched position, it is she who holds the threads of the story, does or does not let her two companions speak, arranges the remarks that could construct the future, holding on to a power—that of creation and the quest for an initiation. The work criticizes the state of stagnation and suggests the creation of a new race and a new language, banking on the contribution of a transformation of the arts, a renewal of the role of the mask that appears during ceremonies—rites of passage, weddings, funerals—and reconnects mankind to the hieratic, illuminating its journey. By resuming her ancestral function and giving it meaning again, the author finds a new potential and links creativity to the sacred, past to present, while keeping current needs in mind.

The composition draws from various areas, gathering horizons, styles, arts, and outlining the entirety of experience and human feelings. The theater, present through dialogues, stage directions, stage settings, is connected to the poetic, to myth, to journal writing; and the text alludes to the plastic arts, music, and dance to define a universe composed of a broad set of colors, sounds, gestures, and forms.

The text blurs boundaries and presents ambiguity. The reader must go beyond what is stated, beyond the initial meaning, and discover what is hidden behind the language, behind the tension of the contradictory information provided. The characters have multiple faces. Grozi is a long way from representing "White-Intellect," and the narrator isn't always a "misovire"—a term invented by Werewere Liking as a counterpart to the expression misogynist: "[A misovire is] a woman who cannot find an admirable man. [. . .] I've been criticized by some who said that the word didn't exist. They would have preferred 'misandrist' or who knows what other term. I prefer a term that comes closer to misogynist" (Magnier, "À la rencontre de . . . Werewere Liking," 18). The narrator has a complex relationship with men, whose thoughts form the structure of her own arguments. She blames them for a presumptuous attitude, an ostensible lack of self-examination, and irresponsible actions. But she also knows how to enhance their moments of perceptiveness and selects segments of their discussions by withdrawing and falling asleep when their words bore her, thus breaking through their logorrhea—a trick that allows her to control intrusions and redundancies and that illustrates the power she has over her environment.

The textual structure relies on snatches, like a game that disobeys what is lawful, links ideas, is sarcastic, entertains, calls upon the *non-finito* to remain within the creative flow of the possible, open to life. The voids that come out of the fragmented structure not only refer to the political and social situation in which the characters are trapped but also inscribe ritual elements and segments that reclaim lost energy and transform society. In line with the approach of this study, the present chapter will analyze the processes that break up the narrative and then examine the significance of these breaks within the text, enigmas caused by assembling disparate elements that respond to the complexity of a concrete situation. Thus we will first see how the text is splintered by looking at the elements peculiar to the style of writing, elements that we have called "textual signs": title, chapter title, game displays, journal form, final dating, dedication, theatrical characteristics, and combining of words. This will be followed by an analysis of the distinctive features of orality under the name "characteristics of the oral art"—dialogues and monologues, musicality, verbal art, riddle, myth—and end with the unspoken, which in part refers to ritual. Then I will discuss the novel *Orphée-Dafric* to trace the impact of an initiatory and composite form of writing.

We shall see that the various textual signs and references to orality are, at the same time, pathways that lead the reader through the themes discussed, bits and pieces, leaps, impasses. They upset the expected linearity and create a tangled route, inviting the reader to enter other worlds and become involved in an initiation with the narrator. The clusters and transitions fragment the story, inscribing flaws and reconstructing methods.

Textual Signs

The **title** *It Shall Be of Jasper and Coral (Journal of a Misovire . . .)* tells us that the principal character, the one who writes the journal/logbook is a woman: "misovire." The project of keeping a journal is put into question by the suspension points and parentheses—an additional piece of information, whose significance will be revealed as the reader delves further into the text; moreover, it is grafted onto the phrase "It Shall Be of Jasper and Coral," which defines the new race ("it").

The title returns throughout the text like the melody in a composition of themes and variations, sometimes providing additional information: "It shall be of jasper and coral / It shall be of breath and fire" (5).[1] Grozi scatters these segments like a refrain in order to designate the new race: "They will be free and strong and beautiful / They will be of jasper and coral . . ." (21). And the narrator does so in her journal: "For the Race of jasper and coral / A Race with a new breath of life of speech of the Word . . ." (79). These scattered repetitions pick up on the structure of a fragmented musical montage that links the elements of the composition by means of invisible threads.

The **chapter title** "Fore Word" on the text's first page instantly situates the song-novel beyond language. The words suggest other ways of communicating, possibly gestures, signs, sounds, or prelanguage cries. Conscious of stagnation, the narrator chooses to remove herself from the gloomy analyses that have become clichés and seeks to skirt the paralytic state of language, gathering together the frailties in order to set the human being free and remove all meaning from the word early on.

Game displays are other textual signs the reader encounters. The playful framework encourages entertainment, pleasure, reversals, fantasy, imagination, and allows us to go beyond what is real: "Let's play a game in which we amass every weakness every blockage every veneer every bit of ugliness and every stray impulse. Let's superimpose. Let's pile it up. [. . .] There it is: the word no longer has any meaning" (3). Countless perspectives are stacked up that mimic a splintering to give some energy back to language, some significance to worn-out terms, disregarding existence. The game is explained right away, and the reader is guided through the twists and turns of the composition:

> In our game there will be no magical solution, no dogma. Our heroes will leave us unsatisfied: they won't go far enough (imagine the new race already there!). They're groping, they're fluttering, purring and snoring! And with them an incredible woman, frail in flesh, following them only with her gaze her ear and from afar, stalking the power-word that will formulate and give shape to her dream, a fiery dream inside a body she fears is nothing but "meat." . . . A *misovire* in short! She gets lost in their clichés, tries to hook on to an "elsewhere-otherness" and finds herself to be nothing but a mixture of aspiration-inclination and of ill-accepted nonassumed experience. And she goes scudding along from failure to frailty, from a "false start" to a "betrayal" without ever managing to get her "journal" under way. But she still doesn't choke! . . .
>
> As I was saying, a people never falls into complete bankruptcy.
>
> And of all the many truths regarding Africa and Humanity, there is one I insist on prophesying:
>
> "There shall be born here
> From our groping our stammering
> [. . .]
> And the *misovire* I am now shall encounter a misogynist
> [. . .]" (4–5)

The voice is that of a woman, and the text "plays" as it moves from one register to another: from a discourse in which the narrator is missing to a narrative where she reports on her observations (in the novel and in the journal). The text offers two entities that are sometimes dissimilar, sometimes unified. One provides clarification concerning the progression of the story and gives depth to the characters, while the other conveys personal insights and superimposes the pages of a private journal that at times "gets under way" and at times blends in with explanations concerning the problems of becoming. The narrative interrupts the plan and goes beyond the scope of the journal embedded in the song-novel. The title *It Shall Be of Jasper and Coral (Journal of a Misovire . . .)* indicates the distinctive nature of the work—a journal/logbook that is not written for a public. However, the ellipsis that puts the project into question suggests ambiguity. The passing from "she" to "I"—a movement of detachment and fusion with the speaking subject—reproduces distance and union with the hieratic and with the "I" who transcribes the quest for an identity in motion, deliberately blurring the reading.

In the passage quoted above, the first-person plural—"our," "us"—specifies various people, depending upon the situation. "In our game" includes a variety of individuals: Babou and Grozi, who are designated as "our heroes," the narrator, the author, and the reader, whom the text addresses with the words "imagine the new race" and who is invited to discover the discursive traps while adhering to the concepts mentioned—"there will be no magical solution no dogma." The accumulation of negative turns of phrase—"there will be no," "they won't go," "without ever managing," "but she still doesn't choke," "never falls"—on which the text is constructed inserts negation into the narrative and into the syntax, and does so by following the principles of the game, namely, by gathering "every blockage" (3). The present expresses apathy: "snoring." It suggests the possibility of a fall, even if avoided ("never falls"), and distractedness ("gets lost," "goes scudding along"). Gradually, there emerges from the discourse a "prophetic" "I" which is that of a woman. The future proclaims new and better times.

Games liberate and allow disparate elements to come together, to disobey rules and modify them over time, to paint a seeming chaos, to put all possibilities on stage, and to overturn any limitations. They call upon the reader's imagination and, in turn, invite him/her to juggle the ideas presented.

The **journal form** is employed as well, and nine pages of the logbook are scattered throughout the text. The project is sometimes interrupted by Grozi and Babou, and sometimes put aside to grapple with the narrator's thoughts concerning her desire to write a private journal, a project that will be abandoned definitively by the end of the narrative when the narrator finds that she is not yet ready to assume such a task. An extension of the movement of something traced-erased, of an idea proffered and immediately expunged or contradicted—a process of nuance, an accumulation of contrary positions, give depth to the project and to the characters (after all, as was stated earlier, the narrator wasn't always a misovire and Grozi not necessarily a "White-Intellect").

The text precedes the inserted journal. The latter begins on page 15 and will consist of nine pages—a sacred number that will occur again in *Orphée-Dafric*—and nine themes or preoccupations that are both personal and universal. Here we find a reflection on a dedication, the search for an exergue, woman, the need for a new language, criticism, choice, friendship, equilibrium, and, finally, the importance of silence—the moment to abandon the journal. The reader never knows whether the journal actually gets under way and when and if it comes to an end, since it spills out into the narrator's words and fits into the song-novel. In any event, an outline is proposed. Subjects are developed on each page of the "journal-golden logbook" strewn throughout the work, a substitute for the usual division into chapters. The term the woman uses, "journal-golden logbook," explains her project, giving her life meaning. The writing (book) illuminates (golden) her journey, leading to silence—the quest for an initiation.

Different comic effects are scattered throughout the text, among which is the **final dating.** The last page of the song-novel coincides with the end of the journal, and the narrator specifies place and date before turning to silence. But the precise time is extreme and thus comical, as is the adverb "quickly," which suddenly suggests the feeling of running out of time:

> Page 9
> Quickly
> Retreat to a hermitage
> The cure for clichés for complexes
> The bath in the sacred word that contemplates itself in silence
> Weighs words and places deeds
> Here and now on page 9 . . . .
>
> Tour Sarah
> 6 November 1981
> 3:09 P.M. (115)

The nine minutes (a sacred number, as mentioned above), reflecting the brevity (model of the exergue) of each of the nine pages, are a *mise en abîme* of the art of condensation, of the essence sought—"I would confide the essence of nothingness or nothingness and the essence" (7–8)—thus immediately showing the importance of silence. Yet, when the narrator proposes to choose words, she doesn't recommend that the subject remain entirely silent. She valorizes the exergue, proverb, image—the oral art that feeds the whole work through familiar expressions, through the use of metaphors, rhymes, and repetitions. And it is not the logorrhea of Babou and Grozi that keeps the narrator from writing, as she had suggested, but her own demands, her need for perfection and for withdrawal in order to outdo herself.

The **dedication** is introduced on the first page and resolved as the story develops. The journal will not be dedicated to Babou and Grozi, as originally planned, but to the next race, which will be perfection incarnate, running the risk that it will never see the light of day. Thus, the narrator strives for a model that demands exceeding oneself, opening up to what is possible, to the unknown, to the dream, to utopia.

The **theatrical characteristics** are innumerable. The journal's formulation is wrapped in a theatricalized story that explains the narrator's thinking about her intention to write. Her project is put forward from page 7 on, a deviation from the writing of the journal: "Every morning I grab some pencils, notebooks I'd like to keep a journal-golden logbook in which I would confide the essence of nothingness or nothingness and the essence" (7–8). The daily recurrence of a gesture ("Every morning") that doesn't reach execution ("I'd like," "I would confide"). The use of the conditional implies the need for something that is absent in the present. On the final page of the novel, the reader learns that the narrator must first go through an initiation, a retreat, to find the ability to start writing. The journal is constantly interrupted, and the few pages that are presented rupture the novel.

The stage directions that surround Babou and Grozi's dialogues also suspend the verbal discourse to convey the protagonists' internal feelings: "Grozi (more and more pompously): Well then . . ." (21). "Oh! Children of mine . . . / (once again caught up in his own enthusiasm)" (21). Supplementary information on a character's behavior, his attitude in the face of a given situation, his irritations and impulses. This staging allows the reader to come closer to the oral performance via the transcription of elements that lie outside language, surrounding the conversation: gestures, expressions, attitudes when faced with the elaboration of a thought, the interaction of the two actors.

> Since the sound properties of the word are lost in their transcription, the narrator attempts to reconstruct the characteristics of oral production by commenting on volume, flow, intonation, accent, mannerisms, pauses, and silences of the account presented. In relationship to the word, this *commentated discourse,* which so often accompanies the reported discourse, consists of a metalanguage whose scope is equivalent to the complexity of its representation. (Van den Heuvel, *Parole, mot, silence,* 50)

Grozi appears a few pages after the song-novel begins. He is talking to himself: "I wanted . . . I would like . . . I would have liked . . . An adventure . . . No! something else, . . . an encounter that's it! I would have liked an initiatory encounter . . . / He hesitates . . . Then he turns away furiously. What did I do to him now?" (6). The theatrical staging comes across through the punctuation and structure of what is uttered. Hesitation is expressed by countless ellipses, repetition, changes in verbal tense: "I wanted . . . I would like . . . I would have liked . . ." The fact that he speaks out loud is indicated by quotation marks; the pauses, by ellipses; the tonality, firmness, accentuation, by capital letters, exclamation, and interrogation marks.

Other theatrical effects are linked to the poetic to render a theme visible:

> He is seated on the cubic stone
> At the door of the sanctuary
> In his left hand the hand of the heart he holds
> The scepter of selection by trial
> His right hand sketches a stimulating and admonishing gesture
> [. . .]
> And we shall no longer be ignored (79)

A thematic rupture appears in the sudden introduction of the question of a work's distribution and the role of the critic. This is an unexpected topic if we see the project as a wish to keep a journal, although that goal is continuously turned on its head. The abrupt changes in themes and styles and the sketch of the critic in the Greek manner break the narrative. The use of an ironic, comic tone makes fun of the omnipotence of this figure, while at the same time indicating the narrator's need to make literary texts known: "And we shall no longer be ignored" is an allusion to the reality that African literature written in French confronts. It continues to be unknown to a wide public: lack of knowledge of texts and topics, an ambivalent relationship to the colonial past, and difficulties with publishing and distribution. Thus, various problems that affect the writer, society, and intercultural exchange in the world's current evolution are introduced and woven into the fabric's texture.

The **combining of words** is another technique used: "*music-words*" (23), "*wide-open*" (24), "to beseech to pray" (35). It moves one word onto another. This clashing, this "non-sense," produces correlation, sometimes mocking: inside prayer, a cry of supplication; inside the opening up to the world there is clarity; in the writing there is the melody of a musical score, like the one sought for *It Shall Be of Jasper and Coral.* By means of a typographic process, the combinations create new meanings. A void, a time for reflection, is inserted to grasp the unique association.

Characteristics of the Oral Art

Dialogues and **monologues** give expression to the voice of the narrator in search of herself, of unknown figures, of Babou and Grozi, of Black-Night who is dead, and they become entangled. Black-Night speaks to the narrator at night, letting mystery creep in with her nocturnal appearance and her name, picking up on the model of the Mvet—a poetic epic sung at night—and showing the power of recitation at night. Her thinking suggests wisdom. She defines the characteristics of the new race: *"healthy body," "more refined Emotions," "thinking . . . more rigorous," "his will stronger,"* and *"his consciousness more open"* (14). She depicts a complex and contradictory whole being: "The curve is not a curve" (13).

The narrator controls, organizes, and selects the pertinent passages. Through poetic language and through the character of Bathsheba—a mise en abîme for the narrator—Black-Night suggests they liberate themselves from the colonizer, from man, from the weight of the ancestors, and from the instilled Christian precepts:

> *And you were taught Bathsheba*
> *You had to love your neighbors as yourself*
> [. . .]
> *And you Bathsheba you believed them!* (47)

As for the interactions between Babou and Grozi, they seek solutions to Lunaï's apathy. Babou comes out with stereotypes, commonplaces, material subjects, and holds forth on trivialities, as defined by Van den Heuvel:

> *Trivial* doesn't merely refer to the "common" or the "crude," but to a specific functioning of systems of cultural codes on the level of the

communication process. A text is *trivial* when, with all the discursive means available, it aims at "speaking" like the public, at satisfying its latent needs, and at corresponding to its "horizon of expectation" as best it can. (Van den Heuvel, *Parole, mot, silence,* 55)

Grozi is entirely different. His speech is lively and excessive, passionate and engaged. He rises up against corruption, expresses the same thoughts on a new race as Black-Night, and adds the need for a new language. He goes against the everyday, the clichés on how to approach the hereafter, and through the verbal achieves pleasure in formulating his ideas:

And from the depths of all his repression from the depths of all his weary
expectations of all his
apathy
Suddenly
Joy gushes forth
A deep-seated joy that does not endure artificiality confusion (89)

A lively energy is one of Grozi's characteristics, which is stimulated and focused by Babou's questions. The value of the spectacle typifies their relationship, which the narrator constructs by choosing the discourse of the two protagonists. By feigning sleep to interrupt their conversation, she coordinates the essence of their verbal exchanges. Either Babou and Grozi are engaged in dialogue and Grozi opines on Babou's questions, or each of them delivers a monologue in which he elaborates previously expressed statements. Grozi's language is poetic. Its structure resembles that of the griot: metaphors, comparisons, assonances, alliterations:

GROZI: Moron! And what about natural colors?
Spirits will no longer be bulls lying in wait for carmine-red
Sheep on the watch for bright-green
Nor chicks attacking pink-candies . . .
They will have the subtlety of the shades of color
They will distinguish the pink-quiver of affection
The mellow-blue of fertility and the cloud-black of the storm
They will feel the warmth of a hand bearing down
The smell of a sifting look
And the weight of a drop of sweat . . .
They will savor the taste of a protecting heart
The perseverance of a love that lights up to give nourishment
They will eat life with fervor . . . (25)

There is a sudden transition from the familiar to the poetic: "Moron! And what about natural colors?" As if the oral word explodes from the written one, the reader hears the irritation as well as the firmness of tone in "And what about." The verbal flight that follows is full of metaphors.

Juxtapositions revive the language and surprise the reader, who at first stumbles over what is said, the discrepancies and the shifts. Then, called upon to restore meaning in order to grasp the fabric, he will have to follow the bits and pieces to reach the destination. Invited to accompany the narrator on her identity quest, the reader follows a journey of initiation toward the first stirrings of a creative act—writing via a range of reflections on the resolve to keep a journal, or on the need for a new language.

Musicality is suggested through repetitions, sound games, alliterations, assonances, and rhyme: *"Alone will be the one to know / Alone the one to dare"* (18), or "Lunaï is a burned-out and weary village. Alas!" (15).[2] Repeated resonance, syllables, sounds like the notes in a melody, reinforcing the word "vil*la*ge" through the interjection of "a*las*."[3] The repetition characteristic of music underlines an expression within a literary text, functions as a reference point, provides the story with a beat, or else drains the word of its meaning by trotting out the same thing to the point of becoming mind-numbingly punishing: "desperately empty boulevard—empty sidewalks houses—empty empty factories empty hotels—empty empty building complexes empty . . ." (28).

Other musical aspects are suggested throughout the song-novel by the insertion of words that are not French—*"soukoukalba"* (7), "Moussa-speaking" (10)—where the context provides meaning, exciting the reader's imagination: an opening up to unlimited possibilities, playing on sound resonances and on the mystery enclosed inside the words. The countless exclamation and interrogation points and the capital letters specify the timbre and musicality of the narrative.

The work is called a song-novel, which in various ways suggests melodies by which to attain other spheres, other emotions, evoking song—an element of the Bassa ritual that Werewere Liking knows so well.

> The Word of the Djingo [a Bassa healing ritual] is mostly sung and presented in the form of refrains that the group endlessly repeats in chorus. For the African, and particularly for the Bassa, the verb is part of the secret domain and its power depends on it; thus one comes across countless

esoteric songs that only the initiated understand. (Hourantier et al., *Du rituel à la scène chez les Bassa du Cameroun*, 16)

In her article "To W/rite in a New Language," Anne Adams shows that the text's musicality (verbal sounds) reproduces the journey of the protagonists, who are traveling through different levels of "revelation" toward "illumination."

The **verbal art** in Werewere Liking's work is connected to the art of the griot. It uses various techniques and rests on the multiplicity of meanings and changes in register. Transitions, suddenly passing from the poetic to the familiar—"muddle-headed" (3), "make pigs of ourselves" (24), "want to lie down and die" (31), "empty babble" (42), "tramps" (53)—in her writing call upon the power of the oral, of dissonances, reactivating the language with an unexpected confrontation of the bizarre and the everyday. To introduce a page of the "golden-journal/logbook" in the middle of the text, the conjunction "so" or the interjection "fine" is often used, reproducing spoken language: "Fine, page 1! To Grozi and Babou, the ancestors of . . ." (15).

The work mixes genres and valorizes phrasings that produce surprise and necessitate the restructuring of the sentence. Substitution of a term or modification of a statement forces the reader, at first, to reread the sentence. The missing word, on which he/she stumbles, is all the more present through its absence and through the dissonant effect that the new term creates. This hole in the textual fabric causes surprise, then promotes a quest so that the puzzle can be solved: "And we shall live happily ever after / And we shall be numerous children" (5). We expect to read: "And we shall have numerous children." This disparity attempts to renew the language and thereby mark a reversal in a cliché. This method destroys stereotypes, plays with the reader's expectations and with linguistic platitudes. These immutable constructions, passed from generation to generation, are reassuring, are reference points for people to find themselves but also places where they may get lost, thereby congealing the language. The narrator frees herself from any illusory refuge or straitjacket. "Willpower has been scattered to the four corners of futility and all energies have been wasted . . ." (15). Five lines later and in a different context, the expression appears in the form the reader knows it: "from every corner of the world" (15). An adjusted slip that distorts normal speech and thus produces a distance from the familiar expression—disappearances, erasures, playing with the reader's expectations and habits. Such a method accentuates the term "futility" and holds the reader's attention, creating empty spaces throughout the work that contain hidden information and copy ritual processes.

The verbal structure sometimes overturns the first meaning of words, slipping from one meaning into another. The town in which the story takes place has unexpected characteristics that are at odds with the name Lunaï, the narrator's choice, which we imagine to be infused with the lunar sign, that of madness: "Since Black-Night's death, it is impossible to imagine Beauty in Lunaï to dream of Love to glimpse Vast Horizons in short it's impossible to attain Vision here . . ." (8).

This technique, which outsmarts the expected, is repeated extensively and is bewildering: "And we we allow ourselves to be pulled along with the masses with periodic crises of conscience [. . .]" (33); "to be pulled along with the masses" is substituted for the familiar having "the wool pulled over our eyes," meaning to be deceived.[4] It draws a parallel between the masses and deception. The connection is made by the emptiness that becomes a central articulation used to convey more effectively tension and reproach. The hole, the flaw, contains data that require the reader to dive, to descend into himself, into history in order to find a meaning, calling upon a revitalization of the language: "Among the most deadly things of Lunaï the word is the worst of all . . . It is a carcass emptied of all content and all meaning an encumbering and depressing carcass older than old" (26). And the text proposes a solution by linking language to the unspoken: "*It will enable the construction of a sturdy bridge between the spoken and the unspoken*" (14). This junction, this collage, is meticulously arranged, as are a recognition and modification of the *void-void* in the text in order to transgress it.

The female protagonist uses language to condemn iniquities, enhancing her remarks with multiple meanings. She hides behind plural meanings, neutralizing and masking her feelings with irony and obliqueness, aspiring to a new language.

The alignment of sentences follows the breath, the griot's form of delivery. Reminders of the oral art are buried in the text, and in order for the reader to interpret the work and give it meaning, he or she must stand in for the griot via the signs provided. Pathways are traced, leaving space for us to participate and develop our own imagination. Entire phrases go on without any punctuation, forcing us to participate in bringing meaning to the text. Anne Adams repeats the explanations of Werewere Liking, given at a colloquium (which has not been published) at ILENA, the Institut de Littérature et d'Esthétique Négro-africaines, in Abidjan in 1983:

> "Descriptive language and the imaginative [. . .], must be liberated from all logical formation and from the restraints of verisimilitude. They should serve to create a series of images intended to provoke an emotional explosion which can liberate the reader, turning him/her into a creator also" [. . .] (thus re/uniting the audience and the artist/writer). (Adams, "To W/rite a New Language," 153)

At times, just like the griot, the narrator addresses her public/reader, gives directions, clarifications, and guides him through the reading or addresses him with questions or comments—"A strong word a word-of-strength that will have to undress the reader carefully and profoundly [. . .]" (39)—or with questions thrown out in any direction: "To whom to what then should you consecrate your life? Why? When? How?" (59).

The person addressed changes throughout the story. In the manner of the journal mentioned in the title and suggested in the text, the writing functions primarily as a mirror from self to self, in which the reader is the double of the person writing. At other times, the narrator speaks to Grozi and Babou, to the men and women of Lunaï, to Africa, or to the whole human race. She involves her reader by using pronouns and shakes him up, going so far as to jostle him with questions and accusations.

The **riddle** is a form the griot uses to get his audience to participate in the story. "[I]f the *myth* is the form that 'offers' an *answer,* the *riddle* is the form that expresses the *question.* The myth is an answer that contains a prior question; the riddle is a question that calls for an answer" (Jolles, *Formes simples,* 105). The answer lies concealed within the question and bothers the person questioned.

> In the form of the Myth, we are the questioners, in the Riddle we are being questioned—and in such a way that we must respond. That is why the Myth carries the colors of freedom and the Riddle those of constraint; that is why the Myth is active and the Riddle passive. That is why the Myth brings relief when the Riddle is oppressive. (Ibid., 105–6)

Werewere Liking presents the riddle while transforming it, listing the standard questions posed by journalists with their limiting and limited objectives. She provides a variety of responses, ridiculing clichés and the ready-made questions that have lost all meaning.

> *Fourth question:* "Could you explain your work to me?" [. . .]

> *The right answers:* "You see this line is Africa in reverse. This sound is the cry of rebellion of the Black Man. This Capital letter after the comma in line 10 is the sign of my grandfather who was hanged by the colonialists in 1900 [. . .]."
>
> *The wrong answers:* "How could I since I don't understand it myself?"
>
> Or else: "Has anyone ever offered you an explanation of your rosary?" (82–83)

By inserting a wholly different style into the text, this detour creates a feeling of discomfort as it voices sharp criticism. The journalist's platitudes and expectations based on what the public wants are turned upside down. Indirectly, the narrator is addressing her reader, challenging his/her possible penchant for gossip and intimate revelations. Two silences are created. The first is revealed by a change in the weave, a break in the style—a sudden insertion of interview snippets in the middle of the text; the second by presenting questions that create holes. These questions are ridiculed, while the text accuses the journalist of persisting in the use of clichés.

As for **myth,** it stems from an interrogation of the human being confronted with the mysteries of life:

> Man asks the universe and its phenomena to allow him to know them; he receives an *answer,* he receives a *response,* a word that comes to meet him. The universe and its phenomena make themselves known. When the universe is thus created for mankind through *question* and *response,* a *form* comes to be that we shall call *myth.* (Jolles, *Formes simples,* 81)

In *It Shall Be of Jasper and Coral,* Hilôlômbi, who created man, gradually noticed the flaws in his creation and tried to correct them one day through the intermediary of Masks. But man didn't want to straighten up, thus igniting the wrath of the gods. Um, the Mask whose mission was to bring civilization, took man's side and fought for him to have a second chance, but his love turned against him and destroyed him. Then a woman, Soo, arrived, who in turn tried to disseminate good, but when she heard an affectionate voice on the way she became frightened of her desire. Nevertheless, she managed to convey the memory of this Knowledge to women, who, armed with this knowledge, elevated humanity. It didn't last very long, however. When Hilôlômbi wanted to reward woman by making all her wishes come true, he was terribly disappointed to discover that she no longer had any demands and was now herself participating in the general sluggishness and corruption.

The myth explains Lunaï's apathy and women's potential, wiped out by inertia. It delays the narrative and goes back to the origins of humanity, linking the human with the divine. It recounts the fall of man and mentions his inability to assume the role given him. A first void is created by going back in time—the incorporation of myth in a novel interrupts the narrative. Then a second void appears in the myth of Hilôlômbi, who describes the absurdity of mankind's eternally repeated exploits.

Myth evokes the sacred and timelessness, firmly rooting man's acts in the past. It relates anew a collective anonymous story, and its insertion in the text allows for a journey through different eras, for the indirect relaying of a message, highlighting humanity's greed and the drives that characterize it, all of which have remained unchanged through the centuries.

> Through myth, the group is taken back to the time of peace and harmony in the society, achieved through positive actions. It is the utilization of material from former times, put to the service of the present, to re-state the relevant questions. In searching out the debilitating, destructive forces, a confrontation between past and present is established, to arrive at an ideal model. Myth: action that reflects on tradition. (Adams, "To W/rite a New Language," 155)

Toward the end of the song-novel, the narrator traces a parallel between her work (the journal or the reflections gathered together in the work) and the myth—the individual's questioning in the face of existence:

> The next Race will search
> [. . .]
> And since they won't find my precious bubbles
> It will find itself
> It will find itself again
> And they will take me seriously
> For at last I will have bequeathed a beautiful myth at least! . . . (113)

The leaps created by these methods deconstruct the narration and put on stage questions and problems in order to exorcise stagnation. Games, theatricality, verbal art, music, visual arts, are brought together and collected in the writing in order to find harmony again, renewing and revalorizing an ancient practice—ritual.

Combinations and the Unspoken

As previously noted, *It Shall Be of Jasper and Coral* refers to the art of the griot through its verbal games, the use of the comical and the ironic—a feast of reversals and distortions—and the joy of sharing and laughter. It entertains while posing crucial questions and examining the journey of mankind. Since the griot is absent, his art is suggested in the writing by the methods discussed above: descriptions of gestures, use of clichés, repetition, rhyme, poetic imagery. The lack of punctuation and the stringing together of words through hyphenation indicate to the reader an approach he might use, giving him the floor by way of questions, objections, asking him to interpret the roles described, to imagine the tone of the verbal interactions or monologues, to make the characters come alive, to enter into the text and provide the silent spaces with meaning. The text encourages him to act, to create, so as not to sink into the same torpor as Lunaï. Relying on linguistic shifts and collages, it interweaves methods and joins opposites.

However, in contrast to the griot, the narrator no longer brings back the value, breadth, and power of the word. She approves a distance from the Ancestors, a questioning—the retreat where she can find herself again. The word has lost its sacred aspect. Sullied, impure, it deceives and calls for modification, so as to recover energy and power. Therefore the narrator valorizes a popular oral form, relayed from generation to generation, that links past and present while at the same time transforming it. She shows the importance of the innocuous, of chatter, since these maintain contact between individuals and remove anxiety. Yet, at the same time she ridicules them when they perpetuate apathy.

She claims to "have bequeathed a beautiful myth at least! . . ." (113). But, as we saw in chapter 3 when referring to the works of Glissant, the myth is enclosure. It closes in upon itself, traces answers, which the text does not do. The latter suggests certain solutions, but many of the responses remain suspended in air. When will the new race see the light of day? What are the components of the new language? The narrator provides data that have been buried in the hollows of the unspoken, in the handling of skillfully uttered bits and pieces. And it is up to the reader to shed light on them, to detect them in the textual discourse and in what lies beyond language. Thus she evades the form of the myth, mentions it without following its principles.

By fragmenting the spoken word, she activates the reader and revitalizes linguistic exchanges, placing her bet on the silences. Her structure is composed of genres, of processes that evoke music, the visual, the theater; it is created by linguistic leaps of drifting fragments, phrases detached from the whole and fractured, having been forced to acquire autonomy. These segments enclose the essence and are allied with other arts in order to attain their full impact.

> GROZI (ardently): In the theater they should stop tempering words by adding purely illustrative gestures that belabor an obvious point. Other vibrations should come into play and move us to the core. The sound of vowels should strike our pituitary and put us back in touch with other worlds. Colors should attack our skin. Smells should make our mouths water. Images should captivate us. Music and rhythm should bewitch us. And silences should allow us to meditate and to widen our horizons. May we receive the ecstasy of the original explosion that created worlds. (73)

Throughout the narrative, Grozi reflects on art and associates it with ritual: "Art is an eternal destruction." / "The reconstruction and the redestruction of form" (41); "Art is a death ritual, an initiation into transcendence over death" (42). Here the writer traces a parallel between the artist and the initiate, both of whom are seeking an "Inner Vision" (45) by which to be creative and to confront obstacles.

> She [Werewere Liking] has been very critical of contemporary African society, where she can see no plan for the future, either in individual lives or within a larger community that lacks political leadership. Therefore, she has devised a personal plan of cultural revival in which art and ritual play a pivotal role. (D'Almeida, *Francophone African Women Writers,* 125)

Thus, we can elicit the following structure from the text:

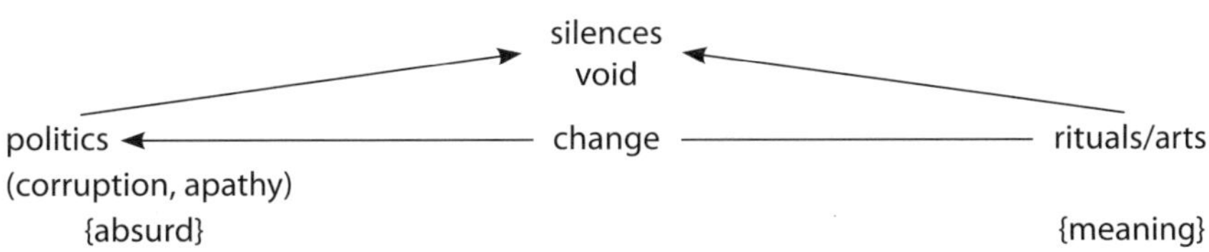

By referring to music, song, the visual arts, and dance, the writer/artist puts him/herself in the text in the place of the person who leads and organizes the rituals. He/she dismantles the events in order to reconstruct them, giving rise to a new form and bridging the gap created by the innumerable abuses. In tangling up these methods, the fracture offers vast silences from which a meaning emerges, contrary to the voids that result from corrupt or indolent systems. The technique allows us to see that, by counting on a new language and on a composite whole, this creation resembles the Menippea described by Bakhtin in *La poétique de Dostoïevski.* It is a genre that shuffles styles, voices, and mixes prose and poetry. It links the burlesque to an ethereal quest, going from Hell to the heights of heaven, expressing a utopia. It navigates through places, worlds, psychic states, exploring the limits and probing existence to trace and test a concept.

> In the Menippea (and that is one of its essential features), the most unbridled, most audacious twists and turns and phantasmagorias are internally motivated and justified by a purely ideal and philosophical goal: that of creating an exceptional situation to provoke and test the philosophical idea (truth) incarnated by the wise man who is searching. [. . .] It is with this purpose in mind that the heroes of the "Menippean satire" ascend to heaven, descend to hell, travel through imaginary lands, are placed in extravagant situations [. . .]. (Bakhtin, *La poétique de Dostoïevski,* 170)

Silence participates in initiation and encourages creativity. It extends in different directions—reminiscence of orality (the art of the griot) and reappropriation of the ritual—describing the political stagnation and psychological states. It invites the reader to participate more actively in the development of the story, to generate and formulate an interpretation.

It is a space from which writing—creation—comes forth. But it is also the expression of an abyss: the inability to formulate, the fear of thinking and saying, the repression of experienced violence, which must be overcome: "Their bloated bodies were found by the dozens, swollen with the pus of not-speaking, blotched with the flagellation of not-questioning" (80); "One idea as good as any void" (85). Silence carries possibilities that are sometimes contradictory. Some silences remain mystifying, such as the silence at the end of the song-novel. The protagonists are looking to give power back to language, "a copious language that can address itself to all our senses" (31), to transmute the *void-void* into the *void-plenty* ("I am the Void that attracts Plenty," 68), but the silence that swallows up the journal and the song-novel stuns the reader. Is it a silence that translates an inability to rise above the male universe, above failure and death, or is it a pause, a time for reflection that allows union with the unutterable and gradually instills the desire to begin an initiation and the inspiration needed for creation? Is it a flight or a withdrawal, the mimesis of the motion of the suggested wave that draws back to remake itself and withdraws again, reassured by its movement? Does writing thus demand the immersion in emptiness?

> In explaining [in *L'espace littéraire*] the specificity of the artistic experience and the ambiguous relationship between "the space of death and the space of the word," by using the myth of Orpheus, Maurice Blanchot explains that Orpheus "doesn't imply eternity and the immutability of the poetic sphere but, on the contrary, [he] links the 'poetic' to a disappearance requirement that goes beyond the norm, it is a call to dying more profoundly [. . .]. Through Orpheus, we are reminded that speaking poetically and disappearing belong to the profundity of a same movement, that the one who sings must risk him/herself fully and perish in the end." (Renard, "Le pouvoir ambigu des mots" [The ambiguous power of words], 18–19)

The writer proposes a descent, a dive into oneself and to the bottom of the abyss, an exploration of the void in the writing in order to give meaning back to language and thus to life:

> This evening's poem that sings of the fall
> And the descent . . . .
> Toward . . . hell you'll say
> And I say toward life
> Warmth lights births and deaths
> [. . .]
> I am reborn out of the ashes (113)

And the abandoned journal is transformed into a song-novel—"reborn out of the ashes"—and sets itself up as book, creation, "script" (the inscription of the stages of the ritual), according to Anne Adams (cited above), in confronting silence. The "stifled" word lies in agitation beneath the word and, scattered in snatches on the page, murmurs and plots so as to seize its interlocutor and also draw him/her in toward a search, a "questioning," a road of initiation.

Having brought up the figure of Orpheus, it is appropriate to discuss Werewere Liking's *Orphée-Dafric* (1981) in terms of the themes elaborated above. This novel follows a similar course, punctuated by rituals in which woman plays an equally central role and where similar discursive techniques come into play to trace the stages of a journey of initiation in order to better confront life.

It is the story of a young man named Orpheus, who is the eldest in a family of ten children and who provides for his brothers' needs. After a three-year engagement to Nyango, he embarks on the test of crossing the river—a traditional and daring practice by which to obtain the gods' agreement—to marry her. Once the wedding is celebrated, the young couple retires, as is customary, and Orpheus falls into a deep sleep. The novel shifts and the reader can no longer distinguish between the dream and the protagonists' narrative. The dream fractures the narrative and dismantles temporality in order to follow a quest and achieve transformation.

The work refers specifically to the Greek myth. Orpheus symbolizes the poetic, music, and enchantment. This hero knows how to tame wild animals and is interested in mysteries. He travels all the way to Egypt to complete his education and be initiated into different practices. He weds Eurydice, who dies the day they are married, whereupon he sets out to find her, crossing through Hell to bring her back to earth. But he loses her forever when he breaks the agreement he had made. In his impatience to see her he turns around before they reach the exit. This failure marks him with a grief that progressively destroys him; he is doomed to wander, distraught, for the rest of his days.

The choice of such a myth sets the narrative in a precise context. Orpheus, poet and magician, sustains the text and with his presence recalls the influence of the arts, the power of wonder, and the combination of music and word. This mythical figure, who moves between earthly and subterranean spheres, symbolizes a descent into oneself and into life. Still, the story changes the myth, rewrites and adapts it to a completely different situation, steering clear of unhappiness. As it passes from Europe (Greece) to Africa it links the myth to the novel, collective and timeless oral recitation to the written word. It is a descent into death, only to rise again to life and free itself from the past, from destiny, from Europe. It is the practice of an initiation quest to acquire knowledge and to better confront life. The myth, resurfacing in the protagonist's nightmare, suspends the story and fractures the narrative. The ageless dream follows the movement of a pursuit, composed of disturbances and certainties, of submergings and resurfacings, of a voyage dark as well as luminous. Orpheus's dialogue with Ngué's wagon inscribes the marvelous, the magic of the tale, and juxtaposes universes and images, depicting the movement of a journey that covets emptiness. The subject is caught in a movement where he vacillates and loses track of his reference points.

Leaps, combinations, passing from the poetic to the familiar, from the dream to the story, from past to present, from Greek mythology to Africa, compound words, and irony launch enigmas from all sides and require the reader to approach and to familiarize himself with new places. At the same time, the writing, fragmented by these intrusions and clusters, throws a critical and revitalizing look upon humanity:

> And so as to die in dying emptiness, they choose to hibernate in luxury; in a burst of gluttony, they became consumers of "Womencarsvillas," of "fridgestereochannelcolortelevisions" that became known as "exterior brands of possibility . . . " So as to die and die alone, they choose to vegetate in "association": they created the Single-Herd-Party. (*Orphée-Dafric,* 31)

Orphée-Dafric is going to evade the *void-void* for a completely different site and, thanks to Nyango, commit himself to an initiation: "Fortunately for me, I am well favored, I have a master: Nyango's love. It will surely guide me to her. I can rely on it completely while I wait to become my own master one day" (ibid., 32). In the myth, as she vanishes Eurydice takes away the sparkle of joy, Orpheus's bewitching power, and his desire to live. This loss destabilizes him and he drifts into nothingness, the meaninglessness of a word that has lost all significance. Werewere Liking reformulates the myth. The character rids himself of non-sense and finds himself again, and going through various stages, raising issues, and undergoing a series of tests (Ngué's wagon, the giant ant, sword, hanging stairs), he acquires the Knowledge that will allow him to confront life.

> Indeed, the initiation completed, Orphée has grown in knowledge, acquired a sense of balance, rediscovered the power of love, the importance of spirituality, and the desire for creativity. He is therefore ready and equipped for a new beginning. Having an acute awareness of what leadership requires, he can become a leader. (D'Almeida, *Francophone African Women Writers,* 140)

He proposes to his companions that they turn the malaise around by immersing themselves in the void in order to prevail over the past, inertia, and political games:

> Leaving from nowhere and from everywhere
> Leaving from it all and from my naughts
> Leaving rooted in my uprootedness
> Developing myself in my underdevelopment
> Rendering literate my illiteracy

Leaving empty from my all too plentiful void
Leaving strong from my weakness
Leaving dead from my deathful life
Walking and living eternally. (*Orphée-Dafric,* 51)

This approach will be taken through a renewal of the arts in harmony with the unutterable forces: "There, on the bloodstain of the virgin Nyango, sits enthroned the twenty-first card of the Book of Thot, impassive witness of the cosmic benediction, the only one capable of permitting true creativity" (ibid., 67). When she awakens, Nyango refers to the Book of Thot, which Orphée-Dafric's father had given her. This figure is central in Werewere Liking's writing: it symbolizes the utterances the writer seeks.

> Thot, the Egyptian god of writing and exchange, of the chain of reasoning and the thread of conjectures, furnished the space in which texture moves, grasping and articulating signs in each text and on its epistemological shores. We owe Thot a taste for the game and the advantages of giving ourselves rules. (Battestini, *African Writing and Text,* 418)

Also:

> The king of Thebes refuses Thot's genius because it endangers the stability of the order over which he presides. Thot's proposed texture is a revolution: it provides a cipher whose main characteristic is to enable the intellection of all ciphers, like itself arbitrary and provisional but palimpsest to all the others, finding their meanings in the traces they retain of all those which they are not or are no longer. (419)

This links up with what I have suggested for *It Shall Be of Jasper and Coral,* where the writing counts on an eclectic whole, playing with styles, arts, and words and creating puzzles to translate the questioning, the losses, the outbursts of the protagonist, contravening rules and moving between spaces, processes, and cultures.

This attraction to the hieratic located outside the religious—the subject will "become my own master one day" (*Orphée-Dafric,* 32)—counts on the void in order to create. Orphée-Dafric and Nyango are aware of the importance of knowledge: the art of joining ancestral practices, rituals that have been relayed through the centuries, to new and individual approaches, breaking with tradition, and choosing one another freely. They rearrange methods and possibilities. And by using a language, an artifice, that takes its distance from reality and the characters' needs, the text plays with the shifts to transcribe a metamorphosis, reconciling the human being with himself, overcoming the existential, historic, cultural, and verbal impasse.

In this context, Roland Barthes raises the following paradox:

> [The] writer is placed by his writing in a contradiction that offers no way out: either the object of the work is naively in agreement with the conventions of form, literature remains deaf to our present history, and the literary myth is not surpassed; or else the writer recognizes the vast freshness of the present world but has only a splendid dead language available to give an account of it [. . .]. (*Le degré zéro de l'écriture* [The zero degree of writing], 63)

Werewere Liking seeks to skirt this problem by calling upon the unspoken that asks the reader to follow Orphée's journey into Hell. She plays with dissonances and juxtapositions and tries to escape from a rigid, imposed language. She revivifies the writing by initiating the reader into rituals and puzzles, and puts him in contact with other regions: the magic of the verb, the poetic of the beyond. She urges him toward the crossroads of worlds, continents, eras, propelling him toward being tested so that he, in turn, can avoid the snares of the Greek Orpheus's fate and risk the unknown, connecting forms of knowledge, defying received ideas, upsetting the fixed forms of language, and empowering the imagination.

7 Tchicaya U Tam'Si

The Madman and the Medusa—Games of Inscription and Erasure

Tchicaya U Tam'Si was born in 1931 in M'Pili, Congo. His name reflects his destiny: "little leaf that speaks for its country." At the age of fifteen he left for France, where he joined his father, Jean Félix Tchicaya, the deputy for Middle Congo at the French National Assembly and a political fighter for the National Congolese Movement, which played a central role in the struggle for decolonization.

Tchicaya later returned to Africa, to Leopoldville, where he worked side by side with Patrice Lumumba, director of the newspaper *Congo*. Subsequently, he held a position at UNESCO until his retirement in 1986. He died of a heart attack at the age of fifty-seven on April 21, 1988.

For many years he devoted himself to poetry, publishing several collections, among which are *Le mauvais sang* (Bad blood) (1955); *Feu de brousse* (Brush fire) (1957), for which he received the grand prize in literature from the AEF (Afrique-Équitoriale Française); *À triche-coeur* (With cheating heart) (1960); and *Le ventre* (The belly) (1964). He also published a book of folktales, *Légendes africaines* (1966); a collection of short stories, *La main sèche* (Dry hand) (1980); two plays, *Le Zulu* (1977) and *Le destin glorieux du Maréchal Nnikon Nniku, prince qu'on sort* (The glorious destiny of Marshall Nnikon Nniku, prince consort); and four novels: *Les cancrelats* (The cockroaches) (1980), *Les méduses ou les orties de mer* (1982) (*The Madman and the Medusa,* translated by Sonja Haussmann Smith and William Jay Smith, 1989), *Les phalènes* (The moths) (1984), and *Ces fruits si doux de l'arbre à pain* (The sweet fruit of the bread tree) (1987).

In his writing Tchicaya avoids easy outs and illusory safe havens. "Nations, people die of their fixed identity. In life change is necessary. I want to be a civilization, not a relic" (Tchicaya and Bekri, "Dialogue Sud-Sud," 57).

MUCH LIKE Werewere Liking and Abdelwahab Meddeb, Tchicaya U Tam'Si scatters a large number of empty spaces through his writing and connects neglected practices and eras. *The Madman and the Medusa* looks at historical events and elements of Congolese cosmogony, including the art of divination, in order to investigate the past, using techniques of orality—themes that will be dealt with in this chapter.

But, whereas we elicited the following diagram from *It Shall Be of Jasper and Coral,*

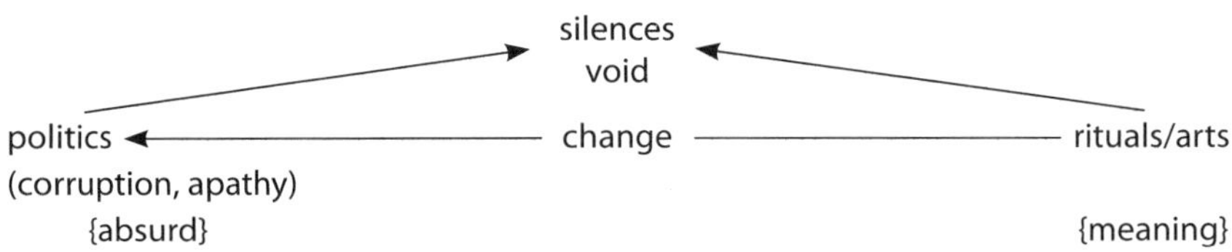

The Madman and the Medusa places emphasis on passing from one void to another, on the interchangeability of these empty spaces:

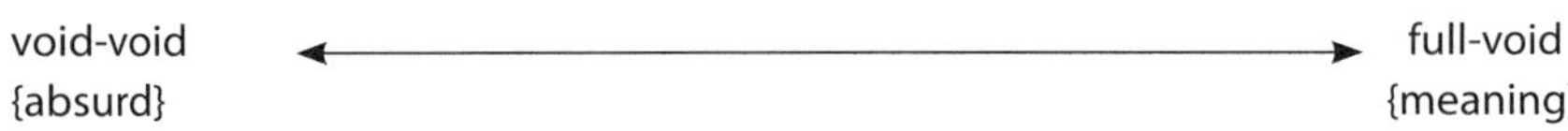

A situation that seems to have a meaning can suddenly change radically and become absurd: the alleged detective, as we shall see, doesn't bring his investigation to an end; the art of the diviner can falsify facts. This playful act of shifting conceals the information provided and obscures the narration. Consequently, the text calls upon the reader to distinguish the events and uncover the political issues and hidden interests.

Tchicaya U Tam'Si situates his works in the specific context of Congo, speaking out against abuses and oppressive customs, dealing all the while with problems that move beyond borders. He seeks to clarify the present by turning toward past events, and he evokes the various traumas that have scarred and destabilized the region: slavery, colonization, rebellions, dictatorships, plots, and internal conflicts.

We should note that, from the sixteenth to the nineteenth centuries and with the help of local lords and courtiers, European slave traders stripped first the coasts then gradually the interior of the continent. The slave trade assaulted and uprooted hundreds of thousands of Congolese to the Americas, depopulating large numbers of villages. In addition, in the nineteenth century, as legal slavery drew to an end, colonization appropriated the region's natural resources and instituted the practice of forced labor. At the Berlin Conference (1884–85), Europe agreed to allocate one part of the Congo to France (Congo-Brazzaville) and the other to Belgium (which later became Zaïre and then the Democratic Republic of Congo). This agreement divided the two banks of the Congo River, which had previously united numerous populations: "Thus the river, which until then had been a crossing point, a hyphen between two sister populations falling under the same political authority, became a frontier" (Aissi, "De la colonisation à nos jours" [From colonization to the present time], 45). Foreign companies settled in the territories and seized their wealth without devising a middle- or long-term plan, but imposing new alienating structures. It resulted in a systematic pillaging of possessions—a violence to which Gide's *Le voyage au Congo* (*Travels in the Congo*) and Céline's *Voyage au bout de la nuit* (*Journey to the End of the Night*) attest.

> These enterprises, envisioned as colonization companies, having to work to establish the infrastructure and the conditions needed for the colonial exploitation, in exchange for exorbitant advantages contained in the conditions of contract, turned out in practice to be like simple commercial enterprises, engaged in pillaging the natural resources and perpetrating scores of brutal acts against the native people. (Ibid., 46)

Colonization caused the collapse of the local social and economic organization. It exacerbated ethnic differences and encouraged conflicts that often proved deadly. In 1959, for example, the rivalry between the Lari and the M'Bochi was the cause of two hundred deaths. Upheavals and inequalities became the motivating force for revolts and propagated an increase in injuries, which African writers condemn as they combat silence and broach the issue of injustices and crimes committed against the African people.

The Madman and the Medusa, a novel published in 1982, is the fragmented account of a dramatic search for three friends, Elenga, Muendo, and Luambu, who one after the other suddenly disappear within three days. Visions, memories, dreams, rumors, are linked together to construct an investigation that rests on erasures, silences, questionable disappearances, and disquieting repressions. The narrative is endlessly interrupted to show the difficulty in determining true motives. The presumed deaths of the three characters at first point to false leads, reassuring to some. Enigmas gnaw at the novel, which begins with a mystery: the consecutive death of two of the friends and the coma of the third. It leads the "detective," André Sola, to consult a diviner to clarify the matter and reconstruct the facts. Memories become muddled and are lost. Time is fractured and clues are erased:

> "Two men died during the last week of June 1944." "Actually three died. . . ." But the third one didn't die, miraculously perhaps. Who knows?
>
> The three men were, of course, acquainted. . . . When I say that the third one didn't die, I mean not the same week. How and why? If I told you now, you wouldn't understand this strange case any better. . . . (Tchicaya U Tam'Si, *The Madman and the Medusa,* 3)[1]

The text carefully maintains a mystery around the possible death of Luambu. The reader is called on to reconstruct the facts and solve the countless questions by following the events, clarifying the obscurities and the silences, following the bits and pieces, sorting out the information given to extricate the false leads.

Several voices interlace—poetry, journalism, detective story, proverbs, tales—situated between dream and reality, between life and death. The story follows a precise external chronology (from Tuesday the 20th to Saturday the 24th of June) that is completely dismantled by an internal timelessness: return to the past (an obsessive memory that haunts Luambu), words and gestures of the madman, and prophesies. Time is fractured. Through subtle interlocking, the author superimposes various eras that refer back and forth to each other, while the present is shaped by a complex texture that clusters experiences and events and becomes the memory of a people. The work, which takes place during the Second World War, is marked by colonization, recalling other forms of violence that have profoundly undermined Africa. Embedded and repressed, infinite wounds have mutilated the land where the story unfolds and haunt the present.

> Warships, real metal monsters whose terrifying aspect was barely hidden under their camouflage nets, were anchored in the bay instead of berthed at the pier in the harbor, which was not equipped to accommodate them. From one of them a white man disembarked at dusk and came ashore

> near the Songolo, the river of bad spirits, where an accomplice, a black man, a number-one sorcerer, awaited him.
>
> Whoever remembers this event will undoubtedly find a certain similarity with the story that will unfold in the following pages. (2)

The novel refers to various incidents scattered through history. Certain events conceal others, which are either brought up in the discourse or suggested in the silences, providing a dimension to what is suppressed. For example, the French "warships" are a reminder of the first European ships that allowed the slave trade to the Americas to take place: "From one of them a white man disembarked at dusk and came ashore near the Songolo."

Tchicaya U Tam'Si re-records a history that is often erased, cast aside, denied. It constitutes the context that intertwines a true and profound malaise upon which other conflicts are grafted, among them the problem of existence, interrogations, daily obstacles, fears and desires experienced in the course of living life. The political situation accentuates the internal crack and sets in motion the opening up of an abyss, of a non-meaning that destroys the human being as he or she confronts the future. Power subjects the individual to constraints whose fruits he will never harvest. The thread gradually comes undone, condemning colonial power, certain ancient practices, and interethnic struggles. The Vili and the Teche, appointed to important jobs, settle in Pointe-Noire, impose their law, and create tensions in the community that provoke lethal confrontations.

While raising numerous criticisms against various abuses—the colonial power, certain beliefs and situations (consulting sorcerers to decipher events, displaying of sects and false prophets, violence committed in schools by teachers who mimic the acts of the colonizers)—the novel is constructed around visions and premonitions. In this process, the writer substitutes himself for the diviner through the power of his writing and his poetic inspiration, fracturing the narration—from the deep gap springs the image that transgresses the so-ominous absurd.

Thus, we note that the author fragments his story in multiple ways to illustrate the political, cultural, and social context of Congo. He uses the model of the detective story to conduct an investigation into the death of his characters, but gradually dismantles this model as the narrative continues, pushing and shoving, breaking the development of the investigation. Tchicaya also uses elements specific to orality which contribute to breaking up the story, introducing expressions in Lingala, proverbs, elements of the tale, and producing a text that interweaves methods, languages, and arts.

Like Werewere Liking, he sketches the form of a Menippea (see Bakhtin, discussed in chap. 6), skillfully combining oral specificities with the written text, the elements of an investigation with the art of divination, as he slips from one form to another.

The Madman and the Medusa centers principally on investigations—inquiries into the past to discover who is responsible for Muendo's and Elenga's deaths. In the course of the narrative, the author reports on the political context to remind the reader of the events that have assailed the region. The inquiry is carried out by evoking elements that belong to the detective novel while gradually deconstructing it and using visions, the art of divination, and dreams that divulge obscure facts. But in the end the reader is left to clarify the events, by examining the information provided and sorting it out.

By giving information that is open to reevaluation or is concealed, the writer leaves the development of the story unresolved. This process reproduces the state of stagnation that has enveloped the region and, by fracturing the narrative, provides data that the author either denies or instantly erases; hence, the text reflects the struggle, the stagnation, and the impossibility of moving forward that have devastated Congo. The innumerable empty spaces in the work reproduce the sense of absurdity that results from the context in which the characters are ensnared. Nevertheless, by way of the poetic and the use of the word, the text suggests a way out and defies the meaningless void. It appeals to a whole Congolese cosmogony, to a concept of the universe, to the art of the diviner, to dreams, and to oral techniques: speech, local expressions, proverbs, images. This study will thus first analyze the processes by which an investigation is attempted, and then the elements of the poetic writing that build on the methods of oral art, so as to understand the shifting games practiced by the writer, who uses one form and then distances himself from it—thereby obscuring the narrative.

Investigations

The detective story allows for "enigmas" to occur around the main plot, which centers on the disappearance of the three protagonists and, secondarily, on returning to the "enigmas" of history—deletions, erasures, buried facts. Tchicaya makes use of the plan of the detective story only to subsequently and skillfully deconstruct it throughout the narrative.

The detective story relies on a labyrinthine plot, sometimes surprisingly complicated, in which countless data lead to a dead end:

> The mysterious detective novel, in which one seeks to discover the identity of the perpetrator, is constructed as follows: on the one hand there are several easy solutions, tempting at first sight but which, one after another, turn out to be false; on the other hand, there is a completely unlikely solution, which one won't reach until the end and which will turn out to be the only true one. (Todorov, *Introduction à la littérature fantastique,* 54)

These data create suspense, implicating the reader in the story so that he will identify himself with the detective or supervise his inquiry. This genre stimulates the reader's attention and encourages him to participate actively in the search for the guilty party. It is made up of false leads that capture his interest. After countless adventures, the plot ends up in an unexpected situation, unless the reader himself has managed to discover the mystery and "catch" the criminal.

Tchicaya U Tam'Si uses these techniques to arouse the reader's interest and play with his expectations. He handles the threads of the plot and, with various twists and turns, delays the puzzle's solution as long as possible. However, he seeks above all to puncture the silence to shed light on the past and rewrite history in order to neutralize its destructive power. First of all, he discards the false accusations around the deaths of Muendo and Elenga and Luambu's coma. Then he ends up with the description of an oppressive political situation and depicts the consequences of colonialism. The fragmentary character of the indications and enigmas, augmented by the detective story approach, create flaws that mirror the political and social events as well as what is kept silent, the fears of the inhabitants, the speculations, the rumors—empty spaces that conceal the truth, leading to false leads.

Thus the novel slowly moves away from the detective story, which rests on a system that is strictly that of a thriller. It does so by way of a detective who turns out to be unfit for such a task, and by the presence of other methods that advance the investigation: visions of the madman, consultation of diviners, and dreams. Let us take a closer look at these interlocking methods.

First there is the presence of the **detective.** The alleged detective, André Sola, is frail, unstable, and surprisingly naïve. As a result of his vacillating, he obfuscates the situation and falsely accuses Luambu: he must find a scapegoat, an obvious motive, tangibly related to the killings of Elenga and Muendo. Vulnerable and clumsy, he can no longer see the truth, blurring events and refuting valid motives and political context. Without noticing it, he prefers his own predictions and becomes unable to perceive reality.

Thus, his role as a detective is gradually derided. Sola doesn't want to see the failings of the colonial system and therefore cannot identify the facts. In addition, he gets lost in Christian beliefs, superstitions he hasn't questioned. He himself is manipulated by dogmas and rituals that submerge him in the void: "He had brought back with him a bottle of holy water wrapped up in kraft paper. With a bough he had sprinkled the guy's place, which in fact didn't look more ominous than any other place in the office" (121). The "bottle" is "wrapped up"—a contortion that hides a malaise. The sentence is left hanging, interrupted without any typographical marks: "the guy's place." This discontinuity—the reader doesn't know what "the guy" is doing—accentuates Sola's confusion and shows his inability to follow his own thinking to the end, as well as his lack of basic information. His speech, his actions, are made up of silences, of the unspoken, blanks that translate his ramblings, his imbalance, his confusion, and his many fears. Despite the diviner's indications, he persistently gets bogged down in false leads. He throws no light whatsoever on the facts and indiscriminately absorbs all rumors: "André Sola seemed to be always present wherever the conversation was about the dead and the coma that happened the next to last week in June. He was gathering every detail that might allow him to understand what had happened" (68).

Nevertheless, he is the only character who tries to discover the truth and to brave the mystery openly. He is aware that opacity will end up by destroying everyone: "André Sola felt his throat tighten: he had to find a clue; he had to unravel this affair, which was not only an enigma, a mystery, but a dangerous threat to him and to others" (7).

However, the novel caricatures the role of the detective and ridicules a function designed to discover the perpetrator. Under colonialism, crimes committed by Europeans went unpunished and were even encouraged in order to spread terror:

> The oppressor's government can set up commissions of inquiry and of information daily if it wants to; in the eyes of the native, these commissions do not exist. The fact is that soon we shall have had seven years of crimes in Algeria and there has not yet been a single Frenchman indicted

> before a French court of justice for the murder of an Algerian. (Fanon, *The Wretched of the Earth,* 92)

The guilty one is untouchable, invisible. Consequently, it is pointless and even dangerous to reveal his identity. Besides, Sola talks nonsense and clutches at religious teachings that bring about his ruin. His ineptitude, his inabilities, hide the true facts and cause more harm, showing that the role he assumes as a detective turns against him: by braving an inaccessible system—colonialism—he can only plunge into madness. His analyses and thoughts never end up with a solution.

In order to better expose the facts, the author draws on the irrational as a subterfuge. The text uses visions: consultations with diviners; portentous dreams of Elenga, Mazola, and Luambu; the "madman's" predictions, which see beyond the trouble, rifts, and obsessions. The visions give meaning to the existence of Luambu, who will recover and go back to continue on life's journey. By putting together signs, he calls on the reader to discover the events as reflected by the signs scattered on the path of life: "Where can you walk when there are threatening signs everywhere? Where can you look without losing your eyesight, blinded by seeing more than is allowed?" (107)

The novel maintains a link with the beyond, the invisible, and evokes ancient practices that belong to a whole Congolese cosmogony. Let us analyze the three methods that call upon the irrational: consultations with the diviner, the madman's prophesies, and dreams.

Through the **diviner** and divination, the author suggests a mode of deciphering to the reader—the art of gathering fragments. We can draw a parallel between the signs of the diviner and writing.

> Cartry (1963) mentions "veritable tablets of writing" and talks of "writing to be read"; apropos the graphic signs of the Gurmanche geomancians of Burkina-Faso, he does not hesitate to publish in the *Journal des Africanistes:*
>
> "It behooves us to ask about the ultimate raison d'être of this system of signs, which from many points of view constitutes a veritable writing. These fragments of calabash preserve the geomancian's ritual inscriptions from the failures and corruptions of memory and guarantee the correct execution of sacrifice." (Battestini, *African Writing and Text,* 44)

The structure of the novel rests on a similar fragmentation and on the image to translate facts. It alternates themes and destroys the temporal linear progression (from Tuesday the 20th to Saturday the 24th of June). It begins with consultations of diviners—a trick of the author, a magical setting that carries the reader to a world beyond what is seen.

> In other words, through a radical shift, in literal and symbolic fashion, of the character and context of problem solving, the divination process is used to introduce a mode of cognition different from the cultural norm, whatever that might be; and then, even more important, the divination session creates a synthesis of the non-normal and normal modes as the plans of action are developed between diviner and client. (Peek, *African Divination Systems,* 205)

Using divination allows the author to go beyond the facts and gradually to uncover injustices and fears. It is used as a literary technique: structural model (assembling snatches) and narrative process.

The detective is generally bounded by a specific procedure and police methods that help him to make progress with his investigation. In *The Madman and the Medusa* the diviner replaces this structure of information, surveillance, and control. He constructs the narration and allows the truth to come out, even if it wasn't grasped by André Sola, who had consulted him.

> Suddenly the surface of the water in the gourd divides into two parts, sunlight and dark. The parts are equal. There is soot on the path in front of them, more in front of the woman. . . . They are fugitives, they are running away. "He had a serious problem with a white man named Martin!" André didn't take in the sense of the seer's pronouncement. (35)

The diviner heartily disapproves of André Sola's behavior: "The smell of incense invades his nostrils. The soothsayer watches him sniff and shakes his head" (35). The diviner doesn't always read through the night and knows his limits while specifying that the elements are within reach and that it's enough to take them into consideration: "The seer could not see or tell what had happened these last days. [. . .] The seer said that one shouldn't try to find out more, and that this death could be explained by what one already knew" (31).

The author uses the art of divination to penetrate the mystery and understand it. Since Sola, tormented by his obsessions, doesn't grasp the diviner's words, the text calls upon the reader to pursue the inquiry by supplying additional explanations.

The elements provided by the diviner allow the reader to have knowledge of the characters' past. Presenting the art of divination calls upon other worlds, other forces by which to contravene the colonial power, the rumors that perpetuate injustices, the false accusations, the personal obsessions (Sola's, for instance), going beyond what is visible and introducing different motives.

> The search for knowledge so prominent in African cultures has a very distinctive character to it. According to Douglas, "Any culture which admits the use of oracles and divination is committed to a distinction between appearances and reality. The oracle offers a way of reaching behind appearances to another source of knowledge" [. . .]. There is truly a "thirst for objective knowledge," as Lévi-Strauss terms it [. . .]. Coincidence is never a sufficient explanation. Answers to all questions are available if, but only if, one uses the proper mode of communication in addressing the correct source of knowledge. (Peek, *African Divination Systems,* 194)

The presence of the diviner shows how important it is to understand signs in order to move forward in life and in the fabric of the text. And it's the writing's *mise en abîme* that dismantles an immediate coherence, an illusory temporality, a predictable world, and that by making a connection with the beyond, fractures the real.

The **figure of the madman** is another way of calling upon the irrational. Our three protagonists meet thanks to the spectacle of a "madman" who was gesticulating and ranting at the fishermen and children on the beach. Standing up to his waist in the sea, surrounded by jellyfish,[2] he condemns the incompetence of humans: "But you don't know any longer where your heart is. How can you find your path in the dark? Why are you coveting what you already have?" (56). A fight ensues, and Luambu, outraged by the violence of the fishermen against the "madman," tries to defend him. Without knowing each other, Muendo and Elenga come to his aid. From that moment on, a deep friendship connects the three men.

Subsequently, the madman appears as a prelude to each disaster. He embodies clairvoyance and is often linked to the jellyfish: "What a strange situation! What is Luambu's understanding of the medusa and the incoherent and uncontrolled speech of the madman who, you know, might not have been so mad [. . .]" (142). They symbolize his nettling vision and the difficulty of being, the all-consuming pain and suffering: "Are they complaining of the rash the medusa gives them? They should walk away from the ocean whose deeps are in turmoil, suffering from God knows what kind of weariness of living" (141–42). The jellyfish are spellbinding and devastating. They burn on both sides. Light, gracious, ethereal, wounding, poisonous—they define the different states produced by the quest for truth the "madman" solicits. His "delirious" speech breaks the narration, pushing the ideas around. He comes straight to the point, and with his prophesies he provides the reader with information.

The figure of the madman allows things to be said disguised as trivia: the "madman" can put everything into question since he is positioned on the margin of society, stands apart because of forms of behavior and speech that know no limits. He violates what is lawful—the constraints and taboos of society, the law—and expresses his thoughts in chaotic ways. His partially incoherent speech allows him both to turn norms and conventions upside down and to escape from repression. Those close to him cannot take him seriously, even if he disturbs the power in place and touches upon crucial problems. Rejected by the community, he is free. Destabilized, he in turn destabilizes others. His strength is rooted in his use of language and the words he utters. Aware of the fact that words are deceptive, he misuses them intentionally, and his delirium is a powerful subversive process.

The "madness" of the character in *The Madman and the Medusa* is a way to break the silences, getting a message across, a piece of wisdom: "Our madman—was he really mad?—was not yet resigned to silence" (57). The madman speaks. This figure presents a detached view of society and its pitfalls. It permits the spoken to be uttered, the silence to be broken, and the events yet to come to be announced through conduct that kindles discomfort. His abrupt gestures, his disorderly words, his bizarre dances, his emaciated body, stand out and cannot in any way leave anyone indifferent. The "madman" is embarrassing, disturbing, and spurs people to look reality in the face, understand his thinking, see his appalling body. At the core of the novel, he presents an eccentric and off-center point of view that differs from the commonly heard noise, thereby enlightening the reader.

The insertion of **dreams** extends the use of the irrational. Elenga's dream, reported by the diviner during a consultation with André, plunges the reader back into Elenga's childhood. This is a literary trick to create a flashback, drawing a parallel with his father's destiny and showing the difficulty of avoiding the traps of history. Additionally, nightmare functions as a premonition, a *mise en abîme* of the art of divination: the diviner examines Elenga's dream thoroughly and then reports it to André. This structure makes it possible for the dream to announce the father's death and to state the son's journey and the presence of danger. The literary mechanism rummages through the past in order to look toward the future.

Mazola (Elenga's sister) describes to Luambu (with whom she is in love) a nightmare which she had the previous night and which announces the coming disasters to the reader: soldiers are cracking down on the strikers of the Congo Ocean Railroad System (CFCO) with arbitrary shooting rampages. Inscribed in the fabric of the text, the dream disregards rumors and censorship: the causes of Elenga's coming death will be kept silent by the administration. This is the writer's skillfulness: by valorizing the dream, the vision, the unconscious, the poetic image, by alternating words with the unspoken, he depicts the pain and the price of the rebellion, bringing out the actual facts.

These visions, which are a means of moving away from reality, interweave with other connections, bring in other solutions, infuse perceptiveness to contravene the malaise and the everyday dramas—they symbolize the role of the poet. Luambu finds the way back to life through the words of Julienne, his deceased wife. He connects with the past, with the beyond, with the word to liberate himself from the malaise that haunts him: "Before he fell into a coma, he heard a voice that he recognized without any doubt. It was the voice of Julienne, who said: 'He who looks life straight in the eyes will not lose face. . . . Love life'" (214).

By using the dream, the writer unveils other motives and guides the reader toward a better grasp of the facts. Thus, he provides Luambu with the means by which to return to life again. This fragmented process, which conveys some information that needs to be deciphered, is a *mise en abîme* of Tchicaya's writing that calls upon other techniques by which to construct his narrative and report history. His novel assembles information in snippets, following the dream, and requires that the disparate elements be organized in order to interpret them.

Thus we have seen that our "detective" André Sola does not mention the incongruities or notice the deadlocks and false leads at all. He relies on rumors that, by definition, amass contradictions, combine fears, desires, and dreams from a variety of individuals. According to the gossip making the rounds, Luambu's clothing, when he's stretched out on the grave of his two friends, is described as white and then, a few pages farther along, as black without Sola realizing it: "Note that they readily accepted the fact that the third man, wearing a white T-shirt, white canvas shorts, white socks, and espadrilles, was found lying on the ground between the graves of the two others" (3). Then, a little later: "When they found him lying on Muendo's grave, all dressed in black, in his sport shirt, trousers, socks, and espadrilles (others swore that he was wearing patent-leather shoes), he was holding a knife with a golden blade in his left hand" (11). Thus, the reader is called upon to replace André Sola. Erasures, textual shifts, and empty spaces placed by a narrator who has more precise data than Sola are going to attract the reader's attention and require him to run the inquiry in order to clear the mix of unresolved questions and elements, and more than anything else to avoid the alleged detective's clumsiness. For the narrator provides the reader with much supplementary information of a sort that guides him to present the facts and separate the false accusations, the hesitations, thrusts, and limitations of the characters; to understand the motivations of Sola, of Elenga's uncle, and disconnect them from those of Mr. Martin and his kind. The silences call upon the reader, while also reproducing the political context and thereby thrusting him/her in turn into history's chasm.

Luambu is invisible or in a coma; the details are immediately changed and the vagueness persists: "The event, it is clear, took place in June 1944. That could well be a hundred years ago . . ." (13). The account takes place during the Second World War: a description of ships and soldiers, specificity provided by the date "June 1944" but rendered instantly vague by adding the phrase "that could well be a hundred years ago." The events repeat and the violence continues beyond any exact date. The elements of the investigation are imprecise: "When was it? That's it . . . no . . . wait a minute! That's right, it was Wednesday. No, Thursday" (15). But the story provides leads. Allusions guide the careful reader to coming events, indicating the path, the psychological state of the characters, and their destiny: "Did he see Luambu making a vague gesture of retreat from Mazola who wants to bite into the jujubes of the tree on each side of his body. Muendo is a plank that is going to be cut" (142). The reader receives much information, if he remains attentive. He learns of coming events that have been surreptitiously slipped into the fabric of the story. Thus Muendo's death will be caused by the saws he handles every day in his work: "Muendo is a plank that is going to be cut."

The text gives information and then renders it doubtful, erases it, denies it, thereby demanding that the reader become involved in sorting out the data. The diviner suggests a mode of reading that the writer picks up on, scattering images throughout the text (water from the jar) that the reader must decipher. Philip Peek clearly traces this connection: "Divination systems create configurations of symbols (verbal or material) whose correct order or pattern must be revealed" (*African Divination Systems,* 202). A little later he writes: "Not only does divination reveal the basic patterns underlying human activities; it also reveals individual life patterns and relationships with others. Divination produces a narrative of a client's life and a correct history of the event in question" (203). And it is up to the reader to read the images created and see the possibilities without simplifying historic events or the traits and struggles of the characters. Nevertheless, he will never reach any certitude—the narrator provides no answer but opens up a world of possibilities.

Thus, on the one hand, the detective story creates a mysterious atmosphere, appealing for the reader's help to expose the murderers and shed light on the facts. On the other hand, this kind of dismantling allows for the system to be deconstructed. At the same time, it allows for a perception of the world it ridicules (an entire police system), to outline a more complex context in which the human being finds his strength beyond what he/she can understand, beyond the real, by way of visions, dreams, and prophesy. By developing other methods, using the art of the diviner—the reader of signs and dreams—Tchicaya fragments his narrative, providing elements of Congolese culture and cosmogony, all the while questioning them, modifying them, adapting them to the needs of the present. He shows that reading the past is an arduous task, which requires that a variety of investigations be made and numerous signs deciphered.

Techniques Borrowed from Oral Art

The author also fragments his writing by another process: with techniques borrowed from oral art, creating many leaps that enrich the fabric and direct the reader via techniques—such as repetition—that enlighten and confuse him at the same time. Tchicaya U Tam'Si, the "little leaf that speaks for its country," transcribes proverbs, borrows narrative characteristics from the tale, and uses the griot's practices in order to construct his story: repetitions, musicality, and images.

> It isn't difficult for me to remember evenings of my childhood, which were in fact the first school I attended. Legends taught us to be brave, tales to behave better, riddles and proverbs to learn how to have a conversation—up to a point in any case. Indeed, it was under the tree of "palavers"—kapok or mango tree—that everything else was learned: "important knowledge"—jurisprudence, rhetoric, and politics too. (Tchicaya U Tam'Si, *Légendes africaines,* 13)

The author brings together ancient collective knowledge, while mingling it with living contemporary local expressions, intense thoughts, sagacious exchanges that divert the commonplace through laughter and, in passing, jostle it with rumors. The evocation of the oral style inscribes sometimes a collective knowledge that interprets a perception of the world, and sometimes a spontaneous exchange, lively or brooding, an obsession, in time with the events that have marked the Congolese land. Tchicaya's writing evokes history, mindless states, raids, and goes wild: a jerking, dissonant, convulsive tempo recording the stops and starts, the wavering, and the conflicts that have set Congo ablaze. Let us examine the characteristics of orality and the way the author uses them.

The **tale** is a ruse, as Édouard Glissant has noted: "These cultures begin immediately with the tale which, paradoxically, is already a practice of diversion. What the tale diverts this way is the propensity to attach itself to a Genesis, it's the inflexibility of filiation, the shadow cast by the founding legitimacies" (*Introduction à une poétique du divers,* 63). This form flouts reality, using enchantment, metamorphoses, magic, and normally is found in some faraway and imprecise era: "Once upon a time."

Through the marvelous and timeless, Tchicaya distances himself from the events: he seems to withdraw from what is real in order to criticize it more vehemently, or to let the reader know indirectly about the events to come. The novel begins by placing the account that will follow in a distant period that is not clearly defined: "This story took place about the time when, so they said, a white man used to wander at night through the Native Village of Pointe-Noire and with a magic wand turn men, women, children, and dogs into corned beef, which people called monkey meat" (1). The writer uses techniques from the tale, inserting magic and metamorphoses as he sheds an ironic look on colonialism.

The first chapter, titled "Elenga," appears well after the beginning of the story, which one might call an introduction and which is reminiscent of the griot's presentation before he embarks on his story, changing techniques as he goes, just as Catherine N'Diaye does (see chap. 3, above). This section situates the narrative. The first chapter, which begins on page 21 of the book, calls upon the techniques of the tale to describe the character of Elenga by recounting his childhood. It mixes dream and reality, the animal world and the human one. Having placed the actor in a seemingly magic universe, the author suddenly moves away from it and brings harmful signs into view that corrode the atmosphere and lead us toward a profound uneasiness—Elenga's dream becomes a premonition: "A huge flame consumes both the totem pole and his father, mingling the sting of the rope with the smell of burnt wood and charred flesh and filling his lungs with its choking irritant" (28).

Throughout the narrative, the author refers to the tale for the construction of his plot. This genre allows him to carry the reader into an atemporal universe where he can, at one and the same time, bring up a truth, a fact (such as the colonials' abuses early in the novel), and also dismantle a world closed in upon itself—the tale is based on a self-contained structure. It engenders closure, and the writer recalls it: "He tried to remember the story in which one is surrounded by invisible walls and cannot imagine coming out of the nightmare!" (171).

Tchicaya plays with a form, long practiced, that subverts reality to propose a path, to clarify a situation. But he also withdraws from it by offering no way out: the characters don't turn into animals or heavenly creatures to escape from the events, they quite simply die, not managing in any way to defy the forces that get away from them. The novel looks harshly at reality in order to better subvert and transform it. The writing, nourished with orality, is used as a magic wand to illuminate the facts and overcome them. And the tale is one way of approaching the oral word. Thus, the author calls on it, then turns away from it, playing with the gaps and the shifts.

The **proverb** breaks up the narrative. It interrupts the fabric by juxtaposing a compact phrase that contains carefully pondered collective knowledge. In its brevity, it contrasts with the narrative descriptions and is striking in its abundant use of images, like the metaphor, as it refers to a believable body of knowledge that originates from the community. When it is created by the author, the proverb simulates the specificities of ancient and anonymous knowledge. It inscribes a rupture: a shift to the observations of a community, to a saying beyond any time reference that refers to the visual, to popular knowledge, so as to provide a better way to tolerate life and convey observations.

The proverb suggests transformation through indirect language and the use of images. In a narrative context, it reflects the cultural foundations of a community—an insertion that fragments the fabric to remind the reader of the framework in which the story is unfolding. It is the transmission of an ancestral idea that traces a meaning outside the text. The subtlety of the constructed image penetrates the reader and, in snippets, guides him through the novel: "You are thundering and spouting around here, but it's all for nothing, you want to start sowing seed when it's not yet the season!" (82). With this sentence, in which all is stated both indirectly and clearly, Elenga cuts short a long argument with his uncle (who has become his adoptive father) on the subject of his sister. He has recourse to the proverb to impose his point of view and bring the discussion to an end.

The thought introduced by "It is said" is linked, by the proverb, to a collective knowledge located beyond the story: "It is said: 'Face life and it will watch you live; if you don't face life, it will not take care of you!'" (196). The light comes from the voice of Julienne, Luambu's deceased wife, who imparts to him a version of the same proverb: "He who looks life straight in the eyes will not lose face. . . . Love life" (214). The novel ends with these words, leaving it up to the reader to resolve the enigmas. The proverb illuminates and guides the reader. It is a form that feeds the text by referring to a thought that comes from afar and conveys an approach to the world. It contributes to fragmenting the fabric of the text by inserting a short compact sentence, and indirectly transmits an idea, an opinion.

The writer adjusts phrases, plays with orality by evoking tale and proverb, which he changes to adapt them to the novel, linking past and present, counting on the multiple meanings characteristic of the art of the griot. This approach breaks up the narrative, gives the reader additional information to be discovered, and shares images created by an entire community.

Repetition, a technique used by oral art, strengthens the subject at hand, emphasizes the depicted emotion, and focuses the reader's attention on the developed theme, creating reference points, functioning as a reminder, and giving rhythm to the story. It is also by means of repetition that the author explores the manifold meanings of a term and "modulates" the word, playing with the language:

> [. . .] to the *Bilanda Laï,* those hotheads [*têtes*] who stepped off the train each time it arrived at the station.
>
> He had come to talk. But either he couldn't find the right words or he was afraid to articulate them. "This strike is bad, very bad." He was ducking the issue [*baissait la tête*] when events were taking a turn for the worse. Hadn't he been one of the employees who reacted against [*tenaient tête*] the sound advice of the authorities? (15)

The word *tête* (head) is used three times in this passage, each time with a new meaning. The repetition of the adjective "bad" substantiates what's been said. With this reiteration, the reader feels the weight that afflicts the character.

The repetitions play a role not only in sentences and paragraphs but also from page to page and chapter to chapter—repetitions here anchor, solidify, and connect the whole. Echoes of elements that typify a character or a situation are tracks of reading that create a counterpoint melody. For example, "'Ho, a child!'" (24) is picked up by "It's the bullet, ho! He's a child, ho!" (143). These repetitions emphasize important data. And an observation proclaimed by a diviner, "He had a serious problem with a white man named Martin!" (35), reappears much later without necessarily providing Sola with a real explanation: "It was while telling himself this that the gossip whispered once long ago came back to his mind: 'This man used to work for a white man named Martin'" (193). Under other circumstances, repetitions offer an opportunity for clarification if the reader—in contrast to Sola—manages to grasp them: "They had realized that one 'stopper' wasn't enough" (37), and a page later: "Modesty led him to say 'stopper,' brazenness led him, feet firmly planted on the ground, to say: MONEY" (38).

In the detective story, enigmas are revealed gradually and repetitions are a way of coming back to facts and observations, displaying them, changing them, challenging them, and thus consolidating the textual structure through recurrences and refrains.

Repetitions also convey the anguish a character feels: "'André confirms that Muendo is dead. But how did it happen? How? This morning he was in perfect health when he left for work to make money and feed his wife and children'" (17). A character's words translate astonishment, vertigo, and internal disquiet through repetition and interrogation:

> Poor, poor Rosalie! But she wasn't the worst off. What about Muendo's wife, a widow now, whose child had been born in the throes of her grief. Don't tell me that it isn't an evil omen on which no light can be shed. But where is the light? Oh, Lord, pity our wretchedness. André, find out, you must find out. And then there is this stranger . . . whatever his name is. (18)

The exclamations and questions that indicate the vocal tone convey the turmoil. The use of the negation weighs the sentence down, evoking the imbalance of the situation, which so profoundly assails the character. He even forgets the name of the "stranger." Voice, hesitation, the expression "whatever his name is," are signals to be understood, which indicate that one must go beyond the events and rumors to clarify the situation. The writer is depicting the confusion, fear, babbling, and vertigo that overwhelm the characters. Repetition gives rhythm to the text and involves the reader more deeply in its fabric, clears the way, and provides signs.

Multilingualism is often present in a "francophone" African text, whether in a veiled manner,[3] or through onomatopoeia, slang, or expressions in other languages that are sometimes not translated. These methods evoke a situation that arises from a multilingual context, inscribing vernacular language into a written language—French—and reminding the reader that the author is juggling several cultures. In addition, they saturate the writing with characteristics specific to the place where the story develops: "'*kebe ku fua,'* which translates as 'danger of death'" (181). Or: "*Bu longu bu yenda toto-lô siba bula nien*! / There is light at the ultimate borders of the world!" (162). Passing into Kikongo or elsewhere into Lingala offers the reader the chance to be in contact with these languages, no matter how briefly, to savor their sounds, imagine unknown combinations of consonants and vowels, evoking other cultures. These passages energize and enliven the text. When a translation is not provided, the author is calling on the reader's imagination. Sometimes the expression humorously reflects the void in which the character has been thrown—for instance, in this description of Sola in his religious enthusiasm: "He hung on to his desk with the last of his strength, invoking the spirits of the departed who are under our feet and our Father in Heaven. 'Ah, *Zambi Abkulu*!'" (195). These are words that must remain mysterious to convey a force, but in this framework they also denote a criticism. The author sustains mystery, ambiguity, playing with and counting on their contribution and *métissage,* weaving in meanings, and encouraging the reader's imagination.

Onomatopoeia ("haaaan!" [*Les méduses ou les orties de mer,* 25],[4] "snap," 93), sentences that reflect spoken language ("whatever his name is," 18) or evoke clichés ("Mr. Husband of mine work all week. The month was tough," 40), simplify the narration and recall clichés only to make fun of them: "When they get tired of munching on greens" (1). Shifts, leaps, and various assemblages fragment the fabric, and irony indirectly conveys criticism of colonialism.

Slang, everyday speech, infuses life, actualizes, inspires immediacy; it leaps from one riverbank to another, from literary language to lively and crude direct exchange. The reader stumbles on the changes in register. Inventions, detours, collages, adjust the language to a social, cultural, geographic, and emotional context, revealing its complexity.

The **dialogues** and **monologues** reproduce exchanges and internal thoughts, debates, discussions with others or with the self. The tonality is implicit in the punctuation, repetitions, and selected terms. It is a theatrical stage setting—an illusion of hearing the protagonists' words unchanged. It simulates a live broadcast with its blunders, awkward moments, its fervor and freshness—the liveliness of spontaneity.

Luambu's monologues give the reader an opportunity to better understand the situation. This character does not say very much. Living on the margins, rebelling against customs and injustices, he can easily be the target of an accusation. Thus, his monologues throw light on the facts by exposing his intimate thoughts. Passing from the first- to the second-person pronoun shows the disparity that Luambu maintains with himself—the past tears him apart.

Monologues are also a way to communicate the difficulty of telling. The dialogues between Elenga, Muendo, Luambu, and Mazola are filled with silences, which are surrounded by a discourse on the inability of conveying feelings, preoccupations, for fear of diminishing them or betraying their intent: "The words are so weak" (105); "[. . .] throws loose words into your mind so that you don't know which ones to use and when, for they don't come spontaneously!" (115); "The way he told the story could reveal inner feelings that he didn't have, or about which he wasn't sure himself" (114). The dialogues and monologues are useful to the development of the textual fabric and help the reader better evaluate the situation. The unspoken doesn't conceal the enigmas in order to hide the perpetrator but expresses the limitations of language. The way a speech is received is unpredictable, revealing the frailty and the traps of language.

Tchicaya devotes many sections to **rumors.** One of the chapters is called "Rumors: Chance." They follow from no reasoning or scrutiny; they are dangerous and hide the true answers: "What are we all doing? Joking when evil is threatening" (50). But, just as in Werewere Liking's *It Shall Be of Jasper and Coral,* their recurrence in the text shows that they fulfill a human function by maintaining contact between human beings, and their triviality reproduces voids—a musical hackneyed phraseology, an everyday purr.

> Just as in trivial conversation, the textual discourse withdraws from its informational function (the account) to be nothing but a resonant *link,* established by the address, by the "tropes" of imitated voices that hurl words devoid of meaning, stuttering, "empty chatter." As the emotional

sub-conversation, the text can contain a "sub-text" that, like a shadow, introduces the unconscious between the words and, like a voice-over, gives the discourse a certain musicality and very special energy. (Van den Heuvel, *Parole, mot, silence,* 62)

The chattering often takes place between unfamiliar voices that interrupt the development of the story. These innocuous words, made up of questions, repetitions, interjections, disagreements, and overlapping speeches, connect people and articulate the fantasies of some of them: "When an event is reported, each person in turn adds an unlikely detail to make it more truthful" (14). On this issue let us look at Van den Heuvel again:

> The gossipmonger allows the individual to join the *group.* [. . .]
>
> Saying nothing, basically empty, pure *word,* the speech of the gossip comes close to being *noise* or, as Blanchot says, to "human rustling." Through its relational value, this "noise making the rounds" becomes the *pleasure* that circulates. (*Parole, mot, silence,* 212)

Such statements assemble the collective deliriums: "The whole population of Pointe-Noire, shocked by the news of those deaths that last weekend in June, had fastened on that coma and had let its imagination wander deliriously in order to hide an unspeakable terror" (12).

Rumors support illusions that cover up the true motives, dragging the inhabitants into complacency, into the enjoyment of blather, and into deception. The novel repeatedly puts malicious gossip on stage to divert the reader (who is called upon to replace the detective André Sola) from his/her inclinations and possible expectations, and from the false leads that push aside the truth. The narrator condemns the detrimental effects of chatter, all the while playing with the impulsive and thoughtless value of such exchanges where the word, under cover of the naïve, the spontaneous, leads the malicious gossip astray. Overtaken by the pleasure of the verbal exchange and by fear, human beings lose their way and cover up the facts, thereby prolonging the murkiness that exculpates the guilty.

The author inscribes African oral characteristics, Congolese expressions, and proverbs into his French-language text. He makes spaces, eras, and methods coexist. He connects the past to the present, orality to the written, enchantment to reality. Thus he presents a situation in its complexity, its combinations, and its intertwinements.

In its multiple forms, orality enriches the novel, breaking the fabric, and showing the power of the word:

> Writing is truly saying things: expanding into the world without scattering or diluting oneself, and without being afraid to exercise the powers of orality there, which are so appropriate for the diversity of all things, repetition, rehashing, the circular word, the spiral scream, the breaks in the voice. (Glissant, *Traité du tout-monde,* 121)

The word causes wonder, illuminates the human journey, maintains the relationship between individuals. But as we have seen, it can just as well mislead the one who hears it (such as the malicious gossip that contributes to obscuring the facts). The poet also reminds us that the word is as ambivalent as the unspoken. The griot knows the power of his art that enlightens people by transmitting knowledge created across the centuries and, at the same time, manipulates them. Therefore the text invites the reader to recognize its range and distinguish its many forms, to discard the gossip so as to reveal the illusions, to understand the repetitions so as to bring out the facts.

Inscriptions and Erasures

In conclusion, the fragments refer to breaks caused by history, and to the confusions and voids that result. The text criticizes rumors, human tendencies, and outlines modifications—such as Elenga's rejection of the suitor his uncle had picked for his sister. And since Sola's investigation is on the wrong track, the author relies on visions, which will reveal the facts and indicate the path to be taken.

The many snippets create voids, some of which are absurd, such as the deaths of Elenga and Muendo. The silences are a double-edged sword. Some of them, concealing crimes, stir up the question "A secret [. . .] What crime does it hide?" (41) or express the inability to speak, the need to keep secrets: "The world one makes oneself is a mystery that should be kept secret . . . otherwise it might stab you and knock you down. Life is a strangler!" (39–40). Still others lead to possibilities and carry the future: Luambu goes back to living, disregarding the absurd by breaking the silence that had taken hold of him.

> Any liberation begins with words and, as Africa consists of people to be liberated, the first one to speak falls into the mouth of prophecy. Although

> he would disagree, Tchicaya U Tam'Si is a prophet. There are a thousand and one ways to be a prophet: express things that do not belong to us alone, express pain, joy, hope, memory, the dream of an entire people. (Sony Labou Tansi, "Tchicaya U Tam'Si," 83)

Tchicaya the writer takes on the function of the diviner, no longer plumbing the water's depth in the jug, but that of the world in order to comprehend the human being's journey. He casts a look from which the strength of childhood and imagination emerge, investing the visual to better disintegrate the humiliating and lethal unspoken words. The text shows the need to read signs/writing so as to move through existence/the textual fabric, pushing misdeeds aside to find the path. The textual discontinuity translates uncertainties, wanderings, rebellions, cracks, losses, and vacillation and subverts ready-made notions to head for the unforeseeable, the intangible of existence.

Luambu symbolizes the writer. He realizes that he is being used by Mr. Martin when he copies the false data the latter gives him, and he brings this work to a close: "A leaf from the tree against which he had bumped fell on his shoulder, then at his feet [. . .]. The leaf was answering his question [. . .]" (175). Like the leaf that falls on Luambu, the book answers the enigma and, in order to do so, carefully alternates language with the unspoken: "In a sense, silence is a new language, the purest form of statement, which bases communication on a 'full' interlocutory situation that, accompanied by an unbearable 'void,' necessarily produces an *implosion* effect" (Van den Heuvel, *Parole, mot, silence,* 84). It is up to the reader to understand its significance and decipher its meaning.

The author runs an investigation that is a quest, which looks at the past to see what mankind will become, opening up to the universe by connecting the here with the elsewhere, the real with the unreal, the past with the present, ancestral practices with current needs. Congolese cosmogony, the reading of signs, and oral art enlighten the reader and guide the narration, linking various approaches in order to insert other languages into the French, the oral into the written, shuffling eras and traditions.

> An equilibrium and ability to endure are revived through *échos-monde.* Individuals and communities go beyond vainglory or suffering, power or impatience, together—however imperceptibly. [. . .] Its results are unpredictable, but the beginnings of the capacity to endure are detectible, coming where formerly there were classicisms. It is no longer through

> deepening a tradition but through the tendency of all traditions to enter into relation that this is achieved. (Glissant, *Poetics of Relation,* 95)

Playing with empty spaces, the writer maintains tension, shifting from one to the other, reminding us that a method doesn't necessarily result in the desired outcome. It would have been difficult to bring up the true facts that surround the mystery of the death of two of the protagonists and the disappearance of the third, for as soon as the novel offers a path to be followed, it rejects it just as quickly. Consultation of diviners and testimonies are insufficient unless the events are to be confronted head on.

Tchicaya calls on dreams and visions, on the art of deciphering signs, and the totem-title symbolizes the imaginary and the pain that results from it. Jellyfish (medusae), with their gracious and voluptuous movement, float by freely. Yet, when they come in contact with man, they burn him. Tchicaya's tale is enchanting, stirring illusions, encouraging the reader to invest the language with images, to steer clear of the absurd of human gestures. He puts the reader in charge of pursuing the journey, of taking into account the violence of the colonial context, of reevaluating the meaning of visions and human imagination in order to see beyond the darkness and trace a better future.

8 Assia Djebar

Women of Algiers in Their Apartment and *Fantasia: An Algerian Cavalcade*—Palimpsest Memory

Assia Djebar, who was born in 1936 in Cherchell, near Algiers, Algeria, the daughter of a Berber-speaking mother and an Arabic-speaking father, has written many novels, plays, and essays. Her first novel, *La soif,* appeared in 1957 (*The Mischief,* 1958). Subsequently, she published, among others, *Les impatients* (1958), *Les enfants du nouveau monde* (1962) (*Children of the New World: A Novel of the Algerian War,* 2005), *Les alouettes naïves* (1967), and after a long silence, *Femmes d'Alger dans leur appartement* (1980) (*Women of Algiers in Their Apartment,* 1992). Then came *L'amour, la fantasia* (1985) (*Fantasia: An Algerian Cavalcade,* 1993), *Ombre sultane* (1987) (*A Sister to Scheherazade,* 1987), *Loin de Médine* (1991) (*Far from Medina,* 1994), *Vaste est la prison* (1995) (*So Vast the Prison: A Novel,* 2001), *Le Blanc de l'Algérie* (1996) (*Algerian White,* 2003), *Oran, langue morte* (1997) (*The Tongue's Blood Does Not Run Dry: Algerian Stories,* 2006), *Les nuits de Strasbourg* (1997), *La Femme sans sépulture* (2202), and *Nulle part dans la maison de mon père* (2007).

She has made two films: *La Nouba des femmes du Mont Chenoua* (1978), which received the international critics prize at the Venice Biennale (1979), and *La Zerda ou les chants de l'oubli* (1982). She has been awarded various literary prizes, including the Maurice Maeterlinck Prize (Brussels) in 1995, the International Literary Neustadt Prize (United States) in 1996, the International Palmi Prize (Italy) in 1998, and the Peace Prize (Germany) in 2000. She was elected to the Académie Française in June 2005.

During the Algerian War, she worked for *El-Moujahid,* the newspaper of the National Liberation Front of Algeria. She studied both in Algeria and in Paris and taught in Rabat and Algiers. As a trained historian she looks critically at the colonial past as well as at ancient practices. Interested in the condition of women, she focuses on memory and turns toward different art forms, especially to music and painting to break the silence, to encourage hearing and seeing. Palimpsest inscription: the written juxtaposes the musicality of the voice with the forms and colors on the canvas, interweaving periods and places, impeding hatred. She taught in the United States from 1995 to 2011 and now resides in Paris.

Assia Djebar's writings turn toward the past to question colonization,[1] to give a voice to women, who are all too frequently pushed aside, and to make known their respective struggles through the decades. In the style of the palimpsest, her writings go back to elements that survive in scattered ways: artists' paintings (Delacroix, Fromentin, Picasso), writings by French officers, accounts by women—mnemonic traces upon which the text is constructed and which allow a return to the events in order to reinterpret them and to put the stress on the distortions, to raise the repressions suffered. The author reexamines the forms of violence inflicted from all sides in order to denounce and overcome them. In an article on Ousmane Sembene and Assia Djebar, Suzanne Crosta writes:

> With rare acuteness, vigilance, and sensitivity, their works record the forces of resistance and liberation vis-à-vis colonialism, the return to Islamic fundamentalism, sexism . . . although they experience, represent, and problematize them in their own way. Whether the project is one of society, writing, or cinema, their personal and artistic journeys give proof of their concern about interrogating the orders of power and their desire to give body to the repressed or eclipsed voices of their people. (Crosta, "Stratégies de subversion et de libération," 50–51)

Djebar reassesses the gaze focused on the Algerian woman (from the outside or inside) by revisiting history. To this end, she intermingles a multiplicity of forms: autobiography, historical accounts, paintings, musical composition, and orality. She also inserts into her texts interviews she did in 1978 and 1982 when making her two films. Many analyses have been done of the references to music, to orality, to song, and to the role of women that appear throughout her work; therefore this study will not dwell on these. It is interested in the reasons that motivate the author to turn to painting, specifically in two works: *Women of Algiers in Their Apartment* and *Fantasia: An Algerian Cavalcade;* it will examine the contribution of the pictorial and its influence on the verbal structure itself, by referring to the concepts laid out in chapter 4 above, in order to deepen the extent of the interlacings outlined.[2]

Women of Algiers in Their Apartment brings together short stories that were written mostly between 1959 and 1979. The 2002 edition contains a supplementary short story, not yet translated into English, with the title "La nuit du récit de Fatima" (2001) and a modified "Overture." Thus, the text lends itself to expansion, growing as the years go by—open to transformations and additions.

Borrowing the title of a painting by Delacroix for her work, Assia Djebar explains her approach in the "Overture" and the "Postface," thereby clearly guiding her reader. She suggests looking at women in a new light by going back to perspectives and images that have been circulating for a long time and have marked them. She shows that Delacroix's painting is ambiguous: it conveys a fantasy while raising a troubling void. The work also turns toward a series of Delacroix-inspired paintings by Picasso that embody liberation, as if the "women of Algiers" were freeing themselves from their imprisonment and discovering the possibility to move again and to act without any constraints "to the beat of the dance of the nude servant woman" (*Femmes d'Alger dans leur appartement,* 10).[3]

The story "La nuit du récit de Fatima," whose title suggests a nocturnal context referring to the tales of *A Thousand and One Nights,* where Scheherazade's words spring up from the darkness, passing themselves off as magic and ruse in order to turn back death, consists of five sections: "Le rapt" (The abduction), "Le petit frère" (The little brother), "L'école" (The school), "L'enfant à donner" (The child to be given), and "L'enfant à donner de nouveau?" (The child to be given again?). These subheads convey additional information and refer to transgression of the law (a young girl, under the yoke of her brothers, accepts being abducted by her future husband), to childhood, education, and the possible repetition of the story and of history.[4] The text promotes a kind of anamnesis by causing concealed events to emerge, letting speak women who will reestablish the connections and differences between generations (much like a theme and its variations in music): similarity of needs, transmission of gestures, weight of the past.

Other stories follow and are grouped in two sections: "Today" and "Yesterday." This temporal reference is unusual, for it does not refer to distinct and separable categories (contrary to what one might think): the present is marked by the past, and the periods fit together. This follows the way the stories are organized, since they are interwoven and do not follow a customary chronology (some were written in 2001, others in 1978, 1959, 1966, and so on)—a blurring of boundaries that continues in the intermingling of artistic forms. These forms are explained, moreover, by Assia Djebar herself, who, by carefully grounding her references, provides paths in her work. This process, interweaving eras, places, arts, proposes an assemblage that by its tangled and fragmented texture rejects any absolutes. This observation can be supported by the author's use of a pseudonym. By choosing a different name (whatever the reasons for this might be), she distances herself from a determined origin—an approach upon which Khatibi dwells in an essay in which he refers to Jean Starobinski's work:

> In the pseudonym he [Starobinski] sees an insubordination against society by which the writer attains the ideal and solitary liberty, on a stage where, awakening to writing, he recasts his identity that is both divided and at the same time rewelded by and in the language, that indestructible link of separation. Perhaps, in order to begin writing, one should liberate a space in the heart of common language, empty it and make it available, certainly by a symbolic patricide, but also in view of a promise, an always anamorphic promise, whose proximity one vaguely perceives with the dis-identification and its lack of reason. A fear of not being understood, enclosed, immured, held back within a first and last name whose law one contests without knowing why. (Khatibi, *La langue de l'autre* [The other's language], 40)

Djebar frees herself on various levels from constraints that would prevent her from creating or having access to the word, seeking a "deterritorialized" place—outside borders.

But let us return to painting, and thus to Delacroix. As he/she reads along, the reader learns that during a short stay in Algiers in 1832 Delacroix had spent a few hours in a harem—a visit that inspired the painting that interests Djebar, one that has become quite famous. She tells us: "Upon his return to Paris, the painter will work for two years on the image of a memory that teeters with a muted and unformulated uncertainty, although well-documented and supported by authentic objects. What he comes out with is a masterpiece that still stirs questions deep within us" (135). Then she recalls that more than ten years later he made "a second version of *Women of Algiers*" (136), which emphasizes the distress it imparts: "Women always waiting. Suddenly less sultanas than prisoners. They have no relationship with us, the spectators. They neither abandon nor refuse themselves to our gaze. Foreign but terribly present in this rarified atmosphere of confinement" (136).

This painting translates at one and the same time the expression of an inevitable exoticism, representative of the exterior gaze that is unfamiliar with the foundations of Algerian culture, and a void that can be attributed to an alienating captivity about which the painter had a premonition. The writer wants to come back to that past to exorcise it while going beyond the exotic image that arises from the canvas—the women's availability and voluptuousness, which are the product of a colonial fantasy and the expression of a certain voyeurism, which Malek Alloula brings out in an essay: "The exotic postcard is the vulgar expression of colonial euphoria, just as Orientalist painting in its early stages was the romantic expression of that same euphoria" (*Le harem colonial,* 29).

Thus the author's reference to Delacroix is motivated by a double reasoning: the desire to distance herself from the colonial vision that the canvas conveys so as to pursue the more concealed aspect of the representation, which suggests a kind of malaise. The women seem to be absent to themselves, and the slightly ajar door in the background reminds one that the painter is violating a taboo by penetrating a place that is closed to the outside world and, above all, to the gaze of the foreigner. Due to this slight opening (infraction), the painting is a questioning: the door opens out onto the darkness (the unknown). Consequently, one comes to wonder whether the representation allows one to go beyond the surface (the exotic desire) toward a familiarity—otherness.

In Merleau-Ponty's terms, mentioned above in chapter 4, the painting is built on the painter's "vision"[5] in that its production is the direct result of the eye and what it sees (in this it differs from photography, which needs a camera as intermediary to capture the image). It causes one to see by the choice of colors and shapes, casting a look that motivates interpretation in the silence of the shapes. By basing herself on this painting, Assia Djebar builds her challenge on a well-known image that has the advantage of raising questions and of making one see despite the taboo. It is the way to go beyond the use of language to valorize vision and in turn to compel the reader to adopt the attitude of "the foreigner." Thus he/she is crisscrossing unfamiliar spaces by passing into another creative form, from writing to painting, and is thereby invited to negotiate the differences to clear a path and decipher meaning: "As soon as one is thrown back into the world of illegibility, one becomes a professional stranger, that is to say a surveyor of passages, frontiers, and smuggling, of margins and passwords" (Khatibi, *La langue de l'autre,* 11). Such assessment allows the writer to report more precisely on the social, cultural, and historical complexity suggested and to better represent its wide-ranging issues.

On the other hand, one should remember that the text pursues an aesthetic that is specific to Arab calligraphy, previously discussed in this study, where the pen in its writing counts on the beauty of the intertwining of different artistic forms (music, architecture, painting, dance):

> Calligraphy obeys a topography of the sign, driven by a space between the utterance of a phrase, that is to say a plastic element of the style and its projection into space, and its adornment as boundary to the thought of meaning. This at the core of every word, every phoneme, all the way to the silent song of the text, redistributed by the calligrapher's line between light and dark (their gradation), the legible, illegible, and unprecedented, imprints of gaze, voice, and gesture [. . .]. (Ibid., 14)

Via this scene Delacroix attempts to capture an atmosphere, replicate a feeling—that sets itself up as an icon. By referring to it, Djebar seeks to liberate women from an imprisonment, due to the projection of an exotic fantasy and patriarchal repression. She counts on glances intersecting to block the evil eye with the visual (the painting) and to overcome evil, insisting on the importance of making others see so as to break the silence about the past:

> [I]n traditional prophylaxis, which still exists, the thing seen, a "person" for instance, is always accompanied by an act that gives one strength, whether good or bad. [. . .] The one who looks at you charitably beautifies your presence [. . .]. On the other hand, the one who casts an "evil eye" on you is a dangerous and jealous individual [. . .]. (Khatibi, *Le corps oriental* [The oriental body], 13)

She provides the reader with a different view of the painting—a *mise en abîme* of representations.

Thus at the heart of the textual structure there are several transitions to be noted. First of all, Djebar's text moves from the first version of Delacroix's canvas to the second representation in order to develop the issues that interest her, those concerning the suffering of women and the role imposed on them. Then the text moves from Delacroix to paintings by Picasso, which are freed from colonization and the imposed restrictions, dismantling imprisonment: "Let's throw wide open the door, all the way in the back, toward the opening of the glimpsed past, but also toward the elsewhere, toward flight or future, no matter which . . ." (*Femmes d'Alger dans leur appartement,* 10). The words will follow this same trajectory, creating "new territories," as Khatibi puts it (*La langue de l'autre,* 31), developing the shift. They will interweave countless threads (testimonies): between storytellers who are voicing their narratives, between painters, between arts. The author moves from one level to another to cut through the darkness and shed light. Moreover, in this scriptural process some critics see a way for the author to discover her own identity. By calling on other gazes and approaches, she leaves the verbal and, in so doing, manages to determine her itinerary more clearly.

> Thus, by using visual elements, and interpreting one of the most important Orientalist paintings depicting Maghrebian subjects, she begins to engage in contrapuntal reading. She follows Said's lead in bringing to light the hidden colonial history that gave rise to nineteenth century painting and literature. However, as a descendant of the women in the harem, and a bi-cultural, bilingual Algerian writer, she can understand whispered conversations in the harem, and reformulate them in the colonizer's tongue. Significantly, as Jennifer Bernardt Steadman explains, Djebar does not position herself as a mere translator or scribe for Algeria's silenced women; the process of collecting women's stories and representing women's voices contributes to her own personal search for voice and self. (Mortimer, "Edward Said and Assia Djebar," 60)

Working on trauma and wounds, she is led by writing to analyze the role that women have been given and thus her own past: "Writing: an *initiation* to an illegible secret" (Khatibi, *Par dessus l'épaule* [Over the shoulder], 69). By collecting material for her works, by listening to women's struggles, she rediscovers the repressions suffered and revisits the places of resistances which set in motion a reflection on her own journey and on her reactions upon confronting history, tradition, and religion.

Djebar's short stories refer to painters not only by mentioning their work: in her verbal descriptions she also reproduces pictorial scenes and sketches physical gestures. For example, seated on the floor, melancholy women listen to each other, their eyes distant, and one of them sighs, hesitates, wants to interrupt this story but it swallows her up, constrains her, despite the *profound melancholy* that threatens to rise in her again [. . .].

She gets up, to cover up her *sadness,* then as she sits down *on the mat* again, prayer beads in her hand, and her *eyes staring in the distance,* she once again becomes a narrator. (*Femmes d'Alger dans leur appartement,* 29)[6]

Here Delacroix's pictorial composition is picked up again through the presentation and melancholy expression of the women. In addition there is the passage via the power of the word—the figure of the ogre who devours ("swallows") before liberating—tracing a parallel with any creative act: "But the story is demanding. It's even what remains, just that silver or ebony black thread, shining in the long night . . ." (*Femmes d'Alger,* 37) or "Won't the thread of the story begin to squeeze me tightly, embrace me, imprison me?" (*Femmes d'Alger,* 49). By turning to painting, she asks the reader to see for himself, to look beyond the presented image—in the hollows of silence. This approach allows for an indirect telling—an "*underground Arabic*" (1); "*An excoriated language, from never having appeared in the sunlight*" (1). And she departs from the use of one language—in this case French—imposed during colonization. On the other hand, transcribing women's stories, which would have been expressed in their dialect and then translated into French, is an additional shift that follows the movement begun between languages, between arts, avoiding any absolutes, which bring closure. The transfer, the displacement, goes beyond the taboos and limitations imposed upon women by society and by beliefs (stating things is perceived as bringing bad luck). Thus it allows for revealing what is supposed to be kept silent.

Transitions, the presence of an intermediary figure, the taking on of other forms, are used often and appear in different ways. In the short story "Women of Algiers in Their Apartment," Ali calls on Baya, a cousin who works in the same hospital, to translate from colloquial Arabic a note his son has left him. Then he asks her to alert Sarah, his wife. By using the visual, French, music, and oral art, the writing goes back to a cultural concept that increases the value of the detour. Besides the storyteller, the griot or the oral artist fulfills this function. He speaks for others, for the community, for a family. It's a matter of containing the destructive power of the word: ". . . words tear you apart, it's true, words tear at you . . ." (42) or "I've always had a hard time with words" (45). Using a transitory figure—otherness—the written allows us to see better and makes for more effective hearing. Let us not forget that this approach goes far back in time: "There is an intermediary between Allah and Mohammed. In the mother's premonitory dream it is the Angel who explicitly announces the first verses to Mohammed" (Khatibi, *Par-dessus l'épaule,* 79).

From one story to the next, Djebar comes back to the painting to modify it. The narrative "Women of Algiers in Their Apartment" begins with a reference to Delacroix:

> *A young woman's head, blindfolded,* neck thrown backward, hair pulled back—*the fog in the* narrow *room prevents one from seeing its color*—either light chestnut, auburn rather, *might it be Sarah? No, not black* . . . The skin seems transparent, *a droplet of sweat on one temple . . . The drop is going to fall.* That nose line, the lower lip with its bright pink edge: I do know it, I recognize it! And the profile pitches sharply [. . .].[7] (5)

Suddenly, after this long staging that picks up the postures and gestures captured on the canvas, the reader realizes that we are in an operating room. These shifts have followed the scattered traces that go back in time. The reclusive women can no longer see, and the exotic projection makes it difficult to understand them: "fog." This past haunts Algerian women, and consequently the text suggests coming back to it so as to overcome it and move forward.

The text also uses other methods to appeal to painting and to construct words in the manner of a pictorial composition: "I finally focused on the *blue tattoo* she had between her eyebrows; a delicate *rosette* that made her look strange. With her many headscarves in *mauve and orange* silk, she seemed like a fierce old queen, come from I knew not where . . ." (*Femmes d'Alger,* 27). The tattoo: a pattern applied to the woman's body to protect her from the evil eye, misfortune, is presented as mysterious. In turn, writing tattooed with visual images suggests an enigma that attempts to report a different version of the past and dodges the real. This woman is elusive, without a specific origin ("fierce . . . come from I knew not where") and is reminiscent of the power of Kateb Yacine's Nedjma.

The women in the story are not waiting. They are active, they react and struggle. Tired, worn out from battle, they continue to be astonishing. The reference to painting grounds the problem and leaves the language to express beyond words, while being wholly transcendent: "'One day we'll take the boat together,' the first one said. 'Not to go away, no, to gaze at the city when all the doors are opening . . . . What a picture! It will make even the light tremble!'" (52). Light symbolizes both the illumination shed upon the past and an inner radiance. The image the author describes functions as a mental icon—deliverance. There are countless instances where visual images appear, mimicking the painter's art: "'Sweet and gentle like wool, winter Ramadan is'" (119) or "'Look at Fatima, she spins wool as fine as a serpent's tongue!'" (125).

In the story "Women of Algiers in Their Apartment," Anne, a Frenchwoman who has come back to Algeria, her birthplace, becomes friends with Sarah, who helps her overcome her despondency. During a visit, Sarah opens the curtains (using the gestures of the woman servant in Delacroix's painting) to let light into the room, in spite of Anne's reaction: "I can't bear the light!" (9). There is the desire to shed light, which recalls the work of illumination of the calligrapher, who decorates the text with images and colors to show the way. Gradually, the women free themselves by exploring the gestures and events of the past through image, word, and music.

Taking further this pictorial reference, which appears in different ways, we should note that Ali, a surgeon, operates on a seriously ill patient, and the procedure proves to be a failure. At the end of the day, he leaves the hospital to forget his woes at the home of a painter who embodies the fringe of society, a political ideal (that turns into a battle). It is a symbolic visit, for this rebellious character, who lives on society's margins, is critical and treats social constraints with disdain.

The terms that pertain to sight in this scene are copious: "What can I tell you, *eyes* of my soul, where do I begin with my miseries, perhaps I should unravel the first thread even from before my birth, speak of her who brought me into the world . . ." (*Femmes d'Alger,* 15). The word passes through the eye (sight)—simulating the painter's work and reminding us that language is born from the image (hieroglyphs, as discussed in chap. 4)—and expresses nostalgia, the desire to return to the "original" place.

The power of the gaze occurs frequently in the text: "She scrutinized people all at once, *a look* that went right through, then lost interest" (105), or: "To him she seemed like a kind of mountain hawk because of her bony, prominent nose, her *eyes* set slightly apart, outlined in kohl, bird's *eyes* indeed" (106). The look allows for seeing beyond the surface and penetrating phenomena. Delacroix "knew how to *observe*" (136). And numerous descriptions borrowed from the painter's work appear in touches, in colors: "The sea breeze: grey and green. A blue trail disappearing in the west" (53). At times the art of drawing suggests healing: "I will follow the trace of your wound" (56). It allows the outline of the wound to be seen in order to be freed from it.

Another characteristic that brings the text close to painting is the presence of an "Overture" and a "Postface" that function as a frame—a border that demarcates the work by providing paths that open out onto possibilities. The text consists of a series of short stories written at different periods of time. They focus on the lives of different women and generations, offering a profusion of perspectives in order to dismantle a restricted, totalizing look—one like the panopticon Foucault describes in *Surveiller et punir* (*Discipline and Punish*). It is exactly that gaze that she wishes to deconstruct—"Yesterday, the master made his authority felt in the closed, feminine spaces through the single presence of his gaze alone, annihilating those of other people" (138)—or that of the stranger who casts an alienating gaze. The mounting of images and views overcomes obstacles (imprisonment, veiled women, projections) to offer different possibilities by following the painters' path: Delacroix, and then Picasso, who "reverses the malediction, causes misfortune to burst loose, inscribes in audacious lines a totally new happiness. A foreknowledge that should guide us in our everyday life" (149). Even if Djebar is wholly conscious of the road yet to be traveled, referring to the countless repressions that have once again befallen women these past decades: "From my exile on, undoubtedly to bypass the savage night that returned in the tearing apart of a century's ending, in so many places on this earth [. . .]" (*Femmes d'Alger,* 10).

We shall now examine *Fantasia: An Algerian Cavalcade* (1985), which retraces French colonization from its beginnings to the Algerian War for Independence and describes the violence that was committed to subjugate the population. The novel is divided into three sections. The first one intertwines segments of the capture of Algiers in 1830 with the narrator's childhood, centering on the theme of love; the second part deals with uprisings and repressions that took place over the following decade, as well as with personal moments in the narrator's life; the third recounts stories of women and their contributions during the Algerian War. The novel tackles a large number of issues that present women's battles, their attitudes, their demands, thus bearing witness.

> The practice of testifying leads to honoring the past. Actively. It is an honor in the form of dissidence, clarification, and judgment. In retrospect, the past becomes mummified, keeping us at a distance. Therefore one must break through the silence. That is how I, in turn, would like to gradually increase access to the past, separate its situations according to

their historicity and singularity, even though the discretion of those who are gone sends the writing back to the powers of silence and oblivion. (Khatibi, *La langue de l'autre,* 24)

To shed light on history, Djebar counts on the musical (rhythm, resonance, songs) and the visual to make one see differently, since this allows her to reveal what lies beyond language. In an interview, she mentions the importance of these connections to her work: "When writing *Fantasia,* I definitively settled my score with the French language. Painters were my mediators" (quoted in Zimra, "Disorienting the Subject in Djebar's *L'amour, la fantasia,*" 151). She interweaves several "memories," several pasts: a distant past that begins with the arrival of the first French colonists in 1830; a more recent historical past of the war against the French from 1954 to 1962; a personal past, that of the narrator, who transcribes events from her childhood and reflections on love, on writing, and on the use of the French language.

To evoke the period beginning in 1830, the author draws upon archived writings originating primarily from French sources: "Thirty-seven witnesses, possibly more, will relate the events of this month of July 1830, some fresh from their experiences, some shortly afterward. Thirty-seven descriptions will be published, of which only three are from the viewpoint of the besieged [. . .] (44).[8] Or: "The senior officers in particular are infected by a veritable scribblomania. They start to publish their memoirs the following year; the chief of general staff is the first, followed shortly afterwards by others" (44).

Artists, too, are part of the expedition that will capture the first moments of the conquest: "When the squadron left Toulon, there were four painters, five draughtsmen and about a dozen engravers on board . . ." (8). Personalities who were famous in Paris, such as the theater director Merle, are there to describe events and report back to the French capital, attesting to the boldness and courage of their people when faced with an enemy that does not capitulate easily. For the recent past described in the novel, Assia Djebar turns to stories about the Algerian War that women told the narrator years later.

Thus the author assumes the task of combining and intertwining various pasts and various periods, constantly questioning the ability of the French language to inscribe events, transcribe memory, and so to determine and capture the anguish without obscuring, erasing, or deforming history and the suffering endured. The text questions the use of the invader's language to describe the abuses and relate the extent of the wounds inflicted by colonization, and to reestablish the truth concerning distorted historical facts as reported primarily by that invader. The author wonders how to disregard the voids that so many years of war and violence caused in order to describe the vast number of murders, bloodshed, rapes, and deaths in a language that pushed Arabic and the local dialect aside and that moreover managed to whitewash the most atrocious deeds. We should recall that, to describe the beginnings of the French invasion, Djebar refers to existing texts that were almost all written by the conqueror. Therefore, the writing and the use of the French language require a ruse in order to skirt the lacunae and the problems they engender, for the words are filled with blood:

> And words themselves become a decoration, flaunted by officers like the carnation they wear in their buttonholes; words will become their most effective weapons. Hordes of interpreters, geographers, ethnographers, linguists, botanists, diverse scholars and professional scribblers will swoop down on this new prey. The supererogatory protuberances of their publications will form a pyramid to hide the initial violence from view. (45)

These writings glorify the initial acts of the conquest, disguising the horrors committed and concealing the distress.

> These texts are distributed in the Paris of Louis-Philippe, far from Algerian soil, where the capitulation has fairly quickly legitimized all manner of expropriations: physical and symbolic usurpations! Their words thrown up by such a cataclysm are for me like a comet's tail, flashing across the sky and leaving it forever riven. (45)

On the other hand, when writing is used by the besieged, such as the dey or the mufti, highly placed personalities in Algiers, it is because they are forced to sign an agreement that settles the terms of their defeat. An act of servitude that orders the population to leave its land and possessions. Or again, when "an elderly native" (32) decides to surrender to the adversary "of his own initiative" (32) and returns with written documents, he is then killed:

> As soon as he walks away from the French camp he is killed by his own countrymen, precisely on account of these papers which cause him to be taken for a spy working for the invaders. So, the first written words, even while promising a fallacious peace, condemn their bearer to death. Any document written by "The Other" proves fatal, since it is a sign of compromise. (33)

Consequently, how does one revisit history and restore the memory of a people in order to better understand the catastrophe? How does one use the French language and include the translated stories of women without betraying them? How will other supporting material, such as painting, be able to represent the extent of the obscured context?

We noted that to describe the distant past of 1830 or 1840, Assia Djebar has recourse to preserved writings that come primarily from the French, and she quotes them repeatedly. If we examine the structure of the first two parts of the novel dealing with this period, we see that she fragments the narration or, rather, that she interweaves "tableaus," moving from a distant past to scenes of her own childhood. Thus, the accounts crisscross and fracture any kind of linear narration, thereby reproducing the rupture of a culture and an identity. The entire first part alternates a recent personal past, the narrator's, each one of whose chapters has a title, and a historic past whose sections are indicated simply by a number (no title), emphasizing the emptiness, the incapacity of naming, of clearly defining that period, since so many events and viewpoints have been stifled and kept silent. This alternation between collective and personal past, between distant and recent periods, blurs any temporal linearity and writes rupture into the novel and its literary organization. In the second part the structure is reversed, for the chapters dealing with 1842 have a title, while those that concern the narrator are numbered. Thus we notice a reversal that at one and the same time shifts the empty space (impossibility of providing a title), showing that some events are elusive and escape any understanding. Here the narrator's identity is vague. The elements fade into each other, and the violence of history has repercussions on the environment while it fragments identity.

Let us return to painting, to the construction of these chapters based on the model of a painting. First of all, the evocation of visual art brings in the degree of silence that emerges in the face of the disaster occurring in the land. The image, being something unspoken, reflects a silence—in this case the silence imposed on Algeria's history. The French, since it is primarily they who report on the events, only express a perspective that manipulates the facts and glorifies them to the advantage of the conqueror. Djebar inscribes the theme of erasure, of deletion, by mentioning the enormity of what has been kept silent, for example the interaction between the two parties that, strangely, is described as being made noiselessly: "No sound accompanies this transformation" (6) and again, "The scene is suddenly blanketed in silence" (7)—thus calling on the reader, who stumbles over the incongruity of the phenomenon, to capture its meaning. The confrontation cannot be taking place soundlessly. Nevertheless, suffering here has taken place in silence. The author shifts one phenomenon onto another, obliging the reader to restore the facts, as if faced with a painting.

In the first chapter, the scenes move along in touches and colors as they do in painting: "the Impregnable City sheds her veils and emerges, a wraith-like apparition, through the blue-grey haze," "carpet of muted greens," and again, "The mountain shuts out the background, dark against the blue wash of the sky" (6). The color choices emanate sadness and inscribe fragility. The mountain "shuts out" instead of being a place of refuge. The city's whiteness no longer reflects divine light and is compared to the exotic image that begins to spread over woman: "The city, a vista of crenellated roofs and pastel hues, makes her first appearance in the role of 'Oriental Woman,' motionless, mysterious" (6). It remains misunderstood by the gaze of strangers, who superimpose a fantasy on it, a need for submission. Captain Amable Matterer reports, "I was the first to catch sight of the city of Algiers, a tiny triangle on a mountain slope" (6). The city as it lies there is itself perceived as submissive, so that the published viewpoints are distorted by the need to subjugate.

The accentuation of the contrast between light and dark (peculiar to painting) imparts the tragic: "*I face these images of darkness*" (46), "in the darkness that is slowly growing lighter" (52), "from the still dark horizon" (53), "I slowly emerged out of the shadow of the tragedy" (114), "through which the sun's glare is filtered" (58), "In the light of dawn" (71). Djebar's writing often reproduces the pictorial ("I imagine the details of this nocturnal *tableau,*" 71), or describes with the transparency of a watercolor ("like some vast *water-colour,*" 113), evoking the power of an image: "Adding a vivid detail, a caustic comment, they *fill in* the *picture* of the calamity [. . .]" (154).[9] And then, as previously discussed, there is the reference to the undulating shape of calligraphy to reproduce its movement: "launches *its arabesques* into the blue" (123), "the last faint whine of the muezzin's *arabesques*" (151), "*calligraphie* d'amour"[10] (*L'amour, la fantasia,* 250).

Although the novel mentions the arrival of the painters coming to represent the first moments of the conquest, it does not refer to their work. Rather, it dwells on evoking the absence of pictorial representation when it is a question of discerning the horrors seen. The French painter and writer Eugène Fromentin was interested in painting landscapes that resembled those of his childhood, and onto them he projects melancholic feelings that in no way reflect the reality: "In the North, the scenes that form the subjects for his canvases, the places where he walks with eyes and ears alert, might be one vast game-park that has been over-hunted" (224). He removes the drama that unfolds before his eyes: the slaughter of tribes and animals. While his writings report on very strange events he has witnessed—the murder of a woman during a fantasia, a severed hand found on the ground—he never paints these scenes: "an unexpected hand—the hand of an unknown woman he was never able to draw" (226), as if his painting were withdrawing from this sort of testimony, refusing any kind of complicity.

Fantasia: An Algerian Cavalcade, the title of the novel, also provides paths that link several arts. It refers to the exuberant movement of the fantasia—an equestrian game of Arab horsemen in which the cry is a major presence—but also to music, the *Fantasia* (that of Beethoven), and to painting (a Delacroix canvas by the same title, which represents an Algerian equestrian scene). The reader comes to wonder why the writer uses such terms: while the issues at hand are war and massacres, how can she refer to love (the French title is *L'amour, la fantasia*) and to equestrian games when an uncontrollable break is being set in motion in Algeria? Gradually the reader becomes aware of the way the text is constructed, its attempt to speak out beyond words, produce images that will better reveal the situation. Between the lines, the writing puts forward paths that will explicate the choice of title. At first, confronted with the enemy, the Algerian is fascinated by the grandeur of the fleet and the force of the artillery. He is unprepared, startled. During the battles, on the other hand, the Algerian camp is divided, and the Bedouin tribes attack the enemy as if they were involved in a fantasia, projecting themselves into a theatricalized scene that leads directly to their death: "The Bedouin tribes arrive as if to participate in yet another *Fantasia,* when the less caution is shown, the more attractive the hazards" (16). As for the French reports, they embellish the murderous scenes, even pointing out the beauty that emanates from death, "the terrible poetry" (18), dwelling on eloquent and marvelous descriptions of the mutilated bodies of the defeated and of the confrontations:

> Thirteen days later, back in Oran, Montagnac also writes to his uncle:
>
> "This little fray offered a charming spectacle. Clouds of horsemen, light as birds, criss-crossing, flitting in every direction, and from time to time the majestic voice of the cannon rising above the shouts of triumph and

> the rifle-shots—all this combined to present a delightful panorama and an exhilarating scene . . ." (54)

Through the novel, Djebar attempts to rewrite history, calling upon the imagination (fantasy inscribed in the very title) to transgress the threatening context and distortions. The parallel drawn between war and love (love not only of young women, the narrator among them, but also the love of foreigners for Algeria, which exists as conquest and self-denial) deliberately creates an unease that tries to summon the reader to reassemble the elements. With a critical look, the mirror of a society, it traces provocative parallels that try to arouse reactions and sift through the past, by weaving connections with which to better discern the enormity of the void produced.

The transitions between chapters and storytellers are reminiscent of the art of the weaver, picking up threads that run through the entire work while inserting unique patterns and specific colors throughout the weft or warp. The texture requires both precise assembling and a framework. Through the aesthetic composition, the creator produces an image that refers to an event or a tale in an attempt to grasp a problem: "When one speaks of a beautiful carpet, it is often said that it has a rhythm, that its colors sing, or that the carpet tells a story, a secret, and in passion is open to an erotic thought, a prayer, a supplication" (Abdelkébir Khatibi, in Khatibi and Amahan, *Du signe à l'image* [From sign to image], 54). Djebar's text is rhythmic owing to the recurring themes, repetition, and abundant musical references. The latter appears in various forms: the repertory of Algerian songs that women perform during ceremonies, Beethoven's musical compositions, funereal operas, and so forth.[11] And, of course, there is the rhythm of the body, too—the breath. Some chapters in the first part are "tied" together by a repetition of words. The story "Three Cloistered Girls" ends this way: "an unprecedented women's *battle*" (13). The next chapter begins with the same word: "The *battle* of Staouéli" (14). The section "The French Policeman's Daughter" ends in the French text with the word "*explosion*" (38), which is immediately repeated as the first word of the next chapter. In the third part, each movement is structured the same way, consisting of six sections each.

In the author's use of color, the choice of red is predominant and emphasizes the described context, which is an odd mixture of bloody clashes, suffering, lamentations, desires, different forms of sensuality, and rites (practiced as protection, among them the henna designs on women's bodies). Another parallel worth noting concerns weaving. In the Maghreb this activity is practiced almost entirely by women, "and women in particular have proven their ability to invent or improvise shapes. It is an active reverie that rests on an age-old demanding technique and a strictly coded aesthetics with which the woman fastens and releases the secret of the hands" (Khatibi, in Khatibi and Amahan, *Du signe à l'image,* 15). Djebar's text repeats this process by turning to women (their stories) and the power of the image. Thereby the author composes a work in which points of view, languages, places, and forms enter into dialogue.

In the French the terms *trame* (which has been translated by "pattern") and *chaîne* (which means warp as well as chain) appear in the text repeatedly: "a pattern of French words" (78), "as she whispers her story" (141),[12] "Chains of memories: is it not indeed a 'chain,' for do not memories fetter us as well as forming our roots?" (178). While the words refer here to the creation of literature and the narration, they also refer to weaving. In addition, the production of a carpet was preceded by a carefully chosen and closely followed ritual to encourage inspiration and the project's success. In the text, one woman's statement is minutely woven into that of the other women, and the narrator's transcription into the French language is carefully worked out so that the work will take "flight" as in the "flying carpet," inspired by Scheherazade, who, as Khatibi reminds us, invented that magic flight in order to survive: "it's not an accident that Scheherazade invents the image of the flying carpet: she must live at all costs between the story and death" (Khatibi, in Khatibi and Amahan, *Du signe à l'image,* 62). In *Fantasia: An Algerian Cavalcade* the story is a battle to reestablish facts, give meaning to events, honor the dead who were never properly buried (men and women in smoke-filled caves, outrageous murders and battles), in order to create a mourning ritual.

Here the task of verbal production takes on the ancestral gesture of women who weave the threads of their imagination with their fingertips to exorcise sorrow and ward off the meaninglessness of existence, calling upon a whole range of tones and forms—the power of aesthetics. "[T]he mystery of the carpet is reminiscent of a good detective story. When he discovers a trace, the investigator has a better picture of the 'case,' that is to say all the possible scenarios" (Khatibi, in Khatibi and Amahan, *Du signe à l'image,* 160). The writer is allowed to tell, break the silence, by using ancestral methods to weave the threads and transform the expanse of the void.

As the story unfurls like a carpet, a parchment—any support on which signs are placed to exorcise and protect—an unrelenting commentary on the use of French is presented. The author begins by formulating countless reservations about using this language, followed by tackling the constraints imposed by society, customs that promote silence—words seen as dangerous and as bearers of bad luck: "Only speak of what conforms, my grandmother would reprove me: to deviate is dangerous, inviting disaster in its multiple disguises. Only speak of everyday mishaps, out of prudence [. . .]" (156). Thus silence covers many subjects and women conform to it. French, though, allows for speaking openly without offending one's own people, for the language of the foreigner is not considered to have the same value: "The compliments—harmless or respectful—expressed in the foreign language, traversed a no-man's-land of silence. . . . How could I admit to the foreigner [. . .] that such loaded words defused themselves as soon as uttered [. . .]" (126). On the other hand, she takes the texts of the past and rectifies the information given by the invader, confronting him in his own language, not allowing him to shy away from the stated words under the pretense of not being able to understand them.

Furthermore, it should not be forgotten that language, whichever one it may be, belongs to everyone and that the work of the writer is to use and handle it with insight and transform it as needed: "Yes, who doesn't remember Marcel Proust's lucid phrase: *'Beautiful books are written in a kind of foreign language'*" (Khatibi, *La langue de l'autre,* 28).

By using French made familiar by the rhythm of the mother tongue and of Arabic, Djebar in her writing encourages the reader to move from one site to another. At times the writing manhandles us on purpose, inscribing the contradictions inherent in existence so that the reader will notice them and take the appropriate road. The love letters written by the "cloistered" young girls, criticized by the author (part 1), who thinks they are hiding the loneliness in which they live, can also be seen as an overture. For, just as Djebar's writing presents itself to an unknown reader, these letters are in dialogue about/with the world, weaving networks by which to see differently, and opening up to an exchange. And on the way they (both the letters and the text) allow their authors to become aware of the past in order to unravel it, of their identity by appropriating the use of word and writing, and changing the customs.

By reworking the scattered elements of collective and individual memory, by bringing together ancient approaches and current claims, by weaving many connections, paths are indicated by which to revisit history. The writing, like the trance session at the maternal grandmother's house, intends to free itself from imposed limitations, from constraints, seizing "images" or creating them to move through darkness, joining in voice and music, which reflect the languages of the body, forming a whole that is a journey toward artistic, linguistic, and cultural otherness: "But my sole ambition in writing is constantly to travel to fresh pastures" (63). The images summoned (as in painting, carpets, tattooing) spur one on to go back in time in order to read and decipher the scattered signs—an intersemiotic crossing. Memory as palimpsest is inscribed in segments.

In an article on Kateb Yacine's *Nedjma,* Antoine Raybaud defines writing as palimpsest by considering several characteristics that elucidate the use of the term here. First of all, he characterizes it as a place from which traces of "ancient signs" emerge. Then, referring to modern narratives (including those of Glissant or Rushdie), he sees in them a multilayered organization: "layers of cultures and multiple narratives, and also of multiple ages, places and worlds, each within the others as much as within the modern system" ("*Nedjma* palimpsest," 97). He says that his objective is, to the extent possible, that of restoring what history has erased (dictatorships, wars, colonization, etc.), which ends up in a fragmented collection. Finally, he draws a parallel between this writing and the model Freud proposed in "Constructions in Analysis," where it is a matter of going back from verbal production to the experience by following the thread of narration to re-create the trauma and overcome it.

These definitions show that writing in palimpsest, marked by the historical context, organizes disparate elements: "Thus, it is starting from obliteration and from the fragmentary recovery of the obliterated material as well as from its reconstruction with current experience, that the palimpsest-text question is posed" (ibid., 100). To speak about history, the author reconstructs snippets of found information to grasp what has been lost, pushed aside, or silenced. And, consequently, several possible interpretations appear. Moreover, the palimpsest-text, made up of multiple elements and having survived the course of time, must be clarified, interpreted in the manner of the trace that is central to Arab culture. Meddeb reminds us that the trace plays a crucial role in pre-Islamic poetry and that

> [t]he ancient desert Arabs made an art of deciphering traces, which they called *Qiyâfat al-athar* and which consists of following and recognizing footprints and hoof tracks [. . .]. The mastery of reading traces is also

> needed by guides [. . .]. Without these guides, caravans would have perished and armies would have been decimated. ("La trace, le signe," 28)

Thus the multiplied texture (images, forms of music, writings) of Djebar's works, crisscrossed by many threads, offers traces to be seized—a constellation of lines—so as to be delivered from the void, making reference to cultural and historic entanglements. And sometimes tradition is picked up again, sometimes it is modified and criticized to be adapted to current needs: "the identity of tradition cannot be an identity of repetition. After all, in its original meaning, 'tradition' signifies that which is worthy of being transmitted to be the first principle of behavior that responds to new conditions and times" (Diagne, "L'avenir de la tradition," 295–96). It does not let itself become fossilized here at all.

By leaving language, the two Djebar works analyzed here show and reproduce the talisman: exploded patterns to exorcise an unwieldy past, traces to be followed to find the threads of history and "unravel" the power of destruction. The narrator in *Fantasia: An Algerian Cavalcade* draws a parallel in the second part of the novel between the itinerary of a received letter and the signs to be deciphered therein to uncover the road and take the necessary measures: "The letter bides its time, an obscure talisman" (59).

The presence and simulation of the talisman or of the signs on the women's body (tattoos) seek to change a harmful situation, to protect, to reveal in timely fashion—magical writings that enclose a power, a capacity to transform. It is up to the reader to decipher them in order to better grasp the battles women in Algeria have waged, the turbulent history of that country which, even though it sank into devastating violence whose results resound today well beyond its borders, inspired all of Africa with the strength to demand independence. And even though the influence of literary writing on history does not extend to politics, it communicates and is an act of sharing:

> The poet rules and governs nothing. He has no enchanted kingdom whatsoever. His luck and his promise are his inventive spirit [. . .]. Inventing the earth as well as the spirit of the earth. The absolute poetry of vocalizing the unheard-of, of making emerge from the unheard that language which accuses the poet and which he accuses. A language that I must reach, separated from the idiom of my tradition and of my first land. (Khatibi, *La langue de l'autre,* 15)

Freed from all ties and constraints, impervious to compromise (like the painter whom Ali, the surgeon, goes to visit), and withdrawing from any conventions, the writing here shares in the traditions, experiences, perspectives, imaginations—an offering beyond the disparaged encounter with the foreigner. The writing inspires leading a ballet (dance, trance) in the manner of the fantasia (musical composition, painting), urging us to invest creativity, combinations, and love and thereby put a stop to hatred.

وبين كوكب ونقطة المشرق سعة المشرق وبين احدهما ونقطة
المغرب سعة المغرب واضعا الموزنة لها مقنطرات تمر ان وقعتا
في المعدل فانما تمر بقطبيه تنصف كل مدار تمر على قوايم فتساوي
الليل والنهار تقريبا الا ان ادرا فيسمى الدورة ولابيا وان انطبقا
على قطبيه انطبق عليه وكانت السنة يوما وليلة ويسمى الدورة
جويا وان ما لا عنه شيئا الا وجنوبا نصفه بعد وان نقع
احد قطبيه تحت الاخر بعد الميل يسمى الدورة حمائليا وما يشتمل
من المدارات اثنين فوقانيا وتحتانيا بعدهما عن القطبين كبعدها
عنها منحطا نصفهما عن المتوسط بين الفوقاني وقطبه فيكون ابد
الخفاء قاطعة المتوازي مختلفين يختلف بهما الليل والنهار الا ما
فالفوقاني قوس نهار الكوكب والتحتاني قوس ليله والواقع منهما بين
بينهما بين ميليته مار بنقطتي المشرق والمغرب يعدل بها و
ضعفه يساوي التفاضل من نصف المدار وكل من قوسي الليل
والنهار السابعة نصف النهار وهي التي غايات ارتفاع الشمس و
وصولها اليها ويكون واسط بين النصف الشرقي والغربي كان
باقطاب الاولى والسادسة قاطعة لها على نقطتي الجنوب والشمال والو

Conclusion

Since its birth in 1921 with *Force-Bonté* by Bakary Diallo, African literature written in French has gone through various well-known phases. At first it was influenced by European literature: travel accounts and the countless clichés these texts conveyed. Then it went through a phase of national claims to rid itself of colonial precepts and find an identity, such as in the writing of Sembene Ousmane. At Independence, it took new paths to bring back very different needs and approaches. It opened up to ambivalence, the unresolved, while frequently expressing a reflection on the role of writing. By dismantling absolutes, transcribing crises and conflicts, this literature inscribes history and political events. By weaving other arts into the writing, by inscribing other languages into the use of one language, it links ancient values to current needs and traces parallels between cultures, revealing practices that are often little known. Thus, to penetrate and analyze these texts, scholars and critics frequently draw on different fields to discover the interconnections and grasp their functions and movements. Chantal Zabus describes the present situation regarding the analysis of African literary texts:

> As the twenty-first century takes its lesson from hybridity, arielism, pidginization, creolization, or Wilson Harris's alternative to all "posts," criticism of African literatures is moving towards increased fragmentation into sub-sub-sets and/or is on the verge of what Said called a "grand synthesis." As a result, it may hook up with both a specialized, context-specific "ideology of difference" and the parallel discourses of e.g. film, "womanism" (as opposed to Euro-American feminism) and anti-Oedipal psychoanalysis. As it is becoming more incestuously comparative and more promiscuously intra- and inter-national, criticism of African literatures is pregnant with a plural horizon of expectation. ("Criticism of African Literatures in English," 141)

This study has followed a similar path, basing its arguments on disparate works that both clarify the approaches that a particular culture adopts toward ritual, oral art, visual image and at the same time deepen reflections that extend across the world concerning the aesthetics of nomadic movement, juxtaposition, or composite order, without dissolving the cultural specifics into a universalizing amalgam.

Following the circulating movement that the writers and artists suggest, this study first of all had to question the split between the Maghreb and sub-Saharan Africa, partially inherited from colonialism. Then, it raised the aesthetic intertwinings, favoring the oralization of the text and the presence of the visual image in the writing. It has sought to show that the authors analyzed use a fragmented writing, transcribing the movement of wandering, deconstructing any absolute, treating the political context from which they spring, removing the structure of established norms, of restrictive and alienating laws. The inscription of visions, prophecies, rites, or quests that will not let themselves be linked to the law of a sacred text and the use of madness suggest pathways that turn away from a singular interpretation and contribute to the creation of silences. These silences pursue the project of "deterritorialization" as described by Deleuze and Guattari in their work on minor literature, cited in chapter 2, and they open onto the unfinished and the unspecified:

> There is nothing that is major or revolutionary except the minor. [. . .] To be a sort of stranger *within* his own language; this is the situation of Kafka's Great Swimmer. Even when it is unique, a language remains a mixture, a schizophrenic mélange, a Harlequin costume in which very different functions of language and distinct centers of power are played out, blurring what can be said and what can't be said; one function will be played off against the other, all the degrees of territoriality and relative deterritorialization will be played out. Even when major, a language is open to an intensive utilization that makes it take flight along creative lines of escape which, no matter how slowly, no matter how cautiously, can now form an absolute deterritorialization. (*Kafka,* 26)

If the erected barriers are preserved, the connections created by the writers are ignored and do not permit access to the wealth of linkages that reflect the geographical, cultural, and aesthetic context of the continent from which the artists draw their imagination. On the other hand, it should be remembered: numerous are the postcolonial writers who rise up against forms of intolerance and enclosure as they seek to present the various aspects of the human being, to open him out to the world, thwarting seclusion, withdrawal, and rejection:

> The place from where the word is uttered, the text is uttered, the voice is uttered, the cry is uttered, that place is immense. But that place can be closed and one can lock oneself inside it. The area from where the cry is uttered can be made into a territory, that is to say be closed by walls, spiritual walls, ideological walls, etc. It ceases to be an "area." The important thing today is precisely that of knowing how to discuss a poetics of Relationship so that, without dismantling, without diluting the place, one can open it up. (Glissant, *Introduction à une poétique du divers,* 29–30)

These writers purposely place themselves in the interstitial space, beyond frontiers, roaming the full expanse of the earth, wandering through the maze, doubling themselves and moving away from the center. They invest the void, traveling across places, periods, cultures, breaking through totalizing thoughts and dogmas, passing from here to the beyond, from present to past, from the visible to the invisible, from one art to another, enriching themselves and moving away from the center. By going to and from the chasms of the earth, these texts cut themselves a path through the darkness, between countries, sites, and processes, as they find, bring back, interlace, and modify distant patterns—scattered fragments in motion that inhabit us. Interweaving the threads that extend across the world, they challenge our limits, broaden our perspectives, as they go toward the recognition of a distant web to which we are connected. Thus they devise our becoming, calling on us to go toward the wholly different and, above all, to take great pleasure in the unknown.

Notes

Introduction

1. A problematic term to be discussed in chapter 1. Since this book has no interest in an overhaul of expressions widely used by theoreticians, academicians, or writers, the term is used for reasons of clarity, albeit cautiously, and by drawing attention to the problems and confusions such expressions produce, which have their share in the creation of false schisms.

2. Although the original word used here is "*circulation,*" this does not have an equivalent meaning in English. However, the implication is not merely "movement" but also a kind of spiraling movement, meaning that it does not necessarily come back full circle but goes about in ways that may overlap and are at times circular.

3. The English word "errancy" does not truly reflect the French word "*errance,*" since the latter refers to the wandering movement of the nomad, while the former generally signifies "going astray" and being "wayward." However, whenever "errancy" appears in the text, the author intends for it to be read as the equivalent of the French term.

1. Circulatory Flow between the Maghreb and Sub-Saharan Africa

1. All quotations that refer to an English book title are taken from the published translated version of the text. The translator's name is given in the bibliography. When the French book title is given, Marjolijn de Jager has translated the quotation.

2. It is difficult to provide an exact number, for many of the languages are currently disappearing.

3. Little correctly notes the contradictions inherent in the use of the term "francophonie." However, it should be mentioned that his suggestion to replace it with "francographie" does not resolve the basic problem in any significant way.

4. As Simon Battestini has observed, the labels sub-Saharan Africa and black Africa are problematic, for they convey the idea of an Africa that is divided (with one part "below" the other) and of two homogeneous parts, which does not in any way

correspond to the situation. "In effect, the descriptive term 'Sub-Saharan' connotes the vague idea of a 'lifeless down-under,' of forlorn geological times prior to the appearance of the human species. The term 'black' is no less abusive, insidious, and loaded with deprecating history. So-called Black Africa has a population whose skin ranges from slightly tanned or bronzed white (frequent among Berbers, Ethiopians and Fulani) to a bluish black (e.g. in West African coastal lagoon fishermen) which may have inspired Matisse" (*African Writing and Text,* 83–84).

5. Painting under glass (*sous verre*) differs from painting on glass in that the painted images appear inverted on the other side of the transparent base.

6. In his film *Quartier Mozart,* the Cameroonian filmmaker Jean-Pierre Bekolo gives the characters special names that allow him to provide valuable information about their personalities, following in the footsteps of a tradition while modifying it to inscribe new approaches that have humor as their goal.

7. Nevertheless, it should be made clear that although combinations have taken place, it is not the elements of Islam in sub-Saharan Africa that allow for a direct tracing of connections with the Maghreb, since Islam originated in the Near East. However, Muslim customs, the interest in Sufism which combines approaches and has recourse to pre-Islamic forms, and the resurgence and circulation of ancient practices sustain the imagination of artists and writers. This does not prevent them from criticizing the misuse of a given practice or, on the other hand, from mentioning its contributions. Thus when faced with religious, political, and cultural elements, many literary texts articulate reactions, which once again allows for links to be made across the continent among authors writing about common themes and similar preoccupations.

8. It should be noted that the cited authors of Independence who work with circulatory flow and exchanges take a different position from the preceding generation, some of whom sought to be reconnected to an origin so that they could overturn the clichés of colonialism and find homogeneity, a cultural unity, again. Thus we differentiate a poetics of identity, as developed by the negritude movement, the writings of Cheikh Anta Diop and Obenga, from a poetics of relation as Glissant developed it, to which he gave the name creolization.

9. An earlier version of this chapter, translated by Marjolijn de Jager, appeared under the title "Maghreb—Sub-Saharan Connections" in *Research in African Literature* 33, no. 3 (Fall 2002): 32–53.

2. On-Screen and Off-Screen Connections

1. In his book *In My Father's House,* Kwame Appiah shows the problems connected with the use of the term "postcolonialism." It doesn't always correspond to a specific definition, for it isn't necessarily possible to establish a clear distinction between the colonial and postcolonial eras. When I use the expression "postcolonial,"

I am referring to the period of Independence, while I fully subscribe to the idea that the transition between these periods is quite often blurred and there is no sudden break either in the political or in the artistic realm, since the transformations are produced over the course of time and not all at once. This is, obviously, an additional element that contributes to explaining the presence of contradictory and disorderly elements in literary texts.

2. Quotation translated by Marjolijn de Jager, since the published English translation was not available.

3. To a great extent, Islam was spread through conquests and the trade across the Sahara. By the early 700s, Egypt and the Maghreb were converted to Islam. In West Africa, Mansa Musa (1312–37) spread Islam by consolidating a relationship with the Maghreb through the creation of research and education centers. However, pre-Islamic ancestral practices were often preserved, and thus numerous methods and ideas have long been intermingled. During the colonial era, Christianity was introduced, a religion already known in Ethiopia by way of the Orthodox Greek monks and practiced by the Copts in Egypt.

4. Moreover, his writing closely interweaves both traditions (see chap. 1).

3. Verbal Flow between Orality and Writing

1. "In contrast with Indian castes, the African castes are guilds, of which there are two: the artisans (blacksmiths and cobblers), and the nonartisans (basically the griots). Griots are musicians, chroniclers, genealogists, praise singers, masters of ceremony, or priests at magic-religious services" (Dieng, "L'épopée dynastique ouest-africaine," 23).

2. Remarks made by Mamemoussé Diagne during the defense of his thèse d'état at Cheick Anta Diop University, Dakar, Senegal, November 29, 2003.

3. I have chosen not to deal with the references to orality in Meddeb's work, for they are presented very differently; Abdellatif El Alami has studied a number of these in his book *Métalangage et philologie extatique (Essai sur Abdelwahab Meddeb)*.

4. Roundtable on December 8, 2003, at the Ninth International Book Fair and Fair of Educational Materials of Dakar (FILDAK), held December 4–9, 2003, at CICES, Senegal.

4. Aesthetic Flow between Visual and Written Art

1. B. Samb Diene, in his thesis entitled "Les ordures ménagères de Dakar. De la diversité chromatique et graphique à l'accumulation de signes: Les signes adinkra" (Household Trash of Dakar: From Chromatic and Graphic Diversity to the Accumulation of Signs: Adinkra Signs), thèse de licence, École National des Arts, Dakar, Senegal, 2000.

2. Since the second part of this citation is not found in the English translation published by Thames and Hudson, Marjolijn de Jager has translated this segment from a more recent French version of the book.

5. Abdelwahab Meddeb

1. I am borrowing Meddeb's words for the title of the present chapter (*Face à l'islam,* 76).

2. Unless stated otherwise, all further references in this chapter are to the novel *Phantasia.*

3. On this subject, see Meddeb's explanations in *Face à l'islam.*

4. A method used in *Talismano,* while *Phantasia* moves away from this approach, referring to a translation instead of using Arabic terms. The approach used in the first novel, though quite different from the second, was a necessary step. However, this study focuses on *Phantasia* to develop an in-depth examination of the themes treated. Undoubtedly, in future studies I will go back to the first novel.

5. The French language has an informal (*tu*) and a formal (*vous*) "you," used according to the situation and the relationship between characters.—Trans.

6. Explanations offered by Abdelwahab Meddeb during a seminar he taught at the University of Geneva, 1989–90.

7. Observation made by Jacques Garelli at a seminar he taught at New York University, 1994.

8. The French words *mot* and *parole* have distinct meanings in French, although they are both translated by "word" in English.—Trans.

6. Werewere Liking

1. Unless stated otherwise, page numbers in this chapter refer to the English translation of the song-novel *It Shall Be of Jasper and Coral.*

2. Although it doesn't show up in the English translation, there are rhymes in the French original: "Seule sera celle qui saura / Seule celle qui osera"; "Lunaï est un village brûlé et las. Hélas! . . ." (*Elle sera de jaspe et de corail,* 27, 23).—Trans.

3. I.e., in French the play between "las" and "Hélas."—Trans.

4. In the original French, the play on words is much more evident, since the words "rouler dans" are found in both expressions. "Rouler dans la masse" (*Elle sera de jaspe et de corail,* 46), "to be pulled along with the masses," is found in the text instead of the usual expression, "rouler dans la farine," to have "the wool pulled over one's eyes."—Trans.

7. Tchicaya U Tam'Si

1. Hereafter, page references to the English translation of Tchicaya U Tam'Si's novel will appear in parentheses in the text.

2. Also called a medusa, as in the title of the novel.

3. In this case the author does not use expressions that are familiar or foreign to the language, but not finding any equivalent in French, he uses roughly approximate terms and provides additional explanations indirectly.

4. Since this term was omitted from the published English translation, I am quoting here from the French version.—Trans.

8. Assia Djebar

1. From 1830 onward, Algeria was colonized by France, which settled there by force, violently suppressing all resistance and frequent insurrections—historic events traced in Djebar's *L'amour, la fantasia.* But this novel isn't limited to that topic, and it condemns all forms of abuse (including those that originate from old customs, religion, etc.) against women, thereby accentuating their courage and remembering their crucial role in the war for Independence (1954–62).

2. To clarify the presence of visual art in Djebar, this chapter turns to the immensely valuable works of Khatibi, at the cultural crossroads (Muslim, Berber, Western, African), entrenched in so many traditions. Reassessing the status granted to women and the need for a feminist struggle are central to Djebar's work. However, these issues have been discussed at length by critics, as well as the influence of music. Following the lines laid down in this study, I would like to examine an equally important problem, which is her treatment of the image and the way in which, even as she renews traditional methods, she changes them to represent what has been kept silent.

3. From the French edition. Unless otherwise specified, references in the first part of this chapter are to the short stories in the collection *Women of Algiers in Their Apartment.* For references to the expanded (2002) edition of *Femmes d'Alger,* where there is no published English translation of certain sections, the French title will be given in the citation.

4. In French, the word *histoire* has two meanings: "history" and "story."—Trans.

5. In French, the word *vision* means both "sight" and "vision."—Trans.

6. Throughout this chapter I use italics in the Djebar quotations to accentuate the terms that relate to the themes being discussed.

7. Since this passage is in italics in Djebar's text, my emphasis here is in Roman font.

8. Unless otherwise specified, citations in the rest of this chapter are to the published English translation, *Fantasia: An Algerian Cavalcade.*

9. In the French original, many more words in this quotation (and in those that follow) relate directly to painting. They have been omitted from the published English translation.—Trans.

10. *Calligraphie d'amour* is found in the French original and can be literally translated as "calligraphy of love."—Trans.

11. In this regard, see the previously cited article by Suzanne Crosta, "Stratégies de subversion et de libération."

12. In French: "La trame de son histoire murmurée" (*L'amour, la fantasia,* 160).

Bibliography

Adams, Anne. "To W/rite a New Language: Werewere Liking's Adaptation of Ritual to the Novel." *Callaloo* 16, no. 1 (1993): 153–86.

Adonis. *Introduction à la poétique arabe.* Trans. from Arabic into French by Bassam Tahhan and Anne Wade Minkowski. Paris: Sindbad, 1985.

"Africanité du Maghreb." Special issue, *Africultures,* no. 13 (December 1998).

Aissi, Antoine. "De la colonisation à nos jours." *Notre librairie,* nos. 92–93 (March–May 1988): 44–49.

Alaoui, Brahim, ed. *Ahmed Cherkaoui: La passion du signe.* Exhibition at the Institut du monde arabe, October 15 to December 15, 1996. Paris: Éditions Revue noire, 1996.

———, ed. *Art contemporain arabe.* Paris: Institut du monde arabe, 1989.

Alaoui, Brahim, and Laila Al Wahidi, curators. *Peintres du Maroc: Belkahia; Bellamine; Cherkaoui; Kacimi.* Catalog of the exhibition, June 25 to September 15, 1991. Paris: Institut du monde arabe, 1991.

Alaoui, Brahim, and Marie-Odile Briot, curators. *Croisement de signes.* Catalog of the exhibition, April 24 to August 15, 1989. Paris: Institut du monde arabe, 1989.

Alaoui, Brahim, and Jean-Hubert Martin, curators. *Rencontres africaines.* Catalog of the exhibition, April 6 to August 15, 1994. Paris: Institut du monde arabe, 1994.

Alessandra, Jacques. *La brûlure des interrogations: Entretiens avec Abdellatif Laâbi.* Paris: L'Harmattan, 1985.

Alloula, Malek. *Le harem colonial: Images d'un sous-érotisme.* Paris: Éditions Séguier, 2001.

Almeida, Irène Assiba d'. *Francophone African Women Writers: Destroying the Emptiness of Silence.* Gainesville: University Press of Florida, 1994.

Amin, Samir. *L'eurocentrisme: Critique d'une idéologie.* Paris: Éditions Anthropos-Economica, 1988.

André-Leicknam, Béatrice, and Christiane Ziegler, curators. *Naissance de l'écriture, cunéiformes et hiéroglyphes.* Catalog of the exhibition at the Galeries nationales du Grand Palais, May 7 to August 9, 1982. Reprint, Paris: Éditions de la Réunion des musées nationaux, 1995.

Appiah, Kwame Anthony. *In My Father's House: Africa in the Philosophy of Culture.* New York: Oxford University Press, 1992.

Arnaud, Jacqueline, ed. *Littérature du Maghreb, itinéraires et contacts de cultures,* vols. 4–5. Paris: L'Harmattan, 1984.

———. *La littérature maghrébine de langue française.* Tome 1, *Origines et perspectives.* Paris: Publisud, 1986.

———. *Littératures maghrébines, itinéraires et contacts de cultures.* Tome 1, *Perspectives générales,* vol. 10. Paris: L'Harmattan, 1990.

———. *Littératures maghrébines, itinéraires et contacts de cultures.* Tome 2: *Les auteurs et leurs oeuvres,* vol. 11. Paris: L'Harmattan, 1990.

"Arts plastiques Maroc." Special issue, *Souffles,* nos. 7–8 (1967).

Asfar, Denis. "*Kaïdara:* Islam and Traditional Religion in a West African Narrative of Initiation." In *Faces of Islam in African Literatures,* ed. Kenneth Harrow, 151–62. Portsmouth, NH: Heinemann, 1991.

Ashcroft, Bill, Gareth Griffiths, and Helen Tiffin, eds. *The Post-colonial Studies Reader.* London: Routledge, 1995.

Bâ, Amadou Hampâté. *Aspects de la civilisation africaine.* Paris: Présence africaine, 1972.

———. *Kaïdara.* Abidjan: NEI-EDICEF, 1994.

———. *La poignée de poussière.* Abidjan: NEI-EDICEF, 1994.

———. *Vie et enseignement de Tierno Bokar.* Paris: Seuil, coll. "Points," 1980.

Bakhtin, Mikhaïl. *Esthétique et théorie du roman.* Trans. from Russian into French by Daria Olivier. Paris: Gallimard, coll. "Tel," [1978], 1987.

———. *La poétique de Dostoïevski.* Trans. from Russian into French by Isabelle Kolitcheff. Paris: Seuil, coll. "Points," [1970], 1998.

Barlet, Olivier. "Les Gnawa, thérapeutes de la différence: Entretien avec Georges Lapassade." In "Africanité du Maghreb," special issue, *Africultures,* no. 13 (December 1998): 15–20.

Barthes, Roland. *Le bruissement de la langue.* Paris: Seuil, 1984.

———. *Le degré zéro de l'écriture,* suivi de *Nouveaux essais critiques.* Paris: Seuil, coll. "Points," [1953], 1972.

———. *Mythologies.* Paris: Seuil, coll. "Points," 1970.

———. *L'obvie et l'obtus: Essais critiques III.* Paris: Seuil, 1982.

Bataille, Georges. *L'expérience intérieure.* Reprint, Paris: Gallimard, 1997.

Battestini, Simon. *African Writing and Text.* Trans. Henri Evans. Ottawa: Legas, 2000.

Bekri, Tahar. *Les songes impatients.* Montréal: Éditions de l'Hexagone, 1997.

Belcher, Stephen. *Epic Traditions of Africa.* Bloomington: Indiana University Press, 1999.

Belinga, Eno. *(L'épopée camerounaise) Mvet, Moneblum ou l'homme bleu.* Yaoudé: Centre d'édition et de production pour l'enseignement et la recherche, 1978.

Ben Jelloun, Tahar. "La mémoire déroutée." In "Postcolonialisme: Décentrement, déplacement, dissemination," special issue, *Dédale,* nos. 5–6 (Spring 1997): 159–63.

Bensmaïa, Réda. "Géographie politique de la littérature: À propos de la notion de 'voyageur professionnel' chez Abdelkébir Khatibi." In *La traversée du français dans les signes littéraires marocains,* ed. Yvette Bénayoun-Szmidt et al., 113–24. Toronto: Éditions La source, 1996.

Blanchot, Maurice. *L'espace littéraire.* Paris: Gallimard, coll. "Folio/Essais," [1988], 2002.

Boughali, Mohamed. *Espaces d'écriture au Maroc.* Casablanca: Afrique-Orient, 1987.

Briot, Marie-Odile. "Chronobiographie." In *Kacimi,* ed. Mohammed Kacimi et al., 168–90. Paris: Revue noire, 1996.

Buci-Glucksmann, Christine. "Le vertical dans l'immanence." In "Le paradoxe des représentations du divin: L'image et l'invisible," special issue, *Dédale,* nos. 1–2 (Fall 1995): 245–56.

Buci-Glucksmann, Christine, et al., eds. *Imaginaires de l'autre: Khatibi et la mémoire littéraire.* Paris: L'Harmattan, 1987.

Butor, Michel. *Les mots dans la peinture.* Geneva and Paris: Champs Flammarion, 1969.

Christen, Anne-Marie, ed. *Écritures, systèmes idéographiques et pratiques expressives.* Actes du colloque international de l'Université Paris VII. Paris: Éditions le Sycomore, 1982.

Cohen, Marcel. *La grande invention de l'écriture et son évolution.* Paris: Klincksieck, 1958.

Conteh-Morgan, John. *Theatre and Drama in Francophone Africa.* Cambridge: Cambridge University Press, 1994.

———. "Myth, Ritual Performance and the Search for a New Theatre in Francophone Africa: The Example of Werewere Liking's *Une Nouvelle Terre.*" In *Black Accents: Writing in French from Africa, Mauritius and the Caribbean,* ed. J. P. Little and Roger Little, 221–34. London: Grant & Cutler, 1997.

Coulon, Christian, and Martin Denis-Constant. *Les Afriques politiques.* Paris: Éditions de la Découverte, 1991.

Crosta, Suzanne. "Stratégies de subversion et de libération: L'inscription et les enjeux de l'auditif et du visuel chez Assia Djebar et Ousmane Sembene." In *Littérature et cinéma en Afrique francophone: Ousmane Sembene et Assia Djebar,* ed. Sada Niang, 49–81. Paris: L'Harmattan, 1996.

Deleuze, Gilles, and Félix Guattari. *Kafka: Toward a Minor Literature.* Trans. Dana Polan. Minneapolis: University of Minnesota Press, 1986.

"Déserts: Vide, errance, écriture." Special issue, *Dédale,* nos. 7–8 (Spring 1998).

Diagne, Souleymane Bachir. "L'avenir de la tradition." In *Sénégal: Trajectoires d'un État,* ed. Momar Coumba Diop. Dakar: CODESRIA, 1992.

Dieng, Bassirou. "L'épopée dynastique ouest-africaine, la construction théorique d'un genre épique." In "Épopées d'Afrique de l'Ouest, épopées médiévales d'Europe," special issue, *Littérales,* no. 29 (2002): 17–37.

Diop, Cheikh Anta. *Les fondements économiques et culturels d'un état fédéral d'Afrique noire.* Paris: Présence africaine, 1974.

———. *L'unité culturelle de l'Afrique noire.* Paris: Présence africaine, [1959], 1982.

Djaout, Tahar. *L'exproprié.* Paris: Éditions François Majault, 1991.

Djebar, Assia. *L'amour, la fantasia.* Paris: Albin Michel, 1995.

———. *Fantasia: An Algerian Cavalcade.* Trans. Dorothy S. Blair. Portsmouth, NH: Heinemann, 1993.

———. *Femmes d'Alger dans leur appartement.* Paris: Albin Michel, coll. "Le Livre de Poche," [1980], 2002.

———. *Women of Algiers in Their Apartment.* Trans. Marjolijn de Jager. CARAF Books. Charlottesville: University Press of Virginia, [1992], 1999.

Ducrot, Oswald. *Dire et ne pas dire: Principes de sémantique linguistique.* Paris: Herman, 1972.

Eco, Umberto. *L'oeuvre ouverte.* Trans. from Italian into French by Chantal Roux de Bézieux. Paris: Seuil, [1965], 1979.

El Alami, Abdellatif. *Métalangage et philosophie extatique (Essai sur Abdelwahab Meddeb).* Paris: L'Harmattan, 2000.

El Maleh, Edmond, and Toni Maraini. *La peinture marocaine au rendez-vous de l'histoire.* Casablanca: Éditions Espace Wafabank, 1988.

El-Moujahid, El-Houssaïn. "Le Maroc et l'Afrique." In *Civilisation marocaine,* ed. Mohamed Sijelmassi and Abdelkébir Khatibi, 50–53. Casablanca: Éditions Oum, Actes Sud/Sindbad, 1996.

Fall, Aminata Sow. *Le jujubier du patriarche.* Paris: Le Serpent à Plumes [1993], 1998.

Fanon, Frantz, *Peau noire, masques blancs.* Paris: Seuil, coll. "Points," 1952.

———. *Toward the African Revolution.* New York: Grove Press, [1967], 1988.

———. *The Wretched of the Earth.* Trans. Constance Farrington. New York: Grove Press, 1965.

Farès, Nabile. *Mémoire de l'absent.* Paris: Seuil, 1974.

Flax, Jane. *Thinking Fragments: Psychoanalysis, Feminism, and Postmodernism in the Contemporary West.* Berkeley and Los Angeles: University of California Press, 1990.

Fu-Kiau, Kia Bunseki. *Le Mukongo et le monde qui l'entourait: Cosmogonie—Kôngo.* Kinshasa: Office National de la Recherche et du Développement, 1969.

Garelli, Jacques. *Rythmes et mondes: Au revers de l'identité et de l'altérité.* Grenoble: Éditions Jérôme Millon, 1991.

Garrigues, Pierre. *Poétiques du fragment.* Paris: Klincksieck, 1995.

Genette, Gérard. *Figures III.* Paris: Éditions du Seuil, 1972.

Gérard, Albert. *African Language Literatures: An Introduction to the Literary History of Sub-Saharan Africa.* Washington, D.C.: Three Continents; London: Longman, 1981.

———. *European Language Writing in Sub-Saharan Africa.* 2 vols. Budapest: Akadémiai Kiadó, 1986.

———. *Littératures en langues africaines.* Mayenne: Éditions Mentha, 1992.

Glissant, Édouard. *Le discours antillais.* Paris: Seuil, 1981.

———. *Introduction à une poétique du divers.* Paris: Gallimard, 1996.

———. *Poetics of Relation.* Trans. Betsy Wing. Ann Arbor: University of Michigan Press, 1997.

———. *Traité du tout-monde, Poétique IV.* Paris: Gallimard, 1997.

Godard, Roger. *Trois poètes congolais: Maxime D'Débéka, J.-Baptiste Tati Loutard, T. U Tam'Si.* Paris: L'Harmattan, 1985.

Gontard, Marc. *Le moi étrange, littérature marocaine de langue française.* Paris: L'Harmattan, 1993.

———. *Violence du texte, littérature marocaine de langue française.* Paris: SMER/ L'Harmattan, 1981.

Grégoire, Emmanuel, and Jean Schmitz, eds. "Afrique noire et monde arabe: Continuités et ruptures." Special issue, *Autrepart,* no. 16. Bondy: Éditions de l'aube, 2000.

Greica et al. *Littérature maghrébine d'expression française: De l'écrit à l'image.* Meknès: Université Sidi Mohamed, 1987.

Hale, Thomas. *Griots and Griottes: Masters of Words and Music.* Indianapolis: Indiana University Press, 1998.

Hammoudi, Abdellah. *La victime et ses masques: Essai sur le sacrifice et la masquarade au Maghreb.* Paris: Seuil, 1988.

Harrow, Kenneth, ed. *Faces of Islam in African Literature.* Portsmouth, NH: Heinemann, 1991.

Heyndels, Ralph. *La pensée fragmentée.* Brussels: Éditions Pierre Mardaga, 1985.

Hourantier, Marie-José. *Du rituel au théâtre-rituel: Contribution à une esthétique théâtrale négro-africaine.* Paris: L'Harmattan, 1984.

Hourantier, Marie-José, Werewere Liking, and Jacques Scherer. *Du rituel à la scène chez les Bassa du Cameroun.* Paris: Nizet, 1979.

Husin, Jabbar Yassin, and Xavier Person (interview); Claude Ollier and Anne Roche (texts). *Abdelwahab Meddeb.* Poitiers: Office du livre en Poitou-Charentes, 1993.

Hussein, Mahmoud. "L'individu postcolonial." In "Postcolonialisme: Décentrement, déplacement, dissemination," special issue, *Dédale,* nos. 5–6 (Spring 1997): 164–74.

Irele, Abiola. *The African Experience in Literature and Ideology.* Bloomington: Indiana University Press, [1981], 1990.

Jabra, Ibrahim Jabra. "Calligraphie et art moderne dans le monde arabe." In *Croisement de signes,* curated by Alaoui Brahim and Marie-Odile Briot, catalog of the

exhibition, April 24 to August 15, 1989, 25–27. Paris: Institut du monde arabe, 1989.
Jolles, André. *Formes simples.* Trans. from German into French by Antoine Marie Buguet. Paris: Seuil, 1972.
Julien, Eileen. *African Novels and the Question of Orality.* Bloomington: Indiana University Press, 1992.
Kacimi, Mohamed, et al. *Kacimi.* Paris: Éditions Revue noire, 1996.
Kadima-Nzuji, Mukala. *La littérature zaïroise de langue française.* Paris: ACCT/Karthala, 1984.
Kane, Cheikh Hamidou. *Ambiguous Adventure.* Trans. Katherine Woods. New York: Collier Books, [1963], 1971.
Kane, Mohamadou K. *Roman africain et tradition.* Dakar: Les Nouvelles Éditions Africaines, 1982.
Kesteloot, Lilyan, and Bassirou Dieng. *Les épopées d'Afrique noire.* Paris: Karthala/Éditions UNESCO, 1997.
Khaïr-Eddine, Mohammed. *Le déterreur.* Paris: Seuil, 1973.
Khapoya, Vincent. *The African Experience: An Introduction.* Englewood Cliffs, N.J.: Prentice Hall, 1994.
Khatibi, Abdelkébir. *La blessure du nom propre.* Paris: Denoël, [1974], 1986.
———. *Cherkaoui, la passion du signe.* Paris: Éditions Revue noire, 1996.
———. "Croisement de regards." In *L'oeuvre de . . . Abdelkébir Khatibi (préliminaire).* Rabat: Éditions Marsam, 1997.
———. *Le corps oriental.* Paris: Éditions Hazan, 2002.
———. *Figures de l'étranger dans la littérature française.* Paris: Denoël, 1987.
———. *La langue de l'autre.* New York and Tunis: Éditions Les Mains Secrètes, 1999.
———. *Maghreb pluriel.* Paris: Denoël/SMER, 1983.
———. *La mémoire tatouée.* Paris: Denoël, 1979.
———. "Paradigmes de civilization." In *L'oeuvre de . . . Abdelkébir Khatibi (préliminaire),* 69–87. Rabat: Éditions Marsam, 1997.
———. *Par-dessus l'épaule.* Paris: Édition Aubier, 1988.
———. *Penser le Maghreb.* Rabat: SMER (Société Marocaine des Éditeurs Réunis), 1993.
———. *Le roman maghrébin.* Reprint, Rabat: SMER, 1979.
Khatibi, Abdelkébir, and Ali Amahan. *Du signe à l'image: Le tapis marocain.* Published in English as *From Sign to Image: The Moroccan Carpet.* Casablanca: Lak International, 1995.
Khatibi, Abdelkébir, and Mohamed Sijelmassi. *L'art calligraphique de l'Islam.* Nouvelle édition. Paris: Gallimard, 1994.
———. *The Splendor of Islamic Calligraphy.* Trans. James Hughes and E. J. Emory. London: Thames and Hudson, [1995], 2001.

Ki-Zerbo, Joseph. *Histoire de l'Afrique noire: D'hier à demain.* Paris: A. Hatier, 1978.

Klee, Paul. *Journal.* Trans. from German into French by Pierre Klossowski. Paris: Éditions Grasset, 1959.

———. *Théorie de l'art moderne.* Trans. from German into French by Pierre-Henri Gonthier. Geneva: Denoël/Gonthier, 1982.

Kundera, Milan. *L'art du roman.* Paris: Gallimard, 1986.

Lafont, Robert, et al. *Anthropologie de l'écriture.* Paris: Centre Georges Pompidou, 1984.

Leroi-Gourhan, André. *Le geste et la parole.* Vol. 1, *Technique et langage.* Paris: Albin Michel, 1964.

———. *Le geste et la parole.* Vol. 2, *La Mémoire et les rythmes.* Paris: Albin Michel, 1964.

Leymarie, Isabelle. *Les griots wolof du Sénégal.* Paris: Servedit-Maisonneuve et Larose, 1999.

Liking, Werewere. *Elle sera de jaspe et de corail.* Paris: L'Harmattan, coll. "Encres noires," 1993.

———. *It Shall Be of Jasper and Coral* and *Love-across-a-Hundred-Lives.* Trans. Marjolijn de Jager. CARAF Books. Charlottesville: University Press of Virginia, 2000.

———. *Orphée-Dafric: Roman;* and *Orphée d'Afrique: Théâtre-rituel,* by Manuna Ma Njock. Paris: L'Harmattan, 1981.

———. *Un Touareg s'est marié à une Pygmée.* Carnières: Lansman, 1992.

Little, Roger. "'La francographie': A New Model for la 'francophonie.'" *ALA Bulletin* 25, no. 4 (Fall 1999): 28–36.

Lyotard, Jean-François. *La condition postmoderne.* Paris: Éditions de Minuit, 1979.

Magnier, Bernard. "À la rencontre de . . . Werewere Liking." Interview. *Notre librairie,* no. 79 (April–June 1985): 17–21.

Maraini, Toni. "Au rendez-vous de l'histoire, la peinture." In *La peinture marocaine au rendez-vous de l'histoire,* by Edmond El Maleh and Toni Maraini. Casablanca: Éditions Espace Wafabank, 1988.

———. *Écrits sur l'art: Choix de textes, Maroc 1967–1989.* Mohammédia: Éditions Al Kalam, coll. "Zellije," 1990.

———. "Farid Belkahia." In *Peintres du Maroc: Belkahia; Bellamine; Cherkaoui; Kacimi,* curated by Brahim Alaoui and Laila Al Wahidi. Catalog of the exhibition, April 6 to August 15, 1994. Paris: Institut du monde arabe, 1994.

———. "L'important, c'est d'être bien dans sa peau." In *Peintres du Maroc: Belkahia; Bellamine; Cherkaoui; Kacimi,* curated by Brahim Alaoui and Laila Al Wahidi. Catalog of the exhibition, April 6 to August 15, 1994. Paris: Institut du monde arabe, 1994.

Marks, John. *Gilles Deleuze: Vitalism and Multiplicity.* London: Pluto Press, 1998.

Mateso, Locha. *La littérature africaine et sa critique.* Paris: Karthala, 1986.
"Mauritanie entre arabité et africanité." Special issue, *Revue du monde musulman et de la Méditerranée,* no. 54 (July 1990).
Mbiti, John S. *African Religions and Philosophy.* New York: Anchor Books/Doubleday, 1970.
M'Bokolo, Elikia. *L'Afrique au XXe siècle, le continent convoité.* Paris: Seuil, coll. "Points," 1985.
Meddeb, Abdelwahab. "Dialogue." In *Rencontres africaines,* curated by Brahim Alaoui and Jean-Hubert Martin, 61–72. Catalog of the exhibition, April 6 to August 15, 1994. Paris: Institut du monde arabe, 1994.
———. "Épiphanie et jouissance." *Intersignes,* nos. 6–7 (Spring 1993): 137–51.
———. *Face à l'islam.* Conversation with Philippe Petit. Conversations pour demain, no. 25. Paris: Éditions Textuel, 2004.
———. "L'image et l'invisible, Ibn Arabî/Jean de la Croix." *Pleine marge,* no. 4 (December 1986): 29–42.
———. "Ouverture." In "Postcolonialisme: Décentrement, déplacement, dissemination," special issue, *Dédale,* nos. 5–6 (Spring 1997): 11–14.
———. *Phantasia.* Paris: Sindbad, 1986.
———. *Talismano.* Reprint, Paris: Sindbad, 1987.
———. "Tous les déserts du monde." In "Déserts: Vide, errance, écriture," special issue, *Dédale,* nos. 7–8 (Spring 1998): 11–20.
———. "La trace, le signe." In *Croisement de signes,* curated by Brahim Alaoui and Marie-Odile Briot, 28–30. Catalog of the exhibition, April 24 to August 15, 1989. Paris: Institut du monde arabe, 1989.
Memmes, Abdallah. *Littérature maghrébine de langue française: Signifiance et interculturalité.* Rabat: Éditions Okad, 1992.
Memmi, Albert. *Portrait du colonisé;* procédé du *Portrait du colonisateur.* Paris: Gallimard, 1985.
Merleau-Ponty, Maurice. *L'oeil et l'esprit.* Paris: Gallimard, 1964.
———. *Le visible et l'invisible.* Paris: Gallimard, 1964.
M'Henni, Mansour, ed. *Tahar Ben Jelloun: Stratégies d'écriture.* Paris: L'Harmattan, 1993.
Mitchell, W. J. T. *Iconology: Image, Text, Ideology.* Chicago: University of Chicago Press, 1986.
Montaut, Annie. "Des *Enfants de minuit* au *Dernier soupir du Maure:* Histoire de trou." In "Postcolonialisme: Décentrement, déplacement, dissemination," special issue, *Dédale,* nos. 5–6 (Spring 1997): 311–33.
Mortimer, Mildred. "Edward Said and Assia Djebar: A Contrapuntal Reading." *Research in African Literatures* 36, no. 3 (2005): 53–67.
———. *Journeys through the French African Novel.* Portsmouth, NH: Heinemann, 1990.

Mouralis, Bernard. *Littérature et développement, essai sur le statut, la fonction et la représentation de la littérature négro-africaine d'expression française.* Lille: Éditions Atelier reproduction des thèses, 1981.

———. *V. Y. Mudimbe, ou le discours, l'écart et l'écriture.* Paris: Présence africaine, 1988.

Mudimbe, V. Y. *Before the Birth of the Moon.* Trans. Marjolijn de Jager. New York: Simon and Schuster, 1989.

———. *Between Tides.* Trans. Stephen Becker. New York: Simon and Schuster, 1991.

———. *The Idea of Africa.* Bloomington: Indiana University Press, 1994.

———. *The Invention of Africa: Gnosis, Philosophy, and the Order of Knowledge.* Bloomington: Indiana University Press, 1988.

Naïr, Sami. "Les deux regards." In "Postcolonialisme: Décentrement, déplacement, dissemination," special issue, *Dédale,* nos. 5–6 (Spring 1997): 17–30.

N'Diaye, Catherine. *Gens de sable.* Paris: P.O.L. Éditeur, 1984.

Ngandu Nkashama, Pius. *Comprendre la littérature africaine écrite.* Issy-les-Moulineaux: Éditions Saint-Paul, Les classiques africains, 1981.

———. *Des mangroves en terre haute.* Paris: L'Harmattan, 1991.

———. *Écritures et discours littéraires, études sur le roman africain.* Paris: L'Harmattan, 1989.

———. *Le pacte de sang.* Paris: L'Harmattan, 1984.

Niane, Djibril Tamsir. *Sundiata: An Epic of Old Mali.* Trans. G. D. Pickett. England: Longman, [1965], 1994.

Okpewho, Isidore. *African Oral Literature: Backgrounds, Character, and Continuity.* Bloomington: Indiana University Press, 1992.

Oyono, Ferdinand. *Houseboy.* Trans. John Reed. London: Heinemann, [1966], 1969.

"Le paradoxe des représentations du divin: L'image et l'invisible." Special issue, *Dédale,* nos. 1–2 (Fall 1995).

Paris, Jean. *Lisible/visible: Six essais de critique générative.* Paris: Seghers/Robert Laffont, 1978.

Peek, Philip, ed. *African Divination Systems: Ways of Knowing.* Bloomington: Indiana University Press, 1991.

Plaza, Monique. *Écriture et folie.* Paris: Presses universitaires de France, 1986.

Pommier, Gérard. *Naissance et renaissance de l'écriture.* Paris: Presses universitaires de France, 1993.

"Postcolonialisme: Décentrement, déplacement, dissemination." Special issue, *Dédale,* nos. 5–6 (Spring 1997).

Rahal, Ahmed. *La communauté noire de Tunis: Thérapie initiatique et rite de possession.* Paris: L'Harmattan, 2000.

Raybaud, Antoine. *Le besoin littéraire.* France: Éditions du Rocher, 2000.

———. "*Nedjma* palimpseste." *Europe,* no. 828 (April 1998): 94–109.

———. "Résurgence de l'oralité dans le roman maghrébin: L'exemple de 'Nedjma' (de Kateb Yacine)." In *Six conférences sur la littérature africaine de langue française,* ed. Wolfgang Leiner, 89–101. Tübingen: Attempto Verlag, 1981.

Raybaud, Antoine, and Florence Quartier-Frings. "Raconter? (Dialogue)." *Revue française de psychanalyse,* no. 3 (1998): 741–50.

Renard, Pierrette. "Le pouvoir ambigu des mots." In *Tahar Ben Jelloun: Stratégies d'écriture,* ed. Mansour M'Henni, 11–23. Paris: L'Harmattan, 1993.

Riesz, Janos, and Alain Ricard, eds. *Semper aliquid novi: Littérature comparée et littératures d'Afrique.* Tübingen: Gunter Narr Verlag, 1990.

Robbe-Grillet, Alain. *Pour un nouveau roman.* Paris: Éditions de Minuit, 1986.

Roberts, Allen F. *Animals in African Art: From the Familiar to the Marvelous.* Exhibition catalog. New York: Museum for African Art, 1995.

Roberts, Allen F., and Mary Nooter Roberts. *A Saint in the City: Sufi Arts of Urban Senegal.* Los Angeles: UCLA Fowler Museum of Cultural History, 2003.

Roberts, Mary Nooter, and Allen F. Roberts, eds. *Memory: Luba Art and the Making of History.* Catalog of the exhibition, February 2 to September 8, 1996. New York: Museum for African Art, 1996.

Rouget, Gilbert. *La musique et la transe.* Paris: Gallimard, coll. "Tel," 1990.

Rushdie, Salman. *Imaginary Homelands.* London: Granta Books/Penguin Books, [1981], 1991.

Salih, Tayeb. *Saison de la migration vers le Nord.* Trans. from Arabic into French by Abdelwahab Meddeb. Paris: Sindbad, 1983.

Sarraute, Nathalie. *L'usage de la parole.* Paris: Gallimard, 1980.

Sassine, Williams. *Le jeune homme de sable.* Paris: Présence africaine, [1979], 1997.

Schimmel, Annemarie. *Calligraphy and Islamic culture.* New York: New York University Press, 1984.

Sellin, Eric. "Islamic Elements in Camara Laye's *L'enfant noir.*" In *Faces of Islam in African Literatures,* ed. Kenneth Harrow, 227–36. Portsmouth, NH: Heinemann, 1991.

Senghor, Léopold Sédar. *Les fondements de l'africanité ou négritude et arabité.* Paris: Présence africaine, 1967.

Shayegan, Daryush. "L'entre-deux dans la littérature d'aujourd'hui." In "Postcolonialisme: Décentrement, déplacement, dissemination," special issue, *Dédale,* nos. 5–6 (Spring 1997): 291–310.

Sijelmassi, Mohamed, ed. *L'art contemporain au Maroc.* Paris: Édition International ACR, 1989.

Sijelmassi, Mohamed, and Abdelkébir Khatibi, eds. *Civilisation marocaine.* Casablanca: Éditions Oum, Actes Sud/Sindbad, 1996.

Slyomovics, Susan. *The Merchant of Art: An Egyptian Hilali Oral Epic Poet in Performance.* University of California Publications in Modern Philology, 120. Berkeley: University of California, 1987.

Sony Labou Tansi. *Je soussigné cardiaque.* Paris: Hatier, coll. "Poche," [1981], 2002.

———. “Tchicaya U Tam’Si: Le père de notre rêve.” *Notre librairie,* nos. 92–93 (March–May 1988): 83.

———. *La vie et demie.* Paris: Seuil, coll. “Points,” [1979], 1988.

Steiner, George. *On Difficulty and Other Essays.* Oxford: Oxford University Press, 1978.

Sylla, Abdou. *L’artisanat sénégalais.* Dakar: Presses universitaires de Dakar, 2004.

———. *Arts plastiques et état au Sénégal.* Dakar: IFAN/Université Cheick Anta Diop, 1998.

Tagne, David Ndachi. “Werewere Liking: Créatrice prolifique et novatrice.” Interview. *Notre librairie,* no. 99 (October–December 1989): 194–96.

Tati-Loutard, Jean-Baptiste. *Chroniques congolaises: Nouvelles.* Paris: L’Harmattan, 1978.

Tchého, Isaac Célestin. “Échos maghrébins de Tchicaya U Tam’Si.” *Notre librairie,* no. 96 (January–March 1989): 56–59.

———. “Kateb Yacine et le monde noir.” In *Actualité de Kateb Yacine,* ed. Jacqueline Arnaud et al., 85–98. Itinéraires et contacts de cultures, 17. Paris: L’Harmattan, 1993.

Tchicaya U Tam’Si. *Ces fruits si doux de l’arbre à pain.* Paris: Seghers, [1987], 1990.

———. “Dialogue Sud-Sud.” *Notre librairie,* no. 95 (October– December 1988): 56–59.

———. *Légendes africaines.* Paris: Seghers, 1968.

———. *Les méduses ou les orties de mer.* Paris: Albin Michel, 1982.

———. *The Madman and the Medusa.* Trans. Sonja Haussmann Smith and William Jay Smith. CARAF Books. Charlottesville: University Press of Virginia, 1989.

Tenkoul, Abderrahman, ed. *Écritures maghrébines, lectures croisées.* Casablanca: Afrique-Orient, 1991.

———. *Littérature marocaine d’écriture française: Essais d’analyse sémiotique.* Casablanca: Afrique-Orient, 1985.

Thompson, Carol A. “Catalogue Notes.” In *Animals in African Art: From the Familiar to the Marvelous,* by Allen F. Roberts, 103–85. Exhibition catalog. New York: Museum for African Art, 1995.

Todorov, Tzvetan. *Introduction à la littérature fantastique.* Paris: Seuil, coll. “Points,” 1970.

Turner, Victor. *From Ritual to Theatre: The Human Seriousness of Play.* New York: PAJ Publications, 1982.

Van den Heuvel, Pierre. *Parole, mot, silence: Pour une poétique de l’énonciation.* Paris: José Corti, 1985.

Vitray-Meyerovitch, Eva, de. *Anthologie du soufisme.* Paris: Sindbad, 1978.

Yacine, Kateb. *Nedjma.* Paris: Seuil, coll. “Points,” [1956], 1996.

———. *Le poète comme un boxeur: Entretiens 1958–1989.* Paris: Seuil, 1994.

———. *Le polygone étoilé.* Paris: Seuil, coll. “Points,” [1966], 1997.

Zabus, Chantal. "Criticism of African Literatures in English: Toward a Horizon of Expectation." *Revue de littérature comparée,* no. 1 (1993): 129–47.
Zimra, Clarisse. "Disorienting the Subject in Djebar's *L'Amour, la fantasia.*" In "Another Look, Another Woman: Retranslations of French Feminism," special issue, *Yale French Studies,* no. 87 (1995): 149–70.
Zumthor, Paul. *Introduction à la poésie orale.* Paris: Seuil, 1983.

Illustration Credits

Black-and-white illustrations

Pages ii and 100: Mangbetu *pagne,* Democratic Republic of Congo. Beaten and painted tree bark, 168 cm high, mid-twentieth century. © Revue Noire.

Page v: Harp, Ngbaka, Central African Republic. Wood and skin, 87 cm high, late nineteenth century. © Revue Noire.

Page xviii: Kuba cloth, Democratic Republic of Congo. © Revue Noire.

Page 28: Islamic calligraphy, in the style known as *tomar.* © Mohamed Sijelmassi.

Page 58: Calligraphy, interwoven floral kufic script, of the name of Allah. © Mohamed Sijelmassi.

Page 102: Calligraphy by Ibn al-Bawwâb, student of Ibn Muqla. Extract from a Koran dated year of the Hegira 391 (AD 1000–1001). © Mohamed Sijelmassi.

Page 156: *Blolo bla* statue, Baule, Ivory Coast. Wood and beads in decorative sintered glass, 210 cm high, mid-twentieth century. © Revue Noire.

Page 204: Calligraphy, a cosmogonic representation. © Mohamed Sijelmassi.

Color plates

Plate 1. Mnemonic tablet, or *Lukasa.* Luba, Democratic Republic of Congo. Wood, metal, and beads, 33 cm high. Collection of Susanne K. Bennett. Photo © Museum for African Art, New York. The arrangement of beads on the tablet inscribes historic events.

Plate 2. Farid Belkahia, *Aube.* 155 cm in diameter, 1983. Photo © Philippe Maillard. Balkahia, a Moroccan artist born in 1934, draws from the ancient heritage of tattooing and signs found throughout Africa.

Plate 3. Farid Belkahia, *Somalia.* Dye on animal skin, 270.5 x 147 cm, 1994. © Revue Noire. The artist is referring to Saharan scripts, signs, talismans.

Plate 4. Ahmed Cherkaoui, *Saadia.* Oil on canvas, 73 x 92 cm, 1965. Photo © Philippe Maillard. In this canvas Cherkaoui (Moroccan, 1934–67) refers to Arab calligraphy, tattooing, ancient geometric forms, and the structure of the labyrinth.

Plate 5. Ahmed Cherkaoui, *La grande II.* Oil on hessian, 89 x 147 cm, 1962. Photo © Philippe Maillard. This painting is reminiscent of the Egyptian cartouche.

Plate 6. Abdoulaye Konaté, installation. Photos © Jean Loup Pivin and Georges Meurillon/Revue Noire. A Malian artist, born in 1953, Konaté works with signs on fabric.

Plate 7. Gouider Triki. Photo © Philippe Maillard. A Tunisian painter, born in 1949. Secret writing going back to prehistoric drawings.

Plate 8. Rachid Koraïchi, *Encerclement d'une poussière d'Homme.* Etching, 120 x 80 cm, 1986. © Éditart. An Algerian artist, born in 1947, Koraïchi intertwines several writing systems, resulting in a dialogue of cultures.

Plate 9. Mahdjoub Ben Bella. Photo © Philippe Maillard. Ben Bella is from Algeria and was born in 1946. This ethereal dance of signs refers to the palimpsest, weaving, and musical composition.

Plate 10. Abdallah Benanteur, *Embarquement à Tipasa.* Oil on canvas, 130 x 217 cm. Photo © Philippe Maillard. Benanteur is an Algerian painter, born in 1931. The flight of lines in the painting evokes the gesture of writing.

Plate 11. Mohammed Kacimi, *Africa* 2. Acrylic on wood, 98 x 115 cm, 1993. © Revue Noire. Kacimi, a Moroccan artist (1942–2003), presents a work of memory and trace.

Plate 12. Modibo Franky Diallo, *Tissage culture.* 90 x 110 cm, 1971. © Revue Noire. Diallo is Malian artist, born in 1954.

Plate 13. Modibo Franky Diallo. © Revue Noire.

Plate 14. Souleymane Keita, *Le massacre des Tutsis.* Oil on canvas, 174 cm in diameter, 1991. Collection of Bassam Chaito. Photo © Mamadou Touré Behan. Keita is a Senegalese artist, born in 1947.

Plate 15. Souleymane Keita, *Pleine lune à Gorée.* Oil on canvas, 200 x 180 cm, 1986. Collection of Bassam Chaito. Photo © Mamadou Touré Behan.

Plate 16. Adam Henein. Photo © Philippe Maillard. Henein is an Egyptian sculptor, born in 1929. In this piece he works with pigments on papyrus, going back to elements from the Pharaonic tradition.

Index